Majestie

MAJESTIE

THE KING BEHIND
THE KING JAMES BIBLE

DAVID TEEMS

THOMAS NELSON
Since 1798

NASHVILLE   DALLAS   MEXICO CITY   RIO DE JANEIRO

Published in Nashville, Tennessee, by Thomas Nelson. Thomas Nelson is a trademark of Thomas Nelson, Inc.

Published in association with Rosenbaum & Associates Literary Agency, Brentwood, Tennessee.

Thomas Nelson, Inc., titles may be purchased in bulk for educational, business, fundraising, or sales promotional use. For information, please e-mail SpecialMarkets@ThomasNelson.com.

Library of Congress Cataloging-in-Publication Data

Teems, David.
  Majestie : the king behind the King James Bible / By David Teems.
    p. cm.
  Includes bibliographical references and index.
  ISBN 978-1-59555-220-4 (alk. paper)
  1. James I, King of England, 1566-1625. 2. Great Britain—History—James I, 1603–1625.
3. Great Britain—Kings and rulers—Biography. 4. Scotland—History—James VI, 1567–1625. 5. Scotland—Kings and rulers—Biography. I. Title.
  DA391.T44 2010
  941.06'1—dc22   2010020907

Printed in the United States of America

10 11 12 13 RRD 6 5 4 3 2 1

To be a king and wear a crown is a thing more glorious to them that see it than it is pleasant to them that bear it.

—Elizabeth I of England

FOR ALL LOST BOYS

Contents

For a Penny's Worth of Hamlet

1603. There is a discernable hum about the city. The swarm and tread of a long forgotten life, a life far removed from our own—a large, teeming, and animated life, fluid, and slightly opaque, like the Thames that winds ventricle-like through its heart. The market at Smithfield is effuse with a smell that might be burnt brick, tallow, or sea coal.[1] The slow moan and shuttle of livestock. There are the alehouses and ladies of sale. The bear-baiting precincts of Southwark and the great Globe itself, pulsing with life deep in the afternoons. The bustle of theatre cues for a penny's worth of Hamlet.

Her language is as alive as her streets, as deathless and penetrating as the smell, as opulent and full of pomp as the fashions they wear—the silk, the lace, the excess, the ornament. Her English is without rule or harness, feral, wanton, a "hungry creature."[2] And she purrs in the hands of her masters.

This is early modern London, the London of Shakespeare and John Donne, of Francis Bacon and Sir Walter Raleigh, of Sir John Falstaff and Mistress Quickly, of the Mermaid Tavern and Puddle Dock, of Fleet Street and Pudding Lane. "That filthie toune,"[3] as the new Stuart king would come to call it.

It is a lyrical age, the age of the sonnet and the rhymeless pentameter, of pamphleteers and playmakers, of three-hour sermons and two-hour plays. Of severed and unsmiling heads mounted aloft the parapets of London Bridge. An age of child kings, and the pox.

Religion can be dangerous, and spelling is a matter of taste.

And rising out of the clamor, out of the fogs and charred winds, comes her king, our king, as we will refer to him, born some four hundred miles to the north, born in a mask, a man more to be pitied than admired, more to be mocked than loved, a man who sleeps with sermons under his pillow. A prince to be feared indeed, but only for his distractions, for his precarious and bungling politics, and perhaps his bad manners.

But like the tragic Lear, he is every inch a king.

⚜

Truth is, I have no idea what the market at Smithfield was like, or any other London marketplace for that matter—the smell, the movement of traffic, if it hummed or whined. As animated as the above text may be, as alive and as effervescent as any treatment of Elizabethan London should be, as convincingly as I can ever hope to express it, it is an interpretation, a reckoning by way of story. At such a distance, it can hardly be anything else. It is a distillation of sources I have plundered, a kind of translation, I suppose, and as any translation does, it clarifies and teaches us how to perceive. The preface to the 1611 King James Bible says it this way:

Translation it is that openeth the window, to let in the light; that breaketh the shell, that we may eat the kernel; that putteth aside the curtain, that we may look into the most Holy place.

The King James I went looking for was not the King James I found. I went looking for the buffoon, for the jester, the lottery winner who came riding into town in a golden pumpkin, the spoiled boy who could not possibly have replaced the great Elizabeth.

I went looking for the Scot whose tongue was too big for his mouth, who dribbled when he drank, who drank too often, and waddled when he walked even when sober.[4] I went looking for the caricature, for the Saturday morning cartoon. What I found was an uncouth, improbable, and yet somehow enchanting king.

I found all the other as well. With a few exceptions, James is all of that. He is as good as any play. He is an entire theater. And for all the fascination with his mother, the Queen of Scots, or his English predecessor, Elizabeth, or any one of the great spirits that trafficked the age, it is James who fascinates me.

> It is not enough to salute King James as an original—he was also one of the most complicated neurotics ever to sit on either the English or Scottish throne.
>
> —G. P. V. Agrigg, Letters of King James VI & I

The life of James Stuart is a study in contradiction. Intellectually astute, he can dazzle with the polish of his rhetoric one minute, and speak with the vulgarity of a tavern bawd the next. Speaking Latin and Greek before he was five, King James is an amusing mix of bombast and imperium, of sparkle and grime, of smut and brilliance, of visionary headship and blunder.

He wasn't much to look at either. His parents were beautiful, stormy. He was James. Like them, he might have been taller had his body been a bit straighter or the plumb of his legs a little truer. We might imagine the young king with his hands on his hips (a pose he liked), his great hat on his head at a fashionable tilt, a lack of shine on his boots, as he appeared when he first saw Anne of Denmark. Like me, she didn't know what to make of him at first.

We call it the *Jacobean Age* because the Latin form of James is *Iacobus*, that is, *Jacob* (יעקב Ya`aqob *yah-ak-obe'* [Hebrew]; Ιακωβ Iakob *ee-ak-obe'* [Greek]). The biblical Jacob was a twin. He was a dissembler, a man of cunning, a creature of artifice who was chosen to father a great people. I am not sure there could be a more appropriate name.

The Jacobean Age was an age of paradox and wide contrast. Rather like its king. Culture had been split in two for some time, Protestant and Catholic. The kingdoms of Scotland and England were divided, and by much more than a ribbon of land. The mood between them was dark and old. And then there was the hissing match between Elizabeth I and Mary Queen of Scots. Their rivalry was intense, ongoing, and at last, fatal.

The age was tainted with a melancholy peculiar to its poetic spirit, and yet there was sufficient mirth to counter it. For every *Hamlet* there was a *Falstaff*. For every *star-cross'd Romeo* there was a *Bottom the Weaver*. Francis Bacon dedicated his *Novum Organum* (1620), an essential work in the evolution of scientific thought, to the king. How did James respond to Bacon's great work? Like God, he said, "it passeth all understanding."

Even as a child, James was known for a quick wit, and was known to deliver his jests with a straight face. In the midst of a busy school day, James came across the Latin word *vivifico*. He said this word must have come from someone who stutters.

But here is the question. Was King James a great king? Was he an awful king, a neglectful king? Was he a visionary? Was he a fool? Strangely, the answer to all of these is *yes*, which is impossible unless you happen to be James. One writer has labeled him with Attention Deficit Hyperactivity Disorder (ADHD).[5] Another said the king "watched, listened, and spoke simultaneously and sometimes did five things at once."[6] He could get more work done in one hour than most men could in a day.

He was impatient. He was constantly moving. The image tends to blur at times.

But for all his privilege, the great name he was born with, for all the blueness of his blood, the gold font he was baptized in, the silk he slept on, the pomp, the ceremony, *majestie** was not a friend to the boy king.

If he was a "most complicated neurotic," the condition had an early start. Prenatal trauma aside, James Stuart was an orphaned, bullied, lonely, and unloved little boy. Problem is, no one could see the boy. They saw a crown, a name, property of the state, but nothing so large or as animate as a child.

Majestie was a kind of parent to him, and not a very nice one. Demanding, unbending, often cruel, but it was the only parent he had, and, oddly, the one parent he learned to trust above all other things, in spite of the disturbance it made. Filial obligation was bound to majestie alone.

Majestie is ultimately how James Stuart must be understood. Only then do we begin, as I did, to see the visionary, the dreamer

---

*majestie is the Early Modern English spelling of *majesty*. It was also spelled *maiestie*, with the Latin *i* for *j*, as in *Iehovah*. I have chosen to keep as much of the original spelling thoughout the text as possible, simply for its charm, if not for a touch of authenticity. Having little or no formal rule, Early Modern English orthography was a matter of sound. According to Melvyn Bragg in *The Adventure of English*, it was "spell as you speak."

king, the Arthur, the Solomon, the peacemaker, the true king behind the King James Bible.

The Jacobethan* understood majestie in ways you and I are incapable. They knew how to address it, how to approach it, how to serve or how to stay out of its way. The creature Majestie, not unlike the biblical Leviathan, must be approached, if at all, with awe and dread. It is beautiful. It is mysterious. And it is deadly.

> Canst thou draw out Leuiathan with an hooke? or his tongue with a corde which thou lettest downe? Canst thou put an hooke into his nose? or bore his iawe [jaw] through with a thorne? Will he make many supplications vnto thee? will he speake soft words vnto thee? Will he make a couenant with thee? wilt thou take him for a seruant for euer? Wilt thou play with him as with a birde? wilt thou binde him for thy maydens? Shall the companions make a banquet of him? shall they part him among the merchants? Canst thou fill his skinne with barbed irons? or his head with fishspeares? Lay thine hand vpon him, remember the battell: doe no more. Behold, the hope of him is in vaine: shall not one be cast downe euen at the sight of him? None is so fierce that dare stirre him vp: who then is able to stand before me? (Job 41:1–8 King James Bible 1611)

James had a way with the creature that was rare, even among kings. He was the only British monarch to use the title "Majestie" exclusive of all other titles. Others were content with "Your Grace,"

Jacobethan is an academic trick that combines the names Elizabethan and Jacobean. It is convenient when discussing things common to both ages (late Elizabethan and early Jacobean).

"Your Majestie," or "Your Highness." Not James. "Majestie" was all the title he wished to hear.

More than a mere word, institution, address, or the useful metaphor, majestie was an issue of profound belief in which James invested his complete self. His was the tragic belief—that of the artist, the prophet, the martyr, the poet-visionary, the child. He believed thoroughly in his "sparkle" of divinity, as he called it, that thing that separates kings from those they rule.

Majestie ultimately failed him, or I should say his illusions did, for at best, earthly majestie is but a simulacrum, a mimic of that divine majestie that cannot be counterfeited. The King James Bible brought these two realms together and in a single enterprise of translation.

James avoided crowds whenever possible, and yet he could be warm and personable, unguarded. He loved to hear himself talk, and he loved to laugh. Because of the odd mechanics of his speech, his Latin was difficult to understand. And though he put on the fashion of a king, he was often disheveled, as if distraction had dressed him that particular morning. When the Native American princess Pocahontas met James at Whitehall in 1617, he was so understated, so unassuming—that is, he was so much himself—she did not realize he was the king at all until it was explained to her later by someone else.

Afraid of water, he never bathed. He, too, might be known by the smell ("a man of considerable rank" as Shakespeare might have said, though he did not). His idea of cutting back on expenses was to have only twenty-four courses of meat served at his table as opposed to the usual thirty.[7]

No itemized accounting of James, or any basic understanding of him is possible without understanding his attachment to the hunt, or *the chase*, as it was called. Here is a king who fainted at the sight of a drawn sword or a naked blade, and yet loved nothing more than the hunt, the thrill of blood and conquest.

Plus, he thought he looked better on a horse.

At last, I am indebted to the many historians and biographers for whose counsel I am most grateful. Consistency was to be expected, and yet the variance among them, while at times negligible, was at times wide, if not puzzling. Did James preach for three hours on the first day of the Hampton Court Conference, or was it five? Did the baby King of Scots have four "rockers" or seven? Does it matter? What conclusions can we make? Again, it is a matter of interpretation, of translation, proving that even the best biography and the best history is still a work of the imagination. After all, it is a story we've come to hear.

The academic will accuse me of allowing my passions to contaminate my scholarship. I can only hope they are right.

After wrestling with the Angel of the Lord, Jacob walked away from Peniel with a limp.[8] And so, too, comes our king, our imperial Jack. With a gait obscured by childhood rickets (or a drunken wet-nurse), our sovereign comes toward us at a kind of waddle, sidewise and crablike. The same could be said of my earlier perceptions of him. But perceptions change.

David Teems
Franklin, Tennessee

 CHAPTER ONE

Mom and Dad (or An Evening with the Macbeths)

The difference between fiction and reality?
Fiction has to make sense.

—TOM CLANCY

THE COOL ROUND mouth of a gun presses soft against the queen's belly. Not a bad start for a piece of fiction, but it is hardly the beginning you would expect in the biography of a king. Stephen King, maybe. It could easily be a scene from *Titus Andronicus, Julius Caesar*, or even *Macbeth*, but Shakespeare is only two years old. Still, the odd figure King James makes in history begs such a start.

The truth is, if you spend any time with the Stuarts,* you might find yourself staring somewhat dumbfounded at the whole odd tribe, which includes not only our king but also those Stuart

---

*The name was changed from *Stewart* to *Stuart* by Mary Queen of Scots because there was no *W* in the French alphabet.

kings before him, the "former lions"[1] of his blood (if there actually were any lions—a few hyenas maybe, a jackal, a few toads). One Stuart king, James II of Scotland (1430–1460), was blown up by his own cannon. Another, James IV (1473–1513), "connived at the deposition and murder of his own father."[2] Charles I of England (1600–1649) to this day suffers the distinction of being the only English king executed by the very people he governed. The reality is rather dark, and yet it cannot help but entertain.

> No woman of spirit would make choice of such a man.
>
> —JAMES MELVILLE, IN RESPONSE TO ELIZABETH I WHEN ASKED WHAT HE THOUGHT ABOUT DARNLEY, 1565

Then there's mom and dad.

Considering the parents he had—the lovely but unwise, charming but unlucky Mary Queen of Scots, and her second husband, the dashing, spoiled, rash, overconfident, dangerous, and severely misinformed Henry Stuart, Lord Darnley—while conception is no real surprise, it is a wonder our king survived birth at all.

Historian David Willson gives Darnley (dad) no quarter whatsoever, saying that he was "not only stupid, but vain, insolent, treacherous, and debauched."[3] And either to drown his rages, to ignite them, or to simply dull the agony of being himself, he also drank heavily and frequently.

Willson is not much kinder to Mary (mom). While commending her beauty, her enchantments, her "high spirits and reckless daring, her fondness for war and manly sports, her soaring ambition, and the burning passion of her loves and hates," he also says that as a ruler, she was "beneath contempt. Frivolous, extravagant, careless, emotional, utterly self-centered, lacking in judgment and temper, unmindful of the interests of her country, she looked upon the world largely as it advanced or retarded her personal aspirations."[4]

By the time baby James was ten months old, one parent was

dead already—that is, dad—a house blown up with him still in it. He had been convalescing from a complex of ailments, among them syphilis, at the old provost's lodgings in a place called Kirk o' Field,[5] a familiar location he chose himself on the outskirts of Edinburgh within the city walls. Other than a few attendants, he was friendless, laid up in a house with a spirit disposed against him, a house that belonged to Robert Balfour, whose brother Darnley had once plotted against.

Those who knew Darnley were surprised he lived as long as he did, that he actually made it to the age of twenty-one. The blast, or so it was thought, deposited him half-naked in the yard, under a pear tree. His valet, William Taylor, lay only a few yards away, his nightshirt bundled around his waist and his head face down on his arms.* It was an odd sight that suggested it might not have been the blast that killed them at all.

Either way, Darnley was dead. Somebody made sure of that. There was evidence as well that he was strangled before the house detonated under him. According to one source, Darnley may have suspected some treachery (there were plenty with reason enough to be treacherous), or perhaps smelled the gunpowder and was let down from a window by rope and chair. Either way, there was no formal investigation carried out whatsoever.

Other than his own mother and father, few shed any tears for the syphilitic and inebriate Darnley.

> Without maturity or self-control, he [Darnley] was a raw boy dragged to his ruin by evil courses before he ever became a man.
>
> —DAVID WILLSON, KING JAMES VI & I

---

*Much of what we know of the incident was reported by one of Darnley's servants, Thomas Nelson, who survived the explosion.

Because he was dead, somebody gained something, somewhere. So now we cry "conspiracy!" That brings us to the other parent.

Bad boys, bad boys

Not long after Henry's death, Mary was taken away and imprisoned at Lochleven. Perhaps marrying the main suspect of Darnley's murder (James Hepburn, the fourth Earl of Bothwell) three months after the incident was a bad choice. And then only after he abducted and raped her. Of course, less than a month after the alleged rape,[6] Mary created Bothwell Duke of Orkney. (The change in title was a matter of elevation. One was expected to marry closer to one's own altitude. Mary had a thing about height.)[7] They married three days later, on 15 May 1567. Bothwell's divorce from his first wife, Anna Rostung from Norway, had only been finalized eight days before that, on 7 May 1567. Anyway, Mary was pregnant, with little Bothwell twins.

With any other family, that might sound strange.

Mary Stuart was one of those unfortunate women who seem to fall for the same kind of guy over and over—the bad boys. The Earl of Bothwell, hardly an improvement over Darnley, was "high in his own conceit, proud, vicious, and vainglorious above measure, one who would attempt anything out of ambition."[8] But Bothwell had only one eye on Mary. The other was on the crown. It is a temptation difficult to manage, or resist. Power, or that sparkle of earthly majestie, is as much the poison as it is the aphrodisiac. It is also a continuing theme in the love life of the Queen of Scots. Her passion, as imperious as it always was, allowed her few options. It always tended to overrule wisdom.

Not long after Darnley's murder, Mary's former mother-in-law, Catherine de Medici, understanding the delicate balance of women in high places, and in spite of the chafe between the two of them, wrote to Mary, as did Elizabeth I. Both of them pleaded with her to act, to accuse somebody, somewhere, to make at least a show of vengeance, to put some distance between herself and the murder of her husband. A bit of misdirection, anything. Mary did nothing. Or at least nothing that might have been mistaken for wisdom.

Because she did nothing, the accusations began to spin feverishly around Edinburgh streets. And, of course, the spew was aggravated and exploited by the Scot firebrand John Knox* and his fellow pulpiteers. Any chance they were given, at the faintest slip, they all started barking. One popular image, raised on a placard, was that of a topless mermaid with a crown on her head. Below the mermaid was a hare within a circle of swords. The image was easy enough for the people to understand. The mermaid was a common symbol of a prostitute. The hare was part of the Hepburn (Bothwell's) family crest.

In spite of these follies, and before any harm could come to the infant prince, the Confederate Lords took action against Mary at Carberry Hill, just outside Edinburgh. On their banner was a painting of a half-naked corpse under a pear tree and a small child (representing James) praying. A text read, "Judge and avenge my cause, O Lord."

There was no real action to speak of. Bothwell fled the country. Mary, making a show of arms, dressing up** and playing the warrior queen, was apprehended and imprisoned. Being led through the Edinburgh streets, as she was, a vindictive mob cried out, "Burn the whore!" Not long after that, Mary was forced to abdicate her throne, and sign a voluntary demission, surrendering her crown to her son.

Of course, to say Mary was imprisoned needs a bit of explaining. It wasn't prison life as we might imagine, with the usual foul language, metal food trays, and the orange jumpsuit. She was confined

---

*John Knox (1505–1572) was founder and head of the Presbyterian Church (the Kirk) in Scotland.

**Mary enjoyed dressing in men's clothing at times, "which apparel she loved oftentimes to be in, in dancing secretly with her husband [Darnley] and going in masks by night through the streets." Weir, *Mary, Queen of Scots*, quoting *Lennox Narrative*.

nonetheless. Lochleven was accessible only by water, which made it a kind of Alcatraz. But that is where the comparison ends. Lochleven was a castle, and with but a few exceptions, Mary enjoyed all the amenities of her station.

She had serving maids and men to attend her. Her rooms were decked with tapestries, and golden chandeliers hung from the ceiling. Her chairs were upholstered with crimson velvet and cloth of gold. She slept in a large canopied state bed. Her sheets were linen, and were changed daily. As recorded in her household accounts, she enjoyed two courses at dinner and supper. Each course included sixteen separate dishes. That is thirty-two dishes at each meal, sixty-four each day.[9]

As the years went on, and the imprisonment took on a greater severity, she was denied these excesses. And the official word was not "imprisoned" but "secluded."[10] This was the beginning of Mary's long and tragic career as political chess piece, convenient to the Spanish, to the French, to select Englishmen, to Rome, even to the Scots, to the benefit of all, except for Mary herself.

James was eleven months old at the time. He would never see his mother again. Some might say this was to his good fortune. One can only speculate what being raised by the Macbeths might have been like, or what kind of prince might have crept out from beneath their shadow. Still, ask any mother what she thinks.

Beautiful, but shy of harness

To be fair, Mary didn't always go for the bad boys. Her childhood promised something altogether different. Henry II, the king of France, said once, "The little queen of Scots is the most perfect child that I have ever seen." By an arrangement made by Henry when Mary was six years old, she was, at fifteen, married to Francis Valois (the Dauphin of France). As a matchmaker, Henry's motives were more strategic than anything else. With Mary's claim to the English throne, he saw the making of a Franco-British empire.

Francis was fourteen. Two years later, Henry II died and Francis became *Francis II*, King of France. Mary was now queen consort of France. She had been crowned queen of Scots at nine months old at the death of her father, the debauchee, James V, who never saw his child, dying, as he did, six days after she was born. He was heartsick that she was not a boy. "The Devil go with it!" he prophesied, "It will end as it began. It came from a woman and it will end in a woman."[11] He was right. The House of Stuart, a line of Scottish and English monarchs, began with Marjorie Bruce, daughter of Robert the Bruce (Robert I of Scotland) and ended with Anne of Great Britain, covering a span of more than three hundred years (1371–1707).

Little Mary became marriage goods. Having eyes for Scotland, Henry VIII wanted to secure Mary for his son Edward. But Henry never really had a way with women in spite of his series on HBO. Mary's mother hid her the best she could, eventually sending her to France to be contracted to the Dauphin.

Francis and Mary were happy together. Mary was abnormally tall. Francis was abnormally short. She was articulate. He stuttered. She was older than Francis. It was the kind of marital dynamic Mary seemed to thrive in. All the dominoes, all the little tricks of fortune fell right and pleasant for them. Life seemed to glow with a nimbus of soft light, that is, until Francis died of an abscess in his ear two years after being crowned king. Mary and her mother-in-law were not friendly at all. There was too much bristle between them, so Mary went back home to Scotland, a country she truly despised.

She was nineteen, experienced, widowed, and quite Catholic, about to rule a hostile, fragmented, complaining, and quite unCatholic Scotland. Alison Weir describes the Scots at the time as "a proud and tenacious people. Foreign visitors praised them as courageous warriors, but also found them to be uncouth and lawless, hostile to strangers and inordinately quarrelsome. Their way of life was seen as primitive."[12] Scotland was not France.

But there was always a touch of wild about the Queen of Scots. Perhaps it was the return to her native Scotland that set it loose. Like the legend of England's Arthur, perhaps the spirit of the land was not so different from that of its true queen—beautiful, but shy of harness.

A young Jane Austen, most sympathetic to the Queen of Scots, refers to the "openness of her heart"[13] that got her in trouble, and kept her in trouble. Like her son, Mary is a writer's dream, and her story as well seems to straddle that divide between fiction and nonfiction.

Though I use the word delicately, they were *crazy* for each other. At least for a very short but enthusiastic season. She was twenty-three. Darnley was nineteen. Both were lovely. Both were tall. Height was important to Mary. At five feet eleven inches, she was taller than just about everybody. Darnley was six feet one inch. Some sources add another inch or two. He had big blue eyes and full lips.[14] Mary once said of Darnley that he was "the lustiest* and best proportioned long [tall] man that she had ever seen."[15]

Others didn't speak of him with quite the ardor the queen did, but nonetheless they described him as attractive, that he "resembled more a woman than a man. For he was handsome, beardless, and ladyfaced."[16] Alison Weir describes Darnley as "astoundingly good looking."[17]

Both Mary and Henry were passionate. Both were attractive. And like Shakespeare's Juliet, Mary had the power and the brains between them. She would have fared much better had she possessed wisdom to season her intelligence. Her luck turned out to be no better than Juliet's.

---

*lustiest—this is not necessarily a sexual reference. *The Oxford English Dictionary* defines *lusty* as "joyful, merry, jocund, cheerful, lively. *Obs.*" Also means "pleasing in appearance; beautiful. *Obs.*"

Her decision to marry Darnley, like most everything she did, was also counter to the wishes of her cousin Elizabeth, who kept tabs on everything Mary did.

In spite of the soft insistence of Mary's ambassador, Maitland, Elizabeth never formally declared the Queen of Scots heir to the English throne. And you can't blame her. A "second," that is, the next in line, the immediate heir, can be dangerous. Most of Europe considered Mary Stuart's own claim to the English throne stronger than Elizabeth's. Indeed, they considered Mary the true queen. A papal bull issued in 1570 didn't help. This document excommunicated Elizabeth and threatened English Catholics with the same excommunication if they maintained allegiance to the "pretended" queen, the "heretic and favourer of heretics" Elizabeth. Not to mention this bull endangered her life, and with the promise of reward.

Elizabeth never let Mary out of her sight (figuratively speaking, of course, for the two never met in real life).

But if Mary had more power and brains than Darnley, Elizabeth had more than both of them, and guarded her own possession (the throne of England) with care, with savvy, and, of course, with the collective skills of Francis Walsingham and William Cecil.

Elizabeth forbad Mary to marry Darnley. After all, like Mary, Darnley had some claim to the English throne as well, and would only strengthen the Queen of Scots' bid. This particular ban, like many that Mary suffered from Elizabeth, went unheeded. Ruled more by her passions, she did as she pleased. The illusion of power was much stronger than her ability to command it, as the English queen did. Elizabeth even sent an old friend and somewhat reluctant Robert Dudley to Scotland as a suitor to Mary. With Dudley as husband, Elizabeth thought, she could have an accurate accounting of her capricious northern queen. She always called Dudley her "eyes."

But Mary had "eyes" of her own, and they fell elsewhere.

Mary and Darnley were first cousins, and this didn't seem to be a problem. They shared the same grandmother, Margaret Stuart, née Tudor, wife of James IV of Scotland, sister of Henry VIII, Elizabeth's father. Now I am neither qualified, nor do I wish to make comment on that highly suspect tradition of inbreeding. It was the wisdom of the times. The complex genetic tangle, the hidden algorithms in the blood, the odd math, or maybe just the dumb chance of it all, I leave to minds more capable than my own to make the call. Either way, any happiness they might have enjoyed was brief. As the fire that marries powder. The rest is pure tragedy.

A friendless queen

Caution might have saved her. But caution was not one of Mary's endowments. With all the charm at her disposal, making a few friends might have saved her, or at least the right friends. A better marriage might have saved her. The smallest measure of prudence might have saved her. But she is a young woman attempting rule in an unruly, treacherous, scambling, and male-dominated country, in a male-dominated world.

John Knox, author of *The First Blaste of the Trumpet Against the Monstrous Regiment of Women*,[18] fashioned himself as the unnamed ruler of Scotland. He loved to dominate, and this particular trait set him and the Queen of Scots at variance from the beginning. Among other things, his *Blaste* claimed that it was "repugneth [repugnant] to nature" for a woman to rule. Because they were "weake, fraile, impacient, feble and foolishe . . . vnconstant, variable, cruell and lacking the spirit of counsel and regiment" it was contrary to the order of God for them to presume dominion over men. However you spell it, it set the Queen of Scots' teeth on edge.

Knox was also a foot shorter than Mary.

It is tempting perhaps to see her as a fawn among jackals, a friendless queen alone in a deadly maze of power and maneuvering, the foolish young girl who had somehow offended Fortune. In the end, as enchanting as she can be, it's just not possible to feel pity for Mary Stuart. She doesn't let you.

 CHAPTER TWO

A Fawn Among Jackals

... in the womb His hand was over you, that, even there, a
Sonne of wickednesse did you no hurt.

—LANCELOT ANDREWS, Sermon on King James's deliverance
from the Gowrie Plot, 1614

WE ARE NOW back in the bedchamber of the queen, the mother-
to-be, Mary Queen of Scots, where our story began. Other than
name, appearance, and a kind of strained civility, the marriage is all
but over. It took six months to go bad. If that.

Darnley, our poor Henry, was promised the title of Crown
Matrimonial, a gift in Mary's power to give. This act would have
made him a true king in the event of Mary's death. But she has
denied him that gift. Of course she has. In one of her few acts of
wisdom, or what appeared to be wisdom, she refused him. The carrot remained on the stick. Though he was called "King" often, the
only official title Henry would ever enjoy was that of Lord, or even
worse, "the Queen's husband."[1] But not King. Mary even had the
coins reminted. Inscribed once with *Henricus et Maria* (Henry and

Mary), they now read *Maria et Henricus*. But this is only part of a whole list of grievances, both real and imagined.

For Mary's part, she can hardly take his bad behavior any longer, the stomping of his royal feet. It might have been attractive at one time, but the relationship has long soured. David Willson used the word *nausea* to describe Mary's feelings toward her "long man."

The date is 9 March 1566. Mary will deliver in June. She is round with child, with our future king. It is late and she is having a quiet supper with a few of her friends in a little room adjacent to her bedchamber in Holyroodhouse (a royal palace in Edinburgh). Among them is a musician named David. He is dressed in a "gown of damask furred, with a satin doublet and a hose of russet velvet,"[2] a gift from the queen. The mood is light, cheerful. Unannounced and unexpected, her husband, the Petulant, enters her chambers from the privy staircase that joins Mary's room to his room just below. With him are a few of his friends.

There is nothing warm or comforting about this visit. There is no sweetness in the little assembly at all. No small talk. Only anticipation, chill and humorless, and a sudden prickle on the back of one man's neck in particular, the sharp ping of recognition. He understands exactly why these men have come, and whom they have come for. He throws himself suddenly and strategically behind the queen, near a window recess, clutching her garments. He, too, is much shorter than the lady.

Even without the firearms or the lack of manners, the intrusion is a treasonable offense, and the intruders don't seem to care. All they have come for is her attention, which they have achieved rather effectively. Now, with the pistol in place, poised against her swollen flesh, the queen has no choice but to witness the brutal murder of the cowering, whimpering, and terrified little man crouching behind her.

David Rizzio (or Riccio) is a musician, an artist, "ane Italiene . . . a man very skillful in music and poetry."[3] He plays guitar and has a beautiful singing voice. Rizzio has been one of Mary's few distractions against the strain of a doomed marriage and the general weariness of Scottish governance. As well as being her French secretary, Rizzio has been a true friend, familiar enough to wear his hat on this particular occasion in the presence of the queen (which further annoys Darnley).

Though Rizzio has access to Mary's private chambers—and at almost any hour she bids him—and though he exercises this rite of friendship, in spite of how it appears, it is not what you might think. The musician is not much to look at. He is not fair. He is rather homely and misshapen, bent actually, slightly bowed in his back, not unlike his guitar.

There is little about him to draw attention away from his music.

He is "neither handsome nor well-faced."[4] Adam Blackwood writes that "He was a man of no beauty or outward shape . . . evil favoured, and in visage very black . . ."[5] He has nice eyes, but all the sorcery is in his voice, and in his hands.

The most unkindest cut of all

If we feel the need to pity someone, the true fawn among jackals, it might just be this poor guy, this "Signior Davy" as some called him. Darnley played a relaxed game of tennis with the unsuspecting man earlier that same day.

By some bit of bad behavior typical of Darnley, "something so vicious which had taken place at a festivity at Inch Island, too disgraceful to be named in a letter,"[6] Mary had long forsaken his bed, so of course there was talk of her and the homely Italian. Mary may have intentionally antagonized Darnley, at least by some small degree. Such a mind is easily tampered with, and perhaps the sport was more than she could resist. Openly, she gave Rizzio gifts, rich gifts, one of which was a fine guitar—an imported ten-stringed instrument made by a master craftsman, with complex and beautiful settings of pearl, ivory, rare woods, engravings, and delicate inlays.[7]

She had already taken first billing on the coins, and to prevent Darnley from making too many moves on his own, political or otherwise, or to keep him from doling out gifts without her authority, or plundering the exchequer, she decreed that all such transactions had to be signed by both of them. But unlike hers, his signature was actually unnecessary. His seal was sufficient. Mary had such a seal made and gave it to Rizzio. When Henry found out about this—and of course he found out about it, he was meant to—what can we expect?

> That she daylie eschewed his [Darnley's] companie more then [than] other, and professed an open dislyke of his persone; that she rased everie day Signior Davie higher in her favor, and used him with greater familiaritie then was fitt. No! It was openlie said that she tooke more pleasure in his companie then in the King's [Darnley's], her husband's; that she made him sitt at table with her, and had frie [free] access to her bed-chamber, at all hours.[8]

She was in need of such a friend. They shared the same outlaw Catholic faith. And his sensibilities were not only those of an artist or a poet, they were satisfyingly French, as were all Mary's deeper longings. It gave her the solace and retreat of a private secluded world. Rizzio was small medication against the misfortune her life had become.

But now all comfort is gone. He is cringing behind his lady, holding on to her, clinging, clawing at her skirts, and as some reports say, with both his hands on her protruding flesh, as if to appeal to the unborn majestie coiled inside her. It does him little good.

Mary remains composed, queenlike, confident that in her voice rests the power of sovereignty. But Darnley is not listening. He is playing the intractable jealous spouse, and not only that; he has given his consent to the man holding the gun (Andrew Ker of Fawdonside).

Darnley's objective is twofold. He will take the life of the musician, and by savage means. Mainly to make a point. He is openly defiant before his wife, the rightful monarch, the larger spirit and name between the two of them.

If he is fortunate, the queen will miscarry (objective number two). After all, a king sleeps in her womb, a title he covets. He will rid himself of the obstacles, wife and child, if he must.

Regicide is a recurring theme in the Stuart blood.

Of course, the unwitting Darnley is being manipulated by the attending Scottish lords. It is their game. Darnley is somewhat of a tennis ball himself—better dressed perhaps, and with a useful title, but with sufficient bounce to serve their ends. And Darnley is just not the mastermind type. They have fed him thoughts of infidelity, and he has fattened himself. They are wary of the Catholic Rizzio and his influence on Mary. The Italian is in the way.

Patrick Lord Ruthven is the oldest and bitterest among them. He speaks first. The queen actually shows some surprise to see him there. He has been bedridden for some time. His skin is pale, drawn, and a glint of armor is visible from under his gown. There is something dangerous in his voice. "Let it please Your Majesty that yonder man David come forth of your privy chamber where he hath been overlong!"[9] These words set off a heated dialogue between the old man and the queen.

The queen at first thinks he is delirious. He was thought to be dying at home. She asks Ruthven if he has taken leave of his senses. She then turns to her husband sharply and asks him just what he thinks he is doing. His answer is shuffling and uncertain. The musician, still cowering behind the queen, has witnessed all of this. He understands the old man clearly, even if the queen does not.

His voice, once beautiful and soothing, is now rather screechy and unpleasant. His hands, which play with tenderness and skill, are now trembling. He cries out in a broken voice (in his native Italian), *"Giustizia! Giustizia! Madame! Save ma vie! Save ma vie!"*[10] The bully husband pries the gifted fingers loose, and the men with him drag the poor creature away kicking and screaming, out of his mind with terror and anticipation.

In sight of the queen, the helpless man is thrown down near the privy staircase where others are waiting. All of this is in sight of the somewhat ruined dinner party.

The queen was, as she put it later, "struck with great dread" and in "extreme fear of our life."[11] By her own report she just missed a blade herself. She swore she could feel the thrust of someone's arm at her shoulder, just missing her flesh. By salvaging some inward calm, she saved her own life and that of her son.

With the pistol steady, unmoved, and only inches from her first-born, the queen has no choice but to desist, and to watch. She has been warned not to turn her head. The introductions are over, and what comes next is horrific—a mania of swiftly moving limbs and blood, tumbling lamps, large cries, then smaller cries, grunts, and wild breathing. The action is mindless and frenetic, with a *Lord of the Flies* kind of ferocity. One of the attackers is wounded in the confusion. Lady Argyll, a guest of the queen, manages to grab the last candle before it fell to the floor.

Somewhere between fifty-three and sixty stab wounds were counted in the musician's lifeless body, the last being from the dashing young husband himself. The lords make sure Darnley's blade is left in the body.

No longer kicking or resisting, the lifeless singer is hurled down the stairwell and draped over a wooden chest. His body is swiftly dispatched, and buried in a pauper's grave in the Canongate cemetery, near the entrance of the Holyrood Abbey. He was never the point anyway. He was more the whipping boy, the crude entertainment, than the true target of correction. For the rest of her life, Mary was convinced that Darnley had intended to end her life and the life of her unborn child as well, which he might have achieved had he not lost the stomach for it.

To this day, tourists who visit Holyrood Castle swear they can see bloodstains on the floor.

Mary wept for her dead friend, but only for a moment or so. Rage proved the stronger passion. "No more tears now," she said with deadly calm, "I will think upon revenge."[12]

Eggs, anyone?

It's not over just yet. Once the mess was made, all of the conspirators, including Darnley, up and leave, and with all the concern of a hunting party felling a deer. They depart, with the exception of Lord Ruthven and the man who held the gun, Andrew Ker. The old man, winded, weary after so strenuous an ordeal, actually sat down and "called for a drinke," in the queen's presence. Wonderstruck, the queen spoke.

> She askt him how he durst presume to commit that unreverence? But he tooke little notice. "Well," says she, "my Lord, it is within my belly that one day will revenge these cruelties and affronts." This was trulie devyned [divined], as was afterwards seen.[13]

Though Mary was denied the satisfaction of exacting revenge for herself, revenge did return upon the heads of the Ruthvens just as her prophecy suggested. In its time it was swift, it was violent, and it was thorough.

Almost immediately after the little incident with the musician, Darnley, being true to his nature, betrayed his confederates. (Of course, knowing Darnley as they did, they expected as much;

hence, the blade left in the corpse that identified Darnley as the arch-conspirator.)

With the coolness and with the sagacity of a true queen, after all that had happened, Mary talked her now-cringing husband (having been "terrified by the consequences of his own actions"[14]) into deserting the nobles and fleeing with her to Dunbar Castle. He agreed, and at midnight "they took horse." By some trick of misdirection they slipped past the guards, and the little family was on its way.

Dunbar was a twenty-five mile trip, and it was all on horseback. No carts, no carriages. Mary, no less pregnant than she had been earlier, at one point cried out in pain, swearing loudly she could go no more. Darnley, back in the saddle again, literally, and once again the good husband, urged her to continue. Flogging his horse, and then hers, he cried out, "Come on! Come on! By God's blood, they will murder both you and me if they can catch us!" She complained even harder, convincing him less. "Come on! In God's name, come on! If this baby dies, we can have more."[15]

Against her great discomfort, and with vengeance awake and gnawing about her heart, quiet and unseen like the child she carried, they continued on and made all of the twenty-five miles to Dunbar Castle. A few days later, Mary poured out her grief in a letter to her cousin in England.

> Some of our subjects and council by their proceedings have declared manifestly what men they are ... slain our most special servant in our own presence and thereafter held our proper person captive treasonably. But of truth we are so tired and evil at ease, what through riding of twenty miles in five hours of the night, as with the frequent sickness and evil disposition by the occasion of our child.[16] (Mary Queen of Scots to Queen Elizabeth I, 15 March 1566)

Histories are strange things. All the large names doing large recordable things, things kept in dusty chronicles and preserved age to age, only to expose in a given moment just how human these individuals truly are, how the distance between us is not as far as we first thought. The next morning Mary had eggs brought in, and made her and Darnley breakfast.[17] Either she was truly famished after such an ordeal or she was playing a part with a much darker purpose in her thoughts.

At Dunbar she regained power. What friends she had rallied to her, and the conspirators fled to England. Even Knox disappeared for a while. It was that swift. It was that strange. As unstable as it was, power in Scotland had a lot of bounce in those days. Ragged bounce, but bounce nonetheless. It had little choice.

In spite of the rage Darnley incited in the queen, all became quiet as the birth of the child approached. A kind of calm suspended between the pair that had the look of reconciliation. It was one of the few tactical moves by the queen that could be mistaken for wisdom. As one source noted, the clamor "subsided and was replaced by an ominous calm: the child of the disillusioned Queen and her friendless consort was about to be born."[18]

CHAPTER THREE

Rockabye Sweet Baby James

> As departyngis of watris, so the herte of the kyng is in the
> power of the Lord; whidur euer he wole, he schal bowe it.
>
> —Proverbs 21:1, John Wycliffe Bible

"The queen growing great with child . . . reteared [retired]
her from Halliroodhous unto the Castle of Edenburgh, where, upon
the nineteenth day of junji, she brought forth a sone, betwixt nine
and ten a clock in the morning."[1] Even through this primitive and
somewhat mangled English, we know that Mary Queen of Scots gave
birth to a son 19 June 1566, between nine and ten in the morning.

Mom is lying on blue taffeta. An expensive cloth. Of course,
mom doesn't care at the moment. It is blue taffeta soiled with blood,
sweat, and other signs of battle. She is exhausted, beaten, weary with
physical combat. It has been a difficult birth. It was a difficult preg-
nancy. Not because of the child. It had more to do with the marriage
that produced the child.

A small voice cries out at last. A kingdom thrills at it.

According to Sir Henry Killigrew, Elizabeth's ambassador, in a letter to William Cecil, it was "a very goodly child." He commented that Mary was in "a good state for a woman in her case."[2] The infant prince was "sucking of his nourice [wet nurse]. . . . as good as naked, I mean his head, feet and hands, all to my judgment well proportioned, and like to prove a goodly prince."[3]

According to custom, peals of cannon fire thunder from the battlements like a wanton storm. The loud ominous crack that announces the birth of a prince. Five hundred bonfires are lighted. And dad? Dad's drunk. But his altered state has more to do with bitterness than it does with celebration. He tends to seethe, to spoil and wither in his own steam.

When Darnley finally does visit mother and child the afternoon of his birth, around two o'clock, the first thing out of Mary's mouth is, "My Lord, God has given you and me a sone, begotten by none but you!"[4]

On one hand, it could just be the forgiving wife, the hopeful Mary, indeed, the suddenly wise monarch believing the best for her young intemperate husband, giving him room to mature, letting bygones be bygones, giving him her assurances—among them the assurance of paternity—that whatever suspicions he may have had about her and the singer, he has indeed sired a king.

On the other hand, Darnley's rage is a deep one. It is old in him. There is little intelligence in it whatsoever, or discretion, caution, and nothing at all resembling mercy. There is only brute cowardice and loud heedless cries. Mary has witnessed it close up. It has left an ugly stain on her memory, on her associations with her once hopeful spouse.

The ruined boy has blood on his hands, blood that will not wash clean. Darnley enjoyed himself a little too much at the expense of the musician, especially if just to make a point. An offense he will pay for.

At the queen's confession, Darnley actually blushes, and kisses the child. Mary continues, and with the same theme.

> My Lord (Darnley), heer I protest to God, and as I shall answer to him at the great day of judgment, this is your sone, and no other man's sone! And I am desirous that all heer, both ladies and others, bear witness.[5]

Does she stop there? Not quite. With a subtlety much swifter than his grasp, she adds, "For he is so much your owne sone, that I fear it be the worse for him hereafter!"[6]

This little play between mom and dad serves well as a prelude to understanding the life, the complex psychology, and kingcraft of James Stuart. *Merriam-Webster's Dictionary* defines *cat and mouse*, at least in part, as "the act of toying with or tormenting something before destroying it."

Concerning the dead guitar player, Mary has the advantage of certainty. Darling Henry does not. The reference in her statement is a strong one, and it lies just beyond his powers of detection, as if there is a deadly subtext. *Let him steep in his suspicion until he chokes on it. Let it ignite beneath him like the powder that will send him skyward over Kirk o' Field.*

On the night his lodging at Kirk o' Field was blown up, Mary actually visited Darnley, and comforted him. He hadn't been feeling well, probably the result of his advancing syphilis. She attended him, spoon-fed him, spoke soft words to him, even slept for a while in a room above him, only to leave quietly sometime in the night as he slept. Not long after that, he was, as they say, *"hoisted with his own petard."*[7]

After making her address to Darnley concerning his paternity, she turned to his English attendant, Sir William Stanley, and said, "This is the son whom I hope shall first unite the two kingdoms of Scotland and England." Mary was quite the prophetess where her son was concerned. Under different circumstances, what a queen she might have made.

"Why, Madam," Stanley asked, "shall he succeed before your Majesty and his father?"

"Because his father has broken to me."[8]

Darnley, overhearing (as he was obviously meant to) said, "Sweet Madam, is this your promise that you made to forgive and forget all?"

"I have forgiven all, but will never forget! What if Fawdonside's pistoll had shott, what wold [would] have become of him [the child] and me bothe? Or what estate wold you have been in? God onlie knows; but we may suspect!"

"Madam, these things are all past."

"Then," said the queen, "let them goe!"[9]

As Caroline Bingham notes, "it is one of the more consistent lessons of history that things which are all past cannot be let go."[10] And Mary let nothing go. She was convinced that Darnley meant the worse for her and her son, to satisfy his ambition. She was also convinced that her resolve, as well as her strength, was much greater than his. She was right on both counts, and indeed saved her own life and her son's.

After Darnley's short flight over Kirk o' Field, though her marital status improved, her luck never did.

Born in a mask

At the moment of birth, a veil covered the child's face, a *caul*,[11] that is, the amniotic membrane was still intact. In respect to this particular child, we might think it a shield, armor, a mask. Though he rarely spoke of it, as an adult James admitted that his renowned fearfulness had an early start, that he had been in threat of danger, "not only since my birth, but even as I may justly say, before my birth: and while I was in my mother's belly."[12]

Other than the trappings, the name he inherited, the pedigree, and the mask, there were no other signs to mark him extraordinary. The child was baptized *Charles James, Prince and Stewart of Scotland, Duke of Rothesay, Earl of Kyle, Carrick, and Cunningham, Lord of the Isles, and Baron of Renfrew.* The baptism took place Tuesday, 17 December 1566. It was a festive event, filled with all the usual pomp and ritual. At the insistence of the queen, the baptism was Catholic. His godparents were the king of France, the queen of England, and the Duke of Savoy. Of course, they were not there.

Attending notables were the comte de Brienne who represented France, M. du Croc, a Frenchman representing Savoy, and the Earl of Bedford representing England. Brienne attended with thirty gentlemen and brought the prince a necklace of pearls and rubies, and two lovely earrings. Savoy sent a feathered jeweled fan. Bedford brought a baptismal font of pure gold as a gift from Elizabeth.

The Scottish lords, as a sign of soft protest, stood outside the chamber.

The prince was carried into the chapel by the French ambassador, passing between two rows of barons and gentlemen and was "followed by a number of Scottish nobles, all Catholics, one bearing the great cierge [a wax candle], another the salt, another the rood [crucifix], another the basin and laver. At the entry to the chapel the Prince was received by the Archbishop of St. Andrews, attended by other Catholic prelates."[13]

[The baptism] was a defiant last assertion of the dying Catholicism in Scotland, with Archbishop Hamilton of St. Andrews and the Bishops of Dunkeld, Dunblane, and Ross in pontifical robes such as had not been seen in Scotland these seven years.[14]

The Countess of Argyle held up the prince at the font (in proxy for Elizabeth), and the archbishop administered the rites of baptism in the manner of Rome, with the exception of the spittle (part of the rite concerned with renunciation of the Devil and opening of the senses toward God), which the queen prohibited.

Though Darnley was at Stirling Castle where the ceremony took place, he did not show at all. He remained in his room sulking, "boycotting" the ceremony and the parties that followed. He was intoxicated, and not only with drink, but with other stimulants—discontent, injured pride, and chronic incompetence, the nagging thorn.

The festivities lasted three days. Not only did it put a strain on the finances of the kingdom, the Scots had to suppress their usual bad manners in favor of the more civilized French ones. As William McElwee suggests, "Mary allowed herself the illusion that life could still be civilized and urbane, showed off her French and her dancing and her charm, ignoring the sinister little indications of lurking trouble."[15]

Mary stayed cool and kept her own private counsel until her son was born and baptized. Once those formalities were passed, then came the strike that sent the sulking husband skyward.

And this is the nuclear family, the little nest that bred our king.

Miscarriage

On 24 July 1567, Mary was forced to sign a "voluntary demission,"[16] basically, a writ of abdication, a document she swore for the rest of her life she signed under duress, under pressure by the nobles, and that it was unlawful. Just a few days before that, being five months pregnant, she miscarried the twins.

Mary's own actions saved the Kirk (the Presbyterian Church) and the nobles the bother of excess intrigue, or for Knox to wear himself out with more spew. She made their work easy. Her marriage to Bothwell, the miscarried twins (the little Hepburns), and the so-called Casket Letters made her end tidy, and complete. A casket is a small box. This one was silver. Inside the casket were letters, love letters she had written to Bothwell, sonnets and other bits, promises concerning their marriage. These letters confirmed her collusion with Bothwell at the murder of Darnley.

History has put a smudge of doubt upon the legitimacy of these letters, suggesting they may have been tampered with (which happens often in this game of dominance). The communication between Bothwell and Mary in the letters was "discreet and coarse," which sounds like our girl, and from this end of history, we are obliged to weigh such evidence against all of Mary's carelessness, all her indelicate bungling, which only makes the letters seem reliable.

But lost in all of Mary's noise, or perhaps misprized, was her child. In all the play with Bothwell, Mary more or less abandoned James. One writer summarizes this way: "In the strange and unnatural relations of Mary and her son, it was Mary who committed the first great wrong."[17]

She made her own bed, so to speak. Of course, this was only 1567. She had another twenty years to complete her fall. A year later, in May 1568, in one last attempt to regain her slippery reign, she somehow escaped her captivity at Lochleven. She then threw together what supporters she had, an army of around six thousand, including nine earls, nine bishops, and eighteen lords. This was an impressive number considering the cloud over her head. Then, in another show of arms, though brief and decisive, Mary's forces were once again undone.[18]

To escape humiliation, she then made the blunder of her life and fled to England, where an entirely new set of problems awaited her, and with much more consequence than those in Scotland. It was not long until she was captive again, and this time there would be no escape. England was not Scotland. And in spite of her sex, Elizabeth could humble both Knox and his Kirk.

In her latter captivity, Mary was given the best medical treatment, and she was allowed to exercise (under guard, an English guard). But her renowned beauty, like the devotion of her followers, soon abandoned her as well. In time, she became arthritic, and began to stoop. It was said that her face, once so full of life, was now "lined and tight."[19]

All the charm and sway of the beautiful sovereign, the enchantress, was lost, replaced by something a bit more crabby and repellent. Her name was still viable, of course, as durable as names are, and European and Catholic princes sought some employment of that name to their benefit. But Mary, once so easy to adore, was in sharp decline.

Year by year, she put on excess weight, and became more fanatical in religious exercises. Losing touch with reality, she dreamed of deliverance and of regaining a crown.

The nobles left the matter of public opinion to Knox. Mary's adulteries and treasons became the hot sermon topic. And I suspect there is nothing quite so satisfying to the small and loud as bringing down a queen. Again, she made their work easy.

Sadly, Mary's imprisonment was, for the remainder of her truly miserable life, a continuous shuttling from one castle to the next. And as grand as that might sound, her final conditions were hardly suitable for a queen. To ensure that foreign powers had no chance of access to her, she was not allowed to stay in any one place more than two years. From the grand to the not so grand, from the noble to the ignoble, harsh, and desolate. Sheffield, Chatsworth, Tutbury, and at last, Fotheringay.

The loss of the twins was due to elements beyond Mary's control. For the miscarriage of her kingdom, however, she had only herself to blame.

 CHAPTER FOUR

The Most Valuable Life in Scotland

I was little boy lost, and I was little boy blue
I am little Jack Frost but I am warm through and through
It's not easy to hide when your heart's on full view
Oh, tonight, cruel world be forgiving
Oh, for once in my life I am living.

—KATE RUSBY, *The Girl Who Couldn't Fly*, "Little Jack Frost"

ON 29 JULY 1567, James Stuart was crowned James VI of Scotland. He was thirteen months old. Neither his mother nor his father was there for the coronation. Actually, hardly anybody was at the coronation—the necessary officials, a few members of the Kirk, and James. It is not difficult to imagine the mood, beneath the polish of ceremony, of course. Thirty-seven years later, his English coronation was as barren as the Scottish one. I imagine he was just as indifferent.

In keeping with the duality that defined James all his life, having had a Catholic baptism, his coronation was Protestant. Both were forced, aggravated with tension.

The rule of nations and of large ponderous names demands the coronation of a monarch be conducted according to tradition, to old appearances, old rites. And so it was. It was mechanical, rote, passionless. The actions taken against the former queen added a touch of audacity to the little event, if not a specter of doubt, considering Mary's clamor over her "forced" abdication.

Caroline Bingham uses the word *maimed* to describe the ceremony.[1]

The little coronation took place at the Church of the Holy Rood, the parish Kirk at Stirling, on a craggy hillside that rose to the castle. A total of seven attended. John Knox preached the coronation sermon, and used the moment to throw more slime on the absent Mary, his beloved Jezebel.

> The preachers, in fact, meant the new regime to subordinate the whole government of Scotland, civil, and ecclesiastical, to themselves. The nobles were determined merely to keep power and wealth exclusively in their own hands or those of their friends. The child whom they were crowning was to spend half his life freeing himself from these two threatened tyrannies.[2]

Rockers

The Earl of Morton took the coronation oath on behalf of James. He was "to reule in ye faith, fear, and love of God, and maintain ye religion then professed in Scotland." The bishop of Orkney crowned the king.

> Ye Bishope anoynted him on ye croune of the head, shoulder blaides, and palmes of ye handes, saiing certain prayers befor in English tounge. The royal rob was put one him, the croune put upone his head, ye sword to his syde, the cepter in his hand. At ye doing of every one of thess

particulars, ther were prayers made in the mother toung. Last of all ye blessing was pronounced by the Bishope.[3]

So begins the reign of James VI of Scotland.

The lords, satisfied with their work, took the king to the castle. In celebration, there were "fyre works, and shotting of canon, and feasting."[4]

Baby kings and baby queens had been the rule in Scotland since 1406. James V, the grandfather of our king, was crowned king at seventeen months old. His daughter, Mary, was Queen of Scots at six days old. That meant the country was managed by regents appointed to rule in the name of the king or queen. These serial minorities were beneficial to the nobles, who gained both in power and autonomy, wearing the name of the king like a badge. It became the odd and yet unquestioned architecture of Scottish politics.

On one side of the Ryal (Sword Dollar), the coin minted the year of James's coronation as king of Scotland in 1567, the legend reads *pro me si mereor me*, which basically means "for me *if* I deserve it" (emphasis mine). In other words, everybody is happy as long as the boy king behaves and does as he is told. To the Kirk and nobles, the best king was a submissive one. The younger, the better. The Latin gave it weight and validity, making it appear less like a threat. The author? All fingers point to George Buchanan, the king's soon-to-be bully schoolmaster.

The infant king was a bit young to notice any of this. He was placed first in the care of the Earl of Mar, another cousin, a man with great integrity. The king and the kingdom were fortunate in this placement.

His first years were spent at Stirling Castle, a powerfully built and well-situated fortress that rose from the town of Stirling upon its rocky eastern slope. It was the image of strength. Its difficult access made it capable of protecting the "most valuable life in Scotland."

The Countess of Mar, Annabella Murray, was appointed to take care of the child. In this appointment, the king was less fortunate. John Knox, never at loss for a kindness, called her "a very Jesabell" and "a sweet tidbit for the Devil's mouth."[5] Knox was fond of the biblical image of Jezebel. It was a continuing theme in his sermons. Typical of the ambivalence of the age, well into his fifties, if not at the edge of sixty, Knox married two sixteen-year-old girls in succession.[6]

Other than the brief tenure with his own mother, and the wet-nurse Helena Little, whom James later accused of being a drunkard, Annabella was the closest thing to a mother James was to enjoy, a maternity that was dutiful, obligated, and reserved, but neither warm nor loving. The countess was too much in awe of the Crown to do its small owner much good. Indeed, James wrote years later that "My Lady Mar was wise and sharp, and held the King in great awe."[7] She referred to James as "the Lord's anointed."[8]

Annabella also hated the Queen of Scots (which made her the most desirable candidate for the job).

By James's toddlerhood and thereafter, she became more the stern governess than anything that might have resembled mom. Lady Mar was "extremely strict in her notions of upbringing, as a result of which, as contemporaries agree, James was much in awe of her."[9] She did object when he was beaten, which was rare anyway, suggesting that she was not physical in her correction or sharpness toward him.

James never had the simple advantage of anyone he might call "mom." He had four young women (another source says seven) who served as "rockers." They were employed to rock the king in his cradle. And of course the wooden cradle had to have a name, as everything else does in the household of a prince. Sounding more like a famous battle site, or something out of Indiana Jones, it was called the "Cradle of Traquair."[10] With tradition that goes back as far as 1107, Traquair, the estate itself, was originally a hunting lodge for Scottish royalty.

The young king's staff included a wet-nurse (the inebriate Helena) and her attendants, the four (or seven) rockers, two other ladies to tend to the king's clothes, and three men of the King's Bedchamber. His Master of the Household was John Cunningham. Part of Cunningham's job was to ensure that all the help attended worship, that they spoke and conducted themselves in "godly and honorable conversation."[11] They were all to be models of behavior for the king, that he might be shielded from "ungodly and light behaviour that might hurt his Highness's tenderness."[12]

The kitchen staff included a master cook, a foreman, a keeper of the vessel, a turnspit, a porter, a keeper of the larder, and a pantryman. There was one keeper of the wine cellar, and one for the ale cellar. (The allowance for the "king's own mouth daily" were two and a half loaves of bread, three pints of ale, and two capons.) One lady was in charge of the laundry. Three men slept in the royal bedchamber—William Murray, William Bokkes, and Alexander Fargison. The king had a French tutor (a husband and wife team). He had a supplier of coals to keep him warm, a pastry chef, and a string band (four brothers—Mekill "Big" Thomas, Robert, James, and William—who played violin and viola).

The entire household operated closely, and one reason for this was the constant threat of abduction.

Three different sources used the same unfortunate modifier, *gloomy*, to describe the young monarch's bedroom. Decked with black damask—"the ruff, head-piece, and pillows being fringed with black."[13] A large frame with a picture of his grandfather, James V, hung on the wall.

A shell game

With a child king or queen (minority), Scotland was managed (and often mismanaged) by a series of regents, those appointed to rule in the place of a king or a queen. It was true for Mary, for her father (James V), for his father (James IV), and for her son, James VI. Until he took the reins himself, four regents would rule Scotland. And all of them would suffer a similar, and rather grim, fate.

Like his mother, James proved bad luck to these men. The Earl of Moray, Mary's half-brother, was the first to rule. Of course, the word *rule* is a bit misleading. Not having the name, pedigree, or divine right of king, the regent, while not altogether powerless, was still subject to the Kirk and the nobles who were always scheming, always circumnavigating, always playing a bit of a shell game. If you need an image to capture the regent, you might think of a substitute teacher you had in high school.

Moray was assassinated (shot) in 1570, when James was four years old. The next to "rule" was James's paternal grandfather, the Earl of Lennox. The somewhat nervous Lennox was the choice of Elizabeth as well. Elizabeth had strings and pulleys everywhere in the Scottish government. Lennox was shot in 1571, and young James, five at the time, had the added horror of watching him die. James actually loved the old man, or was "fond" of him, as one source said.[14] Love was something James had little experience with.

The third regent was his caretaker, the Earl of Mar. His regency lasted a whole year. It is assumed, and it would be nice to assume, that Mar died of natural causes in 1572, when James was six. John Macleod uses the word *oddly* to describe the death of Mar. Mar had been "nobly treated and banqueted by the Lord of Morton, shortly after which he took a vehement sickness which caused him to ride suddenly to Stirling where he died."[15] Morton became the next regent. Of course he did.

The fourth and last regent was James Douglas, the Earl of Morton. His tenure actually began in 1573, when James was seven. Morton was tougher and more savvy than the other regents. (Moray,

Lennox, and Mar were good men who just couldn't negotiate the tangles and trip wires around them.) Morton had both slither and brains. He also had Elizabeth's backing. He lasted longer than the other regents, but eventually lost his head, literally. And there was nothing the English queen could do except rage. Morton never saw it coming. More about that presently.

The Kirk and the nobles were always scheming and counterscheming, watching, circumnavigating, always playing the game of dominance and advantage. And that is how headship was conducted in Scotland. It was the established order James was going to have to survive, and somehow beat.

All of the regents were related to the king. Lennox, I suspect, might not have wanted the position, particularly knowing its history. Self-interest was the subtext in the royal household. Ambition, far from being a sin, had become a virtue. You might say it was a family tradition, a condition of the blood for which the only cure was usurpation or death by execution or assassination.

Even between sovereigns and their own heirs, treachery was not uncommon. Years later, when James's own son Henry, Prince of Wales, was proving to be everything his father wasn't, and gaining more and more popularity among the people, it was at least suggested by some that it was James who engineered Henry's early demise. It was not very likely that James did any such thing, and history doesn't give this event much merit, but it was suggested by some at the time, if only because such an act was not uncommon.

> No feeling of tenderness, of pity, or regret was ever allowed to penetrate to the boy in his artificial orphanhood to modify his feelings about his mother.
>
> —WILLIAM McELWEE, *THE WISEST FOOL IN CHRISTENDOM*

Such was the condition of James's childhood. The Queen of Scots, in the first year of her exile, sent her son "an ABC* and a pony complete with bridle and saddle."[16] With these gifts, she sent a warm letter addressed to "my dear son, James Charles, Prince of Scotland."[17] Because she did not refer to him as a king, the letter never got to James. Nor did the gifts. When James was three, the parliament at Stirling commanded that there be no contact whatsoever between the king and his mother, except through council.

Now that the young king was Scotland's alone, the going strategy was misdirection, keep him too busy to feel. Fill his day with industry and study, with the emblems of pious and worthy kingcraft. And sift his heart for its queen, his mother, for even there she must be dethroned. The Kirk and nobles had just the man for the job."

---

* "An ABC is a spelling-book, or primer, teaching the alphabet and first elements of reading (*Obs.*); hence *fig.* the first principles, most elementary part, or simplest rudiments (of any subject)." *Oxford English Dictionary*.

CHAPTER FIVE

Greek Before Breakfast, Latin Before Scots

He was, after all, a very lonely, loveless little boy.

—WILLIAM MCELWEE, *The Wisest Fool in Christendom*

AUGUST 1571. PARLIAMENT is summoned in Edinburgh by the ruling Protestant lords. It is more of a show of power against the Queen of Scots, still muzzled and still under guard. The lords basically want all parties to know where power is truly vested. Before the entire assembly, before all the nobles and members of the Kirk, the young king is carried in—the crown, the scepter, and the sword of state before him, all the emblems of sovereignty. The five-year-old James is placed on the throne. The words are formal and a bit oversized in his mouth, but he has memorized them for the occasion. The following text was spoken in the high-pitched solemnity of a small boy:

> My Lords and other true subjects, we are convened here as I understand to do justice, and because my age will

> not suffer me to do my charge by myself, I have given my
> power to my goodsire [grandfather] as regent, and you,
> to do; and you will answer to God and to me hereafter.[1]

Once he finished his oration, his grandfather, Lennox, now regent, addressed the gathering of nobles. Of course, James is paying no attention to the speechmaking. There is little he can understand anyway. He does what all little boys do. He fidgets. He squirms in his seat. His eyes roam everywhere, and eventually he notices a tear in the canopy over the throne.* He reaches up to it "to attain to the hole with his finger."[2] Turning to one of the lords near him, he asks, "What is this place?" He is told that he is in parliament. Once Lennox finishes his speech, James then says, "I think there is a hole in this parliament."[3]

No one misses the statement, as casual and as childlike as it is, or ignores the implications. "Whether God inspired the babe with prophecy at that time or not, I will not dispute,"[4] wrote one commentator.

Much has been made of this little extemporaneous remark by the child king. That very parliament the boy king sat in, as most all parliaments were, was little more than "tempestuous wrangling,"[5] a lot of scratch and hiss.

It was the wisdom of the ruling party to have the boy become conscious of his kingship before any other consideration. They did their job well, and it seemed to work. James was never conscious of being anything other than a king. It was how he was taught to approach and interpret life, how he understood the world. He never knew anything else. Considering this imposition upon his childhood

---

*One biographer said it was a hole in the broadcloth covering a table, another said it was a hole in the ceiling, while yet another said it was a tear in the canopy above the throne. What is essential is that there was a hole in a piece of fabric that got the young king's attention.

psychology, it is difficult to fault him as the adult. It determined the shape of his thought life.

The life of a king, even in a poor, complaining country like Scotland, is far above a mere life of privilege. It is, in essence, even as he would write years later, the life of a little god. But even for a "little god" it was still Scotland. Antonia Fraser uses the words *pathetic* and *bleak* to describe the childhood of James Stuart. And, of course, "highly instructive."[6]

The sapling prince and the bitter oak

Statements James was known to make as a young boy reveal a sharp intellect. He was, even from a young age, able to keep his counsel to himself. Since he had few friends, he therefore had little choice. He had playmates of sorts in the son of the Earl of Mar (John Erskine) whom he called Jockie o' Sclaittis (pronounced *slaits*). There was also John Murray, a nephew of the Countess of Mar, and Walter Stuart, a distant relative.[7]

Young Mar, the king's closest companion, as pleasant as his company was, and as often as they were together, proved to be nothing like a real friend. Also, because of the king's physical weakness and the awkwardness evident in his limbs, in normal rough games he always fell behind the others, particularly in wrestling or other martial exercises. This was perhaps one reason the hunt became so important to him later in life, why he loved it so much. The hunt was an equalizer. It sat him on a horse, on limbs much more dependable than his own.

> He [James] had known but little of emotional stability which is nowadays considered so important to the happy development of a child.
>
> —ANTONIA FRASER, *KING JAMES VI OF SCOTLAND, I OF ENGLAND*

To waste no time, and not to let the royal mind go to spoil, the

boy king was put to rigorous study under the harsh but brilliant tute-
lage of George Buchanan. Buchanan lobbied for the position before
there was such a position. Philosopher, poet, Latinist, Buchanan was
perhaps the best educator to be found, not only in Scotland, but
he had an impressive reputation in the world at large. He had once
been the teacher of the great Michel de Montaigne, the French essay-
ist. Montaigne was about the age of James when he came under the
instruction of Buchanan. Of course, Buchanan was a bit nicer back
then. And a lot younger.

Sixty years older than James, Buchanan was an old man in the
winter of his life, set in his ways, and intolerant of large names or
sapling princes. He was a brutal master with a biting wit. Other than
his great intellect, he had the one particular quality the authorities
admired the most: he hated the king's mother. Backed by the church
he more or less fathered, Buchanan considered it part of the king's
education to malign the Queen of Scots. He never missed an opportunity to wreck what small memory the boy had.

A sympathizer with Knox, and Knox's *Blaste*, Buchanan never let
up. To him, Mary was that "bludy woman and poysoning witch."[8]
The young Queen of Scots had once been a pupil of Buchanan's.
Then he became Protestant the year James was born. That was that.

At first, the great teacher wrote verse about her, praising her wit,
her virtue, and other hopeful things he detected. When she proved
less than his words expressed, that is, when she proved to be herself,
his writing looked to him more like contrived flattery, which made
him despise her even more.

He wrote a piece of scorn called *Detectio Mariae Reginae Scotorum*.
The Latin *detectio* means "disclosure, uncovering, revealing." *Detectio*
is Buchanan's thoughts on the Queen of Scots (*Mariae Reginae
Scotorum*). It was his way of revenge. *British Quarterly Review* says,
"Buchanan's '*Detectio Mariae Reginae Scotorum*' is one of the most
powerful pieces of rhetorical invective ever written."[9]

Buchanan was brilliant, original, unflinching, and unafraid, especially before a "nervous, excitable, overstrung boy"[10] like James. It is amusing, and it reveals something about the boy, but as much as Buchanan tried to make James into his perfect king, James was inclined toward the exact opposite. Newton's law of reciprocal action applies. "To every action there is an equal and opposite reaction." Buchanan considered democratic nationalism the ideal form of government, which he said "proved most conducive of human good."[11] James thought no such thing.

As a teacher, Buchanan was tyrannical, though, by an odd hypocrisy, in his politics he had no use for tyrants. To his mind, a tyrant was one who saw himself, or herself, above the law. According to the *Oxford English Dictionary*, a *tyrant* is "one who seizes upon the sovereign power in a state without legal right; an absolute ruler; a usurper. A king or ruler who exercises his power in an oppressive, unjust, or cruel manner; a despot." James hated the word for an altogether different reason, and the tyrannical Buchanan gave him cause. James would grow into an absolutist king, a creature whom Buchanan despised most of all.

In Buchanan's theory, a king should be a lover of piety, indeed, he should pursue piety, in himself and others, and his life should be the very model for his subjects. His countenance should bring dread to bad men, even as it should be the image of delight to good ones. The king was the father of his people so he existed for his subjects and not the other way around. James accepted these views readily, but for all other facets of kingship he would trust his own instincts.

Buchanan created an adult-sized syllabus for his young charge, and a great part of the education of the king was a knowledge of the Scriptures, being intimate with the Bible. A chapter of the Bible was read and discussed at every meal. In 1588, a Jesuit, James Gordon, said, "[James] is naturally eloquent, has a keen intelligence, and a very powerful memory, for he knows a great part of the Bible by heart. He cites not only chapters, but even the verses in a perfectly marvelous way."[12]

Some of Buchanan's teaching had some stick. Some of it did not.

In 1579, when James was thirteen, not far from the time of his true rule of Scotland, Buchanan wrote a book called *De Jure Regni apud Scotos (The Rights of the Crown in Scotland)*. Dedicated to James, and intended as another tool to instill his political beliefs into the will of the young king, this treatise basically taught that the source of all political power is the people. The king, he asserted, is bound by the power that first made him king, which in Buchanan's mind is not God, but the people. He even taught that it was lawful to not only resist tyrants, but to punish them. Years later, in 1584, when James was a true working king, *De Jure Regni* was condemned by an act of Parliament. It was condemned eighty years later at the resumption of the monarchy under Charles II, and burned by the University of Oxford in 1683. James had no use for his teacher's book.

James believed the people were there for him. He was appointed over them by God alone, and could be judged by God alone.

Poor bird

One day James and his boyhood companion, the Earl of Mar, young Jockie, were scuffling over a sparrow. In the exchange, the bird lost its life. Buchanan, hearing what was going on, went into a rage and gave the young king a box (a slap) on the ear, adding that he was "a true bird of that bludy nest." Fortunately, the young king survived his parents. And as doubtful as it was at times, he survived childhood.

There was a second tutor, much younger than Buchanan, softer, and more agreeable—the one person in the entire brood who offered James anything resembling warmth, and that was Peter Young. Where Buchanan was severe, Young was encouraging. Where Buchanan was hard as flint, Young was pliable. Later in the king's life, the cognitive associations with Young were pleasant, favorable. Those with Buchanan were not. His emotions turned violently fearful at the very thought of the man.

Between these two instructors, the king stayed occupied. The balance between Buchanan and Young was a sturdy one, and though the older man was imperial, Young was necessary. With the king's odd psychology already in the first foundational stages of development, he as easily bounced between the extremes, between Buchanan and Young, Young and Buchanan, from the soft to the brittle. The following is a sample of his day, according to Peter Young. This regimen began when James was four.

> First in the morning he sought guidance in prayer, since God Almighty bestows favour and success upon all studies. Being cleansed through prayer and having propitiated the Deity, he devoted himself to Greek, reading either from the New Testament, or Isocrates, or from the apophthegms [maxims] of Plutarch, with practice in the rules of grammar. After breakfast he read Latin, either from Livy, Justin, Cicero, or from Scottish or foreign history. After dinner he gave some time to composition; and during the rest of the afternoon, if time permitted, he studied arithmetic or comosgraphy, which included geography and astronomy, or dialectics or rhetoric. But these subjects were taken up in turn, not followed all at the same time.[13]

It was a rather grim and somewhat pitiful image, the little boy a slave to his books. Pushed harder than other princes were known to be pushed, James could speak Latin and Greek before he was five years old. When he was eight, Sir Henry Killigrew, Elizabeth's emissary, observed the king often, once reporting back to his queen that he witnessed the young king do something *extempore* (spoken or done without preparation) that he could not help but marvel at.

According to Killigrew, James could "read a chapter of the Bible out of Latin into French, and out of French after into English, so well, as few men could have added anything to his translation. His schoolmasters, Mr. George Buchanan and Mr. Peter Young, rare men, caused me to appoint what chapter I would; and so I did, whereby I perceived it was not studied for. They also make his Highness dance before me, which he likewise did with a very good grace; a Prince sure of great hope, if God give him life."[14]

That Buchanan made the king dance provides a useful image. It was in Buchanan's mind all along to make the son of Mary Queen of Scots into a creature of his own liking. Truth is, Buchanan might have made him "dance" as a young frightened, intimidated boy, but as a young man and as an adult, James didn't have the "legs" for it.

And while the metaphor works nicely, for all his "goodly" shape as a toddler, James was graceless and ungainly into his teens and throughout his adult life. From an accident, it was thought, whether it was being dropped by the soused Helen Little or the more believable version being a case of childhood rickets, the king's right foot was "permanently turned out," set somewhat perpendicular to his other foot. His legs were also weak. This condition forced him to walk with an odd gait. Modern writers love to talk about the king "leaning" on his favorites. Truth is, the king had to lean on pretty much anyone available. It wasn't a matter of preferment, but direction.

Buchanan, for all his tyranny, was nonetheless an effective educator of sovereigns, an architect of great minds (or what should have been great minds). For instance, in an attempt to halt James's early tendency to grant favor whenever he was asked for it, and often not paying attention to the request at all, Buchanan implemented a little test.

One day Buchanan brought the king two stacks of requests. The king—against his distractions, his boredom, and the natural inclinations of a high-strung youth—signed them as usual, and as usual paid no attention to the nature of the requests. For the next few weeks Buchanan went around telling everyone that he, not James, was now king of Scotland. James, amazed, asked Buchanan about it. Buchanan then showed him the signed document, indeed granting him rule over his own kingdom. "Well," Buchanan told him, "here is the letter signed in your hand in which you have handed the kingdom to me."[15] He then instructed the king about the dangers of granting such requests and what damage it could do. It was a good lesson, and a practical device to illustrate it. Whether James amended his ways is doubtful.

Buchanan's methods could be quite brutal, and not only verbally, or academically, but unlike the Mar surrogates, he was not afraid to strike James. The following account is an actual encounter between the Countess of Mar and Buchanan. I like this story, not for its crude language, but for its clear demonstration of the humanity that surrounded James.

One day, young Jack and Jockie were at it again, playing, being loud, pushing it, being boys. But it was late in the afternoon and Buchanan was not in the mood. The old man warned the king that "if he did not hold his peace, he would whip his breech." The king made a quick but unfortunate reply, and did so with enough mockery in his words, enough sting, even against the boyish delivery, to arouse Buchanan's fury. "In a passion," Buchanan threw down his book and whipped the king "severely."[16]

Hearing the boy cry out, the Countess of Mar came rushing in and asked the king what was going on. James told her that his teacher had given him a whipping. She turned to Buchanan and cried out how dare he "put his hand on the Lord's anointed."

"Madam," he replied calmly, "I have whipped his arse, you may kiss it if you please."

It is difficult to measure the impact of such a strong personality upon the king as George Buchanan. As an adult, the mention of Buchanan's name—or if someone entered his presence who had a similar bearing to his old teacher—was enough to make James tremble. Antonia Fraser leaves us with a couple of positive results of his childhood.

> The first of these and the most important was a deep and canny reserve, the ability to keep his own counsel and form his own judgments without necessarily sharing them immediately, which it is impossible not to see as a direct result of his traumatic upbringing. Second was a wry sense of humour, the original pawky wit of the Scots, which one glimpses quite early on in his life.[17]

If, to follow Antonia Fraser's list, there are strong elements of his personhood that took shape during this period in his life, even she admits there is perhaps a third. Having been denied love almost from the cradle, James had within him the almost tragic desire to be loved. Growing within his boyish shell, beneath all the noise of kingcraft, all the intellectual brawn and childish folly, was something untended and unfed.

CHAPTER SIX

A Timid, Friendless Boy

Like to a hermit poor in place obscure,
I mean to spend my days of endless doubt,
To wail such woes as time cannot recover,
Where none but love shall ever find me out.

—SIR WALTER RALEIGH

JOCKIE O' SCLAITTIS attempted to finish a story he was telling, but the tedium and his imperfect French were too much for the royal tolerance. The young king, losing all patience, detonated, and in his own heated and yet perfect French raged, *"I have not understood a single word you have said!"* The mild-mannered Peter Young told the king he should never be angry. The king replied, "Then I should not wear the lion on my arms but rather a sheep."[1]

He had an adult snap even as a kid. Being around Buchanan as much as he was, it could not be helped. Buchanan was infective. He had a poet's grasp of the comeback, and the necessary element of timing. For all his gravity and pounce, he was very witty. Though it was not a part of the formal syllabus, the king's witcraft was nurtured under Buchanan's watch as a kind of ancillary education.

As an adult, James was notorious for the sauce and for the

intelligence of his bite. His obscenities came with a kind of Broad
Scots poetry of their own. Modeled after his famous teacher, James
had a "sour, crabbed"[2] kind of wit, sharp as a pinprick, as swift and
at times as brutal as Buchanan's. Perhaps more so, considering his
station.

As an adult, the king enjoyed particular sport with preachers,
and Puritans.

When James was still a young boy, he learned "to trust nobody
entirely, to keep his thoughts deeply and darkly to himself, and to
preserve his skin at all costs and by guile [deception, misdirection],
since God had denied him the physical qualities to outface the savage, unruly men whom he was called upon to govern."[3] If the close
little ruling community begat savage for savage, they could not have
known nor ever imagined the monster they were creating.

Effective rule is all about strategy and tactics, image enhance-
ment, maneuvering, and the mathematics of advantage. Playing
Jacob to someone else's Esau. Friendships are necessary, and at times
the roll and tumble of a few heads. Cash always helps too, but James
never had much of that. Unfortunately, he was not the strategist
Elizabeth was, nor the tactician. But even she was impressed with
him at times. His mask was as convincing as hers ever was, perhaps
more so by the homely creature it did not seem to hide at all. The
best mask is the one that looks the least like a mask.

If his was a forced education, and it was, it was also a thorough
one that quickened those instincts so necessary to govern. Scotland
was ruled by dogs. James was a cat disguised as a dog. Scotland did
this to him.

Being born a king doesn't always guarantee one will have the
capacity or the necessary aptitude to be a king. James had capacity.
His physical weakness was an advantage, because it belied an intellect that was not weak or stricken in the limbs. This will sound like a
contradiction, but beneath his renowned cowardice was a somewhat

courageous mind. James V, in spite of his debaucheries, had the goods to be a fine king. James VI had the proper instincts to rule, and those instincts were set at liberty not only by the severity of his education, but also by the deadly challenges, the Goliaths that stepped in his path. He survived, and that is an accomplishment in itself. Though he abandoned much of what he learned when he put on the English crown, in Scotland he learned when to keep his mouth shut and when to speak. Plus, he understood the value of a good spy or two. His nest buzzed with them.

Even as a child, the notion of divine right, though undeveloped, was firmly planted in his mind. Imperium ruled him. Indeed, the more Buchanan bullied, the more James proved resilient. For all Buchanan's desire to make James into his ideal king, the resistance created an altogether different creature than Buchanan wanted. Buchanan taught him that the people were the center of government. James thought James was the center of everything. It is a forgivable fault. He never had to dream of being the first. He was king before he could walk.

An old young man

M. Fontenay, an envoy from Mary Queen of Scots, was at court on behalf of the Association, an agreement that, if signed, would make Mary and James corulers of Scotland. The king protested that he would support his mother, even on oath. But he did not. He signed nothing, and the Association ultimately failed.

Fontenay's report is clear and brings us close to its object. A sensitive observer with little to gain, he provides testimony as an eyewitness. If Fontenay found James "slippery," he also thought him fascinating, formidable. He considered James "for his years the most remarkable Prince that ever lived." While that may smack a bit of court schmooze, Fontenay was impressed.

Three qualities of the mind he possesses in perfection: he understands clearly, judges wisely, and has a retentive memory. His questions are keen and penetrating and his replies are sound. In any argument, whatever it is about, he maintains the view that appears to him most just, and I have heard him support Catholic against Protestant opinions. He is well instructed in languages, science, affairs of state, better, I dare say, than anyone else in the kingdom. In short, he has a remarkable intelligence, as well as lofty and virtuous ideals and a high opinion of himself.

He dislikes dancing and music, and the little affections of courtly life such as amorous discourse or curiosities of dress, and he has a special aversion for ear-rings. In speaking and eating, in his dress and in his sports, in his conversation in the presence of women, his manners are crude and uncivil and display a lack of proper instruction. He is never still in one place but walks continuously up and down, though his gait is erratic and wandering, and he tramps about even in his own chamber. His voice is loud and his words grave and sententious. He loves the chase above all other pleasures and will hunt for six hours without interruption, galloping over hill and dale with loosened bridle. His body is feeble and yet he is not delicate. In a word, he is an old young man.

I have remarked in him three defects that may prove injurious to his estate and government: he does not estimate correctly his poverty and insignificance but is over-confident of his strength and scornful of other princes; his love for favourites is indiscreet and willful and takes no account of the wishes of his people; he is too lazy and indifferent about affairs, too given to pleasure, allowing all business to be conducted by others. Such things are excusable at his age, yet I fear they may become habitual.[4]

Scotland was a street thing

When James was twelve, the last of the regents, Morton, a strong-handed man, actually ruled Scotland fairly well. He had the backing of Elizabeth, but once his power began to weaken, Morton felt the only way to maintain that power was to have James establish his own rule, sweep the young king up, and rule in his name. That is exactly what he did. On 8 March 1578, James became official ruler of Scotland, his minority conveniently set aside. Morton took control of the king and of Scotland, and ruled in the king's name. James was once again bullied, and powerless as usual, but this condition was about to change.

Morton's coup did not last long at all, power having shifted to yet another party, or "gang,"[5] as William McElwee calls them. Morton eventually gave up his bid and became a gardener at Lochleven.

Rule was always capricious, flirtatious, uncertain. The word itself didn't mean a whole lot. James was a twelve-year-old boy with a name he had yet to grow into, one that everyone wanted a piece of. If it was no small miracle that he grew to be an adult at all, it might be an even greater one that he was sane when he got there.

> By the time James began to rule Scotland as its sole king, he had survived no fewer than nine kidnap attempts.
>
> —JOHN MACLEOD, *DYNASTY: THE STUARTS (1560–1807)*

Somewhere along the way, Morton, having kept his eye on advantage, saw it once again, put down his gardening tools, snatched the young neurotic boy king, and claimed power once again for himself.

By the time James was thirteen, his natural precociousness, and his instinct for duplicity at last began to work in his favor. The gangs slowly lost their original conviction against the ease in which he was once tossed around. Even English money was thrown at the tribal chiefs to keep James unsettled and jarred loose from any solid moorings. Buchanan pocketed a few pounds himself. Peter Young was the only one not taking any money from the English. James was for so long the steel ball being knocked about from one pinball bumper to the next, and yet with none of the usual satisfactions of the game.

Antonia Fraser's image has a little more teeth. She says, "James's actual person never ceased to be the bone over which these aggressive dogs snapped and quarreled, and that in itself must have been a terrifying experience for a timid friendless boy."[6]

He somehow survived. With each skirmish, successful or not, he observed the power of his name, how the light reflected off his crown tended to blind the eyes of its beholders, how thoroughly it affected those around him. He saw how they respected the creature. He was learning how the game was played. To his good fortune, he was underestimated, and often. But he watched and learned beneath all the snapping and plotmaking that threatened his name and person.

Against all his frailty and the classic fearfulness that would escort him into his adult life, unseen to those around him, the boy king was growing a somewhat sturdy backbone, quietly nurturing his own slither and snap in private. He learned to play both cobra and mongoose.

David Willson, in *King James VI and I*, says: "[James] was growing from a child into a youth, prematurely old and sophisticated in certain ways, simple and naïve in others. Baffling contradictions were appearing in his character."

He had learned three things well: "that royalty carried some magical authority within itself; that no man was truly trustworthy; that secrecy and double-dealing were the only means of self-preservation."[7]

A state of ruin

Sir Anthony Weldon said the reason we have so few paintings of King James is that he would not sit still long enough to have them painted.[8]

James was hardly enamored with his own image, either as a child or an adult. He did not preen himself, nor was vanity his master as it had been with Elizabeth. Granted, he had sufficient illusions about who he was, and lived by them attentively. And he was vain, but his vanity was of a different sort than that of the English queen, or his mother. James had no illusions about his looks, nor the odd geometry of his physical body. Adam Nicolson uses the word *hideous* to describe the king's adult face.[9] But even as a child, he was aware of his lack of physical splendor.

Weldon makes a good point, and in spite of the fact that Sir Anthony nursed a personal grudge against the king for his dismissal from the English court, and while we must look on his report with a cautious eye, and while he at times exaggerates the features of the king almost for sport, there is no reason to doubt his assessment on this issue. There is much agreement among other sources, and taken together we may trust the counsel they provide.

Indeed, the adult king's attraction to beautiful young men, at least in part, had everything to do with the way he perceived himself. A crown should have a king beneath it. The "golden round" should add grace upon grace, that is, it should rest upon an Alexander or an Adonis. But there was only James beneath this one. And no one knew this better than James himself.

As a type of compensation for his physical imperfections, he developed and exercised his academic prowess. What he didn't have in beauty, he made up for in brains. He excelled in this pursuit, being driven, as he was, not only by the verbal whip of Buchanan, but by something within himself. Maybe it was the chase, his obsession with the hunt. Any researcher knows the value of the hunt.

Even as a child he could be sententious. But the exercise of intellect was not enough. Intellect is never enough to compensate in matters of the heart.

He had been denied at the most primal levels of human engagement and these particular issues were about to surface and demand a kind of reckoning. Having been force-fed life instead of being allowed to discover it for himself, his cravings were as deep as they were unsatisfied, made more powerful by their very denials.

Antonia Fraser says the young king yearned "to worship something beyond himself, something fairer, more physically perfect"[10] than that which he had been given. William McElwee concurs, saying, "A natural uncouthness of body and speech was to debar him all his life from looking and behaving as he would have wished. It was that, above all, which made him enjoy it so keenly, and even adore it, in others."[11]

A total stranger to love, James had to salvage what he could from the wreckage of a misbegotten childhood. At thirteen, parts of him lay in a state of ruin. If we refer to our college days and consult Abraham Maslow's hierarchy of needs, James would be suspended, or bound, somewhere between the second and third rung, between the safety needs and the belonging (love) needs. In a poem James wrote as a boy, he referred to his first love as a Phoenix, the mythical bird that rises from its own ashes—the dead and impossible thing coming to life.

It is not easy to explore the love life of James Stuart without becoming distracted. Love is slippery enough for any of us, but for the young king it was an apparition. In the bud of life, when his psychology was still soft clay, he had no suitable models, male or female. His parents were mythical creatures bound in shades, or in Buchanan's venom. He never knew them except by slander, by the odd portrait, or by his own detective work.

Everyone who attended the king was appointed. Choice or election had nothing to do with it. Everyone who was bound to the king was bound by duty, by obligation, by oath, by the taint of their own ambitions, and by allegiance to the state. Love, or anything like it was alien, outside of these considerations.

The people of Scotland didn't love him. He was kept at a distance from them. Sure, at his birth, cannons belched from the battlements. Bonfires lit the night sky. Little bursts of promise and hope for a poor beaten country. Celebration, celebration, celebration. The salve of tradition. But when he was crowned thirteen months later, all the celebration had long been silenced, muzzled. Scotland fell back on its old habits. The people had but a vague notion of a minority king, which after the wash of so much history behind them, they understood that to mean there was no real king at all. It was all name, but no substance, no power. Anyway, the nobles and the Kirk dictated what the people were supposed to think.

Scotland suffered chronic identity crisis, a condition that made the nobles rich, made the church both powerful and pontifical, and made the throne just as they wanted it—impotent. A poor country with a poor self-image, run by pack animals.

The nobles didn't love him. To them, he was a title, a name, a toy of strategy, the means to their own advantage. They stood between him and any natural affection he might have nurtured or enjoyed with his own mother. (Or anyone else for that matter.) They demonized her. She was "the whore." She was Knox's Jezebel. The bedeviled witch.

The Kirk didn't love him. The Christ in their midst was a cold one, more wall than door, a lot of heat but no real warmth. They chose only to bully him into submission, and the worst of all possible evils would be for him to become Catholic like his diabolical mother.

His governess, the Countess of Mar, didn't love him. She feared him. She became stern in her awe of him, and served the state with her severity. She was assigned to him, to "the Lord's Anointed." That was all.

Though the young king engaged in activities with his boyhood friends, he was not their physical equal. *And* he was always the king. Made of glass and passion, privilege and distance. He was *other* than them, separated by name and altitude. He could flare up in a tempest and they would have no choice but to take it. They did not know to love him.

And there was always the threat of abduction around him, which did not help.

Elizabeth pretended to love him, though she played the same game of carrot and stick, anticipation and grab. It was to her benefit as well to keep mother and son separated. As an older King of Scots, Elizabeth gave him a yearly stipend, a promised income of about four thousand pounds, of which she might give three, or two, and the occasional five. James, always broke, like her spaniel, was easily maneuvered by this English Pavlov.

Buchanan didn't love him. Buchanan was Buchanan. Hardened, rimed with age and irritability. The stubble on his chin was like little pricks of iron. The greymetal stuff of his own heart. There might have been some solace, some friendly hope in the warmer, truer, kinder Peter Young.

> He [James] was never really given the chance to love anybody better than himself.
>
> —WILLIAM MCELWEE, *THE WISEST FOOL IN CHRISTENDOM*

Then, in the midst of all this political plate shifting, came the unexpected. The king gave his heart away. It was not property of the state after all. It was his own to do with as he pleased. Love was a thing he had little experience with, and the first steps it took were awkward, like the trouble in his own limbs. Love, and anything like love, had always been kept from him purposely, selfishly, brutally. Yet, like the new worlds being discovered, he had boundless capacity both for conquest and for love.

CHAPTER SEVEN

Speak of Me As I Am

Speak of me as I am; nothing extenuate
Nor set down aught in malice: then must you speak
Of one that loved not wisely but too well.

—WILLIAM SHAKESPEARE, *Othello*, V, ii, 342–344.

TO SOME, HE was the Devil incarnate sent to pollute the mind, body, and soul of the impressionable young king. To some, he was the path to favor. To an optimistic few, he was a means to regain a popish Scotland. Elizabeth was wary. She feared the rise of the old alliance between Scotland and France (Auld Alliance). To most, he became a riddle, or at best, a reason for caution. To only one person was he redemption itself, a savior, a long-awaited oasis.

Esme Stuart, Sieur d'Aubigny, was the nephew of the king's paternal grandfather, the regent, Lennox. The Lennox Stuarts had stakes in both Scotland and France. After Darnley's death, Esme was the next male in the Stuart line.

Having never left France in his life, he may have had reasons to come to Scotland other than by invitation of the king. Mary was always busy trying to reassume her throne. She looked to Esme as a possible agent. Maybe he could entice the king away from Scotland, draw him out, and make it easier for her to reinstate herself. For this purpose, Esme was given "fourtie thowsand peeces of gold, in crowns, pistolets [coins] and angels,"[1] and was advised to spend it as he thought best at the Scottish court. Leaving a wife and five kids behind, Esme arrived in Scotland in September 1579.

James was thirteen.

Not even the unsuspecting Esme could have imagined the reception waiting on him, or what fortunes his presence would unlock. No one else could either. Morton, having moved James in the foreground as he had, was taken off guard by the events that followed the arrival of the king's French cousin. He also had no choice but to take it, to submit to the moment against which he was powerless.

All their lives were about to change in another shuffle of uncertain destinies. And the attraction, the sudden flood of powerful emotion in the young king was immediate. "Into the dour surroundings of the young king he [d'Aubigny] brought color, amusement, gaiety, the grace and lightness of France, as well as a knowledge of life . . . Above all, he brought love."[2]

Within a couple of weeks of his cousin's arrival, James made a formal entry into Edinburgh with d'Aubigny by his side. The multiple names can be confusing. He is *Esme Stuart*. He is also *d'Aubigny*. In a paragraph or two from now he will be the *Earl of Lennox*, or simply *Lennox*.

Esme could only speak French and as if listening to music, the king listened with awe and wonder to everything Esme had to say about the French court. "The boy continually hung upon his arm or leant on his shoulder, fiddled with his rich clothes and jewels."[3]

James enjoyed being taken seriously for a change. He enjoyed, maybe for the first time, being treated like a real king, and being encouraged to act and carry himself as a king. But more than that, the Gallic touches of Esme's speech penetrated the dense mantle of state and came over the heart of the young sovereign with sudden conquest. The awakening attributed to Esme Stuart was far reaching and with a tone of completeness.

William McElwee says that James "loved him [Esme] with a passion and abandon scarcely normal in a boy." An indicator of how complete his early isolation and emotional abandonment had been. McElwee also uses the phrase "hero worship," to define the king's attachment—"[James] fell upon d'Aubigny in a passion of hero worship which transformed his entire life."[4] Antonia Fraser puts it a bit stronger than that:

> There was no question that the touchingly love-deprived adolescent boy did fall violently in love with his elegant and attainable older cousin . . . in essence it was a romantic passion . . .
>
> James grew up with a passionate desire to love and to be loved in the romantic sense, to worship something beyond himself, something fairer, more physically perfect than the stunted progidy's body with which he had been endowed. It is this quality for which James has been harshly judged, for the simple reason that the first love object which came his way was a man. But one can advance the opinion that had an equally attractive woman come his way at the same propitious moment, the homosexual inclinations of King James might never have been aroused.[5]

A barren place

The arrival of Esme Stuart in the young king's life indeed set something loose within the boy, and by a passion stronger than his ability to control or silence it—an honest endowment from mom and dad. For, like the ill-fated Queen of Scots, James was incapable of exercising discretion in matters of the heart. There had been so little movement there. The heart of the boy king was a barren place. He was "in such love with him [Esme] as in the open sight of the people oftentimes he will clasp him about the neck with his arms and kiss him."[6]

James loved d'Aubigny with all the pent up emotion that had never had an object. And he loved demandingly. He expected d'Aubigny to supply everything that he had always lacked and everything that he was now beginning to need: to be the family, his beloved, his friend, his mentor and counselor, and his constant companion.[7]

Esme Stuart was in his midthirties. He was tall and had a red beard. He was well shaped, effecting a noticeable contrast against the king's adolescent and somewhat irregular body. Adonis and, well, James. The stuttering unwashed boy king with ragged clothes (for it was his habit to wear out a garment) and the man of fashion, a "man of wax."

Esme had high cheekbones and a fine straight nose. He was an attractive man, most particularly to James who thought him beautiful. His kind was alien to the Scottish court, or had been since the absence of Mary. He had a "lightness of touch" and a "glamour" similar to that which Mary Queen of Scots brought back from France.

D'Aubigny and his coterie of twenty men brought with them the elegance of the French court. They also brought some not-so-elegant things as well, equally as French, bound with the giddy and irresistible presence of taboo. There was no debauchery like privileged debauchery. Defilement at this altitude of society was an art form in itself.

We can assume the king's body and mind were undergoing the

usual storm of change they must in preparation for adulthood, the restless *sturm und drang*.[8] One contemporary chronicler wrote, "His Majesty, having conceived an inward affection to the Lord d'Aubigny, entered in great familiarity and quiet purposes with him."[9] The writer was disguising his meaning behind gentle speech, but the allusion would not be lost on the sixteenth-century Scot. The Kirk, kicking at the goads, disguised nothing, and said clearly "that the Duke of Lennox went about to draw the King to carnal lust."[10]

This commentary must be weighed against the Kirk's resentment toward d'Aubigny.

To the ministers, Lennox was the source and nurture of the king's moral decline, which, by the sound of it, gave them the appearance of caring fathers. This was never the case. The Kirk cared only for the king as the nobles did, that is, how he figured into the maintaining of their own power. D'Aubigny was a threat to their power. Simple. He was also the alarm to wake that neglected thing within the young monarch the Kirk neither expected nor wanted. And not just love, but something much worse—sovereignty.

Majestie, as much as it may have wanted to exert itself, never had the proper vent. It wasn't asleep so much as it was bound with irons. Majestie in the young king, as eager as it was for expression, was image only—name, but no vitality.

D'Aubigny helped throw off the restraints. He encouraged James in the notion of divine right, and of the absolutism due his station, that of anointed sovereignty, which was to help shape his politics of rule. He showed the young king just how much sparkle his crown possessed. Not that d'Aubigny put the notion in the king's head. Divine right, and absolutism, had its origins deep in the royal idiom, from the first crown, or the first monarch to bound out of the ooze. But with d'Aubigny's support, the king was allowed to indulge it for the first time. And the taste was pleasant, life-altering, and it was associated forever with a passion now alive in him.

We might say that love and majestie rose together from their slumbers.

James no longer tolerated hearing himself the topic of scorn, or taking reproof from the pulpits. For a season, James no longer had sermons preached during meals. It was difficult for the Kirk or the nobles not to see the first signs of a backbone in the boy.

Esme Stuart's presence aroused more than just the ignored or waking passions of an awkward prepubescent male. One of the more remarkable things that d'Aubigny brought to Scotland was a genius for intrigue and deception. His "lightness of touch" was a token of an inward subtlety, one that a young brilliant king like James was not likely to miss.

He had come, or so it was thought, as an agent for the French Guises,* and to possibly win the impressionable king over to Roman Catholicism. But if things were not already strange, and though his presence caused an uneasy shifting about by the nobles and the Kirk, not long after his arrival d'Aubigny did something none of them expected. He converted to Protestantism, and at the leading of the young king. This sudden turn had the Guises, Scotland, and Elizabeth's England scratching their heads.

What was he up to?

James never asked such a question. His was the joy of triumph, of leading his wayward cousin/mentor in the path of his own belief. He was thrilled at the submission it asked of Esme, a submission that became mutual between the two of them. Responding to the king's persuasive reasoning, Esme would even argue a point here and there, ask questions. We do not have to assume the sincerity of his conversion. It never really came to test, and history says nothing further

---

*Marie of Guise was James's maternal grandmother. She attempted to rule Scotland as regent in Mary's absence, but Scotland was hostile to her. The Guises were a powerful ruling family in France at that time.

about it. But he knew it would please the king, and that is what seemed to matter. It was a large boon for the powerless boy. The taste of influence, of leading.

Twenty-four years older, d'Aubigny had an honest love for James, in spite of the ease by which some of his darker political intentions were addressed.

That false Scotch urchin!

D'Aubigny's presence, as suggested above, initiated phase two of an already intense education. The lessons the king learned from him were more pleasantly absorbed, and his attention was acute. One of the things attributed to Esme Stuart was the crude language James began to use as a boy. D'Aubigny was the catalyst, the spark that ignited the king's humor—the naughty and foul.

James acquired a taste for bawdy humor, for innuendo. Though he condemned swearing, the text began to filter into his speech with alarming regularity. Even when he spoke of God he would add a foul word or two at times. Some were shocked. Others hardly noticed. By the king's way of thinking, he had developed such a longstanding relationship with God, he protested that he was "over-homely with the Deity."[11] That is, he and God had somewhat of an understanding.

James was untroubled by conscience where his speech was concerned. The age he lived in and the country he kinged needed a sense of humor, whatever shade it might be. He was once reprimanded by the Kirk, admonished to "forbear his often swearing and taking the name of God in vain." James replied with a reserved and simple, "I thank you," and altered nothing.

> James achieved a florescence of obscenity that contrasted painfully with his interest in holy things.
> —DAVID WILLSON, *KING JAMES VI & I*

It is just another in the long list of contradictions in the life of King James, that if he could recite Scripture to the spellbound, if he could quote entire chapters of the Bible, and he did, he could speak trash with the best of them as well. John Macleod says, "James's language was dreadful. It abounded in blasphemy, sex jokes, and toilet humor."[12] After Esme's departure, the king's continued use of foul language might have been a subtle way to keep some piece of him alive.

❦

Almost immediately, and by an exaggerated, if not distorted generosity, James gave Esme the beautiful twelfth-century Abbey of Arbroath. In 1580, James pressured the current Earl of Lennox, Robert Stuart, to resign. He then gave the title to d'Aubigny. Not long after that, he created him Duke of Lennox, the first and only duke in Scotland. This was an unprecedented acceleration. James admitted Esme to the Privy Council, and "placed in his hands the custody of Dunbarton Castle, the key to western Scotland."[13]

Of course, d'Aubigny's ascension, as fast and as high as it was, caused concern among the ruling packs standing at a somewhat lower step. He had significant presence in government, that is, he had "control over the King's household and the King's ear."

D'Aubigny had seized power effortlessly, and without a single kidnapping. The problem was, and he wasn't shortsighted enough not to see it, d'Aubigny was making enemies as quickly as he was accelerating through and above the ranks.

D'Aubigny (now Lennox), with the hardline, lusty but faithful-to-the-Crown Captain James Stewart, a distant cousin of the king, engineered the irrevocable fall of the regent, Morton. "The Captain [James Stewart], who 'thought no man his equal, was splendidly handsome, with a kind of coarse magnificence about him."[14] Captain

Jamy is both Scotty and Captain Kirk (the starship commander, not an officer of the Presbyterian church). Lennox thought him useful, so he singled him out.

Morton was savvy and strong, and in Esme's thinking, could and probably would foil his good fortunes. The action was deliberate and merciless. He even gave the king a part in the little drama. James went hunting with Morton, and treated him with respect and courtesy. When they returned that evening, the king said to the unsuspecting man, "Father, only you have reared me, and I will therefore defend you from your enemies."[15]

At the Privy Council Meeting the following day, Captain Stewart burst into the room, fell to his knees before the king, pointed at Morton and accused him of conspiring in the death of the king's father, Lord Darnley. Morton and Stewart threatened to break into a swordfight then and there, but were restrained.

The king offered no defense for Morton whatsoever. Lennox stood by and appeared perplexed. Morton was arrested and imprisoned.

Elizabeth tried to intervene on Morton's behalf to no avail. The momentum against him was swift and determined. Morton was sentenced to be hanged, drawn and quartered, but James commuted the sentence to a beheading. The regent was beheaded in Edinburgh on a prototype of a device he had invented the year James was crowned king, a kind of guillotine Morton called *the Maiden*.

Morton's head was "set upon a prick, on the highest stone of the gavel of the Tolbuith [gaol], toward the publict street."[16]

But there were complications for the young king. Morton's was the first death James was responsible for, and not by an application of royal justice but by betrayal, by his own duplicity, and in the power of his own name. The day after the execution, a letter from Morton was brought to the king. He refused to look at it. He then "ranged up and down the floor of his chamber, clanking with his finger and his thumb."[17]

Shortly after Morton's death, Captain James Stewart was created the Earl of Arran. Now power rested with Lennox (Esme), Arran (Stewart), and of course, their badge of conquest, King James. At the news of Morton's death, Elizabeth raged, and called the king names: "That false Scotch urchin! What can be expected of the double dealing of such an urchin as this!" James, even then, probably took it as a compliment.

Gifted as she was, and having an eye for talent, she probably was impressed with the young upstart. Of course, she would have kept this to herself. And James, being the good student of Tacitus, was simply following what became a favorite motto, *Qui nescit dissimular nescit regnare.* (He who knows not how to dissemble,* knows not how to rule.)

With the talented and ruthless Morton out of the way, the last of the regents and the last to rule, d'Aubigny was doubtless the most powerful man in the kingdom. And the lords would have none of it. Murmuring abounded. Plotmaking. Slithering.

It is interesting that no one thought about it before, for who would have guessed that the key to a young king's heart, and therefore the key to power itself, would be something as simple as love?

Better that bairns should weep

The Kirk, not necessarily mourning the loss of Morton, but bristling nonetheless at the effrontery, at such open challenge to their power, and at the presence of such a disquieting influence on the once controllable king, made some daring moves in retaliation. Under d'Aubigny's influence, the king had appointed Robert Montgomery, a minister at Stirling, as bishop of Glasgow. The details of Montgomery, his affiliations, origins, are unimportant, but it was no small appointment

---

*To *dissemble* means to conceal one's true motives, feelings, or beliefs.

nonetheless, and this little move put the revenues of the See in d'Aubigny's pocket.

This was, of course, unacceptable to the Presbyterian General Assembly, and particularly to their chieftain Andrew Melville. Lennox (d'Aubigny) and the Kirk began to play cobra and mongoose with each other, the balance of which was tipped in favor of the Frenchman. They threatened to excommunicate Montgomery, at which the king said, "We will not suffer you."[18] To this, one of the Presbyterian ministers returned, "We must obey God rather than men, and we pray God to remove evil company from about you. The welfare of the Kirk is your welfare; the more sharply vice is rebuked the better for you."[19] James, angry and spitting fire, was almost in tears.

Even the brilliant but sour Buchanan was in on the fun. In a letter to James, he said: "I am forced to be somewhat jealous of you [protective or vigilant of], lest bad company, the fawning foster-mother of all vices, draw aside your soft and tender mind into the worst part . . ."[20]

The only logical thing to do? What they have always done: kidnap the king, eliminate the favorite, tip the balance once again. On 22 August 1582, that is exactly what they did. Ruthven, a name we have already heard, is in play once again. The old man, Patrick (1520–1566), who conspired with Darnley in the murder of the musician, died just before James was born. The present head of the house of Ruthven, his son, William, the Earl of Gowrie, was chosen as leader of this new conspiracy.

Reluctant at first to involve himself in an intrigue against the Crown, Gowrie was told all kinds of things, fabricated things, half-truths, anything to convince him to change his mind: one, that he, too, was going to be tried for the murder of the musician, the long-dead Rizzio. That didn't move him. Then he was told that he was the target of an assassination by Lennox.[21] He took the job. The company of conspirators called themselves the Lords Enterprisers. Having a name seemed to add weight to a cause, give its players legitimacy.

McElwee suggests that Lennox (d'Aubigny) underestimated the strength and resolve of the nobles, and therefore "let go of the only card in his hand—his actual possession of the person of the king."[22] If Lennox was sleeping, the nobles were not. The pack was lying in wait, quiet and unnoticed. James, too, in the overconfidence of youth, and testing the mettle of his kingship after the triumph with Lennox, let his guard down.

The king was hunting with Gowrie in a beautiful elevated range in Scotland called Atholl. Gowrie invited James to lodge with him. The king had planned to return to Perth in expectation of Lennox, but Gowrie and those with him insisted that the king accept their hospitality. The king accepted. Gowrie and the Earl of Mar then began to make complaints to the king, and their speech had the faint but familiar presence of the bully again. It was an old and bitter music. James tried to ignore them. He spent an uneasy night in the castle.

The next morning, the old panic began to quicken in him once again, and James attempted to leave the premises. As he did, the Master of Glamis (pronounced *gloms*) "laid his leg across the door" and, with the same bully in his voice, ordered the young king to stay where he was. Realizing his predicament, all the demeanor of a king and all the late sense of power drained from him, he began to cry. Once again he was alone. Frightened, friendless, and alone.

All Glamis could say was, "It is no matter of his tears. Better that bairns [children] should weep than bearded men." It was said these words "entered so deeply into the King's heart, as he did never forget them."[23]

The Lords Enterprisers pulled it off. It was called "the Raid of Ruthven." History loves to name things, and often gives elevation to events or factions that really deserve none. It didn't matter what they called it, James was now prisoner to Gowrie, Glamis, and the nobles. Power shifted once again, making a ripple that was hardly noticed it was so common.

It didn't take the king long to understand what was to happen to his beloved Esme. Lennox could be dealt with without interference. Like his mother, sorrow mingled with rage, and he, too, like the vengeful queen, vowed justice upon the house of Ruthven, a justice that would indeed be satisfied in time.

His captivity to the Ruthvens was a great humiliation. Even at his age, it was his belief that as God's lieutenant on earth, his subjects should fear and obey him. There was nothing of the kind in their thoughts. Andrew Melville observed, "His Majesty took the matter further to heart than any man would have believed, lamenting his hard estate and mishandling by his own subjects, and how he was thought but a beast by other princes for suffering so many indignities."[24]

To "kidnap" the king was not unlike incarcerating the Queen of Scots. And not to soften the severity of it—for it was always achieved by conspiracy, force, and disregard—but to say James was kidnapped, needs a bit of explaining.

To the kidnappers, it was not rebellion. In the eyes of the law it was, but they *were* the law, and the letter itself was flexible. In their mind, the action against the king was something less criminal than all that. To borrow a modern word, it was no more than a *takeover*, an adjustment of power, but not necessarily criminal.

Kidnapping had even gained a kind of legitimacy over the years. It had become one way of claiming power, of one group achieving preeminence at the exclusion of other groups. The king himself was immaterial. He was merely the image and validation of power. And if this is not strange enough, there had to be at least some level of agreement or acceptance by the king himself. In other words, an illusion was created, one of cooperation. "Unless he lent them something of his authority they could make no use of it; and to get it they had perforce to allow him [the king] some liberty of action."[25] This is where they play Gepetto to his Pinocchio, the high-strung wooden boy. He would basically write and say what he was told to write and say, what image to present.

We still use the word *kidnap* because in spite of what spin the nobles gave it, or the validation of old custom, it *was* a criminal act, treasonable, a violent act against the Crown, and a traumatic one to the boy king. But this was how government was conducted in Scotland.

To the church, this setting aside of the king was cause for celebration. The great despair that fell upon the boy cannot be underestimated. It left a murky imprint, stains of thought and belief he would not easily rid himself of.

A dangerous form of blindness

The three-year Eden that James enjoyed with Esme Stuart was over. To the king it was more about the love than it was the political posturing. Love had become the sovereign over the sovereign, the captain's captain. And now that it was awakened in him, it would not be easily put back to sleep again, tamed, or hushed. More quick than dead, his bond with Esme Stuart and the desperate love it aroused left an imprint. There were two more favorites yet in his future. All three rose swiftly and to a great height. And all three had a steep and tragic fall.

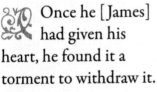

> Once he [James] had given his heart, he found it a torment to withdraw it.
>
> —G. P. V. AKRIGG,
> *INTRODUCTION TO LETTERS OF KING JAMES VI & I*

After his expulsion, d'Aubigny had no friends. He made some attempts at reclaiming his prize—that is, the king—but it went nowhere. Finishing this part of our tale, Arran, the only arm of strength the king had, attempted to save James from his captors, but he was caught and imprisoned. The nobles and the Kirk did a complete work. They knew their job, and executed it well. It was in such treacheries that the factions actually worked well together, in a kind of necessary union. The snarl and the showing of teeth of their usual exchange receded for a common good.

The king was in their power. And as they had always done, they took full advantage for whatever time they could keep it.

At the insistence from those around him, James reluctantly sent Esme a letter demanding that he leave Scotland. D'Aubigny then sent James a letter saying, "I desire rather to die than to live, fearing that in your disdain you have found a cause for loving me no more."[26] Any communication could be dangerous, and the king was watched continuously. One of the gentlemen of the King's Bedchamber, Henry Gibbe, was forced to deliver a letter from d'Aubigny in the "close stool," as it was called.

D'Aubigny had no choice but to return to France. Plans might have been made for some triumphant return to Scotland, a regaining of Paradise, but like a repeat of the abortive childhood experience with his mother, James never saw Esme Stuart again. James Melville wrote in his diary, "Thus were the King and the Duke dissevered, and never saw [each] uther again."[27]

When Lennox (Esme) returned home, France gave the Protestant turncoat a cold reception. He was determined to return, to regain the former glory of his Scottish life, to regain the king, but there was no more time. Esme Stuart was assassinated in May 1583, not long after his return to the continent.

It has been much debated about Esme Stuart's effect on James. As might be expected, the Kirk chieftain Andrew Melville spoke darkly of the relationship, saying that Esme bewitched the vulnerable king, keeping him "in a mistie night of captivity and blak darknes of schamful servitude."[29] A kind of lofty way to suggest a seriously bad influence. To the "mistie night" Caroline Bingham adds that the "King's love for d'Aubigny was a particularly dangerous form of blindness."[30]

> Whatever might happen to me, I shall always be your very faithful servant . . . in spite of all you will always be my true master, and he alone in this world whom my heart is resolved to serve. And would to God that my breast might be split open so that it might be seen what is engraven therein.[28]
>
> —LETTER FROM ESME STUART TO KING JAMES VI, 1582

Time would prove to be the only friend the young king really had. James, after all, had a larger name, a larger title than any of them. In all the scheming, all their arrangements and rearrangements, there was little they could do about that, in spite of their efforts. All James had to do was wait. He had little choice.

His intelligence was also his friend. He was "intellectually mature" at sixteen.

He had been fed the alienation and hardship necessary for the education of a king, as some might say. He was taught the limits of engagement, that detachment so necessary for effective rule. Some of these lessons actually took. And he did have a bit of spine after all, even a bit of a stomach.

Little could they have known it or wished it, but he learned well, and instead of becoming the spaniel (the obedient young dog) of the ruling packs, at seventeen James assumed headship of Scotland and in his own power. Against all the chafe and bristle of the nobles and the Kirk, and perhaps because of them, he learned efficient kingcraft. And much better than they had hoped.

In their design, he would have been a beaten, intimidated king with a broken spirit, a name with no soul, another Edward II of England, or Richard II, who lost his throne for a few bad decisions and some bad company. But James proved to have more mettle than they had suspected of him, having learned the lessons they taught him so well.

For all his foibles, for all the distractions and illusions that got in his way, including the ones he cherished, he was actually good at being a king. Well, like our word *kidnap*, *good* is a flexible word. It will need to stretch for us a bit, but he turned out to be a surprisingly good king.

Because he had once promised it, because he perhaps felt it was the property of the king's all along, a part of Esme Stuart was sent back to Scotland as a gift to the king. His embalmed heart.

CHAPTER EIGHT

You Don't Know Jack

Traine vp a childe in the way he should goe: and when he is
olde, hee will not depart from it.

—PROVERBS 22:6, KING JAMES BIBLE, 1611

INDIFFERENT MAY BE the best word to describe how James felt
about his mother. The years and the distance had done their work.
Fontenay, Mary's envoy to James, said, "At one thing I am astonished.
He has never inquired anything of the Queen of her health, or her
treatment, her servants, her living, and eating, her recreation, or anything similar, and nevertheless I know that he loves and honours her
very much in his heart."[1] Of the love he spoke of, Fontenay is being
optimistic, leaning toward natural affection, something James had
little experience with.

Fontenay was afraid for Mary, and with good cause.

Mary, still under guard in England, had a significant number of
followers, and made noise as often as she could. She never gave up
hope that she might rule again. She refused to call James by any other

title than "Prince." Mary never quite saw the reality for what it was. This perceptual problem was, unfortunately, one of the few things mother and son had in common.

In a letter James wrote to his mother (in cipher) dated July 1584, he assured her of his faithfulness concerning the Association, "which without fail I shall pass."[2] Later, when he denied ever promising such a thing to her, the Queen of Scots was beside herself with rage. She "threatened him with a mother's malediction, declaring she would disinherit him as an unnatural and perfidious son."[3]

After this, he never wrote her again. This is about the same time Elizabeth started talking to James about giving him a yearly stipend of £4,000.

In the same letter above, he told Mary he would "require of the Queen of England your deliverance, for which I wish above all the happiness of this world." James was never convinced, and neither is history, of her sincerity toward him. Mary thought only of her-

Perfidious means "guilty of breaking faith or violating confidence; deliberately faithless; treacherous."

—OXFORD ENGLISH DICTIONARY

self, and of her lost crown. James thought only of himself, and how to keep his crown. If they were alike, and they were, the repulsion is an honest one. By 1584, there was a new king in town, that is, James himself.

God's silly vassal

It was called the *Sovereignty Act of 1584*, a timely little piece of legislation handed down by a king growing more and more into his power. The Sovereignty Act was "Ane act confirming the kingis maiesties Royall power over all statis and subiectis within this Realme."[4]

Parliament declared James head of the Church of Scotland. He and his Privy Council were given jurisdiction over ecclesiastical cases.

The courts and assemblies of the Kirk were dissolved and could not reconvene without royal sanction. And of course, the institution of bishops was confirmed. At seventeen, he was ready to rule. He had had enough, and being raised by vipers gives one an edge. It allows one to think and move very viperlike.

Affairs of state and taunts at the king himself would no longer be tolerated in the pulpits. Of course the Kirk accepted these alterations in government as they had always accepted them, with chagrin, and with a look to the future for the rebound. If history had taught them anything, the balance was always failing. Scotland was a tottering state.

The audacity of this king, the Kirk thought to itself, *to act in his own power.*

And the Kirk pounded its hammer all it could. The little emperor, Knox, was dead, and though he was no longer ranting *Jezebels*, his words had a long and uncompromising echo nonetheless. His voice seemed even stronger from the grave. He had maintained and impressed upon the Kirk and upon all the Lords of the Congregation that the law of God should rule the state, and that a divine rule hardly needed validation or confirmation from a king, or even worse, a queen. Not only that, but monarchs who resisted such rule should be brushed aside. His policy was curiously Roman.

Andrew Melville, one of the chieftains of the Kirk during the reign of James, shaped the theocracy of Knox into a doctrine of two kingdoms, that is, estates *spiritual* and *temporal*. The following was an *in your face* kind of confrontation with the king at Falkland Palace some years later (1596). Melville "wrenched his sovereign's sleeve"[5] and said:

> Sirrah, ye are God's silly vassal; there are two kings and two kingdoms in Scotland: there is king James, the head of the commonwealth; and there is Christ Jesus, the king

of the Church, whose subject James the Sixth is, and of
whose kingdom he is not a king, not a lord, not a head,
but a member.[6]

Melville let the king know that while publicly they would be
compliant, in their hearts they looked only to Christ as king in
Scotland. The Acts of Sovereignty was obviously a source of vexation to the estates spiritual. Melville had the words, the stateliness,
the respect; he just didn't have the power. He may have had a crown
waiting on him in heaven, but there was only one on earth, and it
was the property of the young king.

The Kirk referred to these acts as the "black acts." Many ministers took flight to England, and quickly. This flight concerned James.
He was still young enough to feel the sting of their backbiting, and
the gnashing of their teeth. They had been nipping at him all his life.
And a novice king makes an easy target for slander. It was not difficult to find something offensive to say.

The king's legitimacy was a particular sore spot. The claim was
made, not loudly but widely, that he was the child of the musician, of
the dead Rizzio, and not Darnley's issue at all. This particular slander
cut him deeper than most, and actually made him weep. Anyone
caught saying such a thing was imprisoned. Later, when he was king
of England, it came up again. Because he saw himself as the new
Solomon, some said he was like Solomon indeed, "the son of David."
(That is, David Rizzio, mum's French musician.)

❦

Elizabeth wasn't sure just what to do with this upstart, so she sent
Walsingham. Sir Francis was not impressed. He thought the young
king deceitful, a dissembling peacock with bent feathers and stains on
his doublet. He wrote Elizabeth suggesting that she let the "ingrate

king, this dissembler with God and man, to run his short course to ruin."[7]

There had been so much vacillation, so much bounce, the only certainty was in the mind and resolve of James himself. His title had not changed. His belief in his divine right, in the creature itself, far from losing its fervor, settled deeper and deeper in his conscience. He had learned how immovable and resilient it was. The alliances, however, seen and unseen, had no such stability. Keeping an eye on the king, they had to watch each other as well. Treachery often didn't care in which direction it pointed; it was so much the habit.

> Look not to find the softness of a down pillow in a crown, but remember that it is a thorny piece of stuff and full of continual cares.
>
> —JAMES I OF ENGLAND, *MEDITATIONS OF MATTHEW 27*

Scotland was a street thing.

According to the young king's vision, government and church were harmoniously joined, and in himself. This was the monarch's birthright. The share of divinity he was given at birth was for this very reason, to unite all the warring tribes, spiritual and temporal, into one person. It was a theme he would not depart from. All the schism within his own psychology worked within him and by such a powerful algorithm that union became the driving force in his theory of government.

It was still a play, with acts and scenes, and he executed it convincingly. In spite of the acts, the Kirk thought he was tame, obeisant, maybe even beaten. They let him go hunting without the usual guard. The king was given unexpected levity. The Kirk was certain that their Presbyterianism was safe. "Shrewdly" he stood on Melville's doctrine of two kingdoms, and all to the shock and delight of the Kirk. He actually denied any intentions of making himself the head of the Kirk or even interfering in their affairs. But he insisted that the clergy not intrude with affairs of state, especially with treasonous or seditious sermons. He defended the presence of bishops, which were validated both by the Scriptures and by the early church. He asserted his right to summon or refuse to summon the General Assembly of the Kirk.

This censure of the pulpits was no small matter. If there was ever an agenda to push, there was no more powerful voice than the preacher's. The people could be "tuned" by a savvy pulpiteer. Knox, in his time, and even when he could hardly get to the pulpit without aid, would rattle kingdoms down. Because of this tampering by the king, the clergy heated up. One preacher, James Gibson, claimed it was James all along who was the persecutor of the church. Here is how the dialogue went.

JAMES. What? Call ye me a persecutor?
GIBSON. Yes, sir. So long as ye maintain the wicked Acts against God and the liberty of His Kirk, ye are a persecutor. Whosoever will intrude any tyranny upon the Kirk and maintain the same against the Word of God is a persecutor.
JAMES. What is it that I maintain against the Word of God?
GIBSON. The tyranny of bishops and absolute power.

Gibson went on to say that he had preached before James in the past and was not reproved. To this, the mature king, not the boy, replied, "I give not a turd for thy preaching."[8]

Again, was it crude? Yes. Was it James? Every inch. Gibson was sent to prison.

The issue was that of bishops or no bishops. It was either episcopacy or Presbyterianism. After all the smoke cleared, a compromise was reached. The bishops remained. James had his way. Not fully, but sufficiently. He was eighteen at the time.

This was no longer the boy they could toss about. He had grown heavy in their hands. Their duplicity, all the old tricks and deceit were now recoiling back upon them in the person of the king. His power was not yet fully realized, because power was hardly ever allowed to be fully realized in Scotland. It had always remained inchoate, nascent. Scotland resisted bridle.

His headship was never quite absolute. He was more the first chair, the "first among equals." But it hardly mattered. The back of the Kirk/noble alliance was soon broken. They could still make noise, but at eighteen years old, James learned to think like them, and therefore ahead of them, and that made all the difference.

That troubling question of Mary was about to be settled. The question of James's succession to the English throne was about to be settled as well. We will go over the main details, keeping an eye not so much on the mother, but the son. I have had to be cautious around Mary myself. She has a way of stealing the show.

Big wheels keep on turnin'

As flawed as she was, as capricious, as passionate, as unconquered and untamed, Mary Queen of Scots was *inevitable*. That simply means she was bound to live a large, conspicuous life. Such lives are not often extinguished without a great deal of noise and hers had a large, conspicuous end. Indeed, it was as loud and as boisterous as Elizabeth's was compact and silent. Elizabeth went peacefully in the night. No sound, no struggle. The theaters were closed, inappropriate as playgoing was "in the dying time."[9] London was hush with anticipation.

Mary did not go peacefully in the night. *En ma fin est mon commencement.* (In my end is my beginning.)[10] She embroidered this on the cloth of state. The phrase referred to the martyrdom she began to imagine and cherish in her thoughts. It was strongest among her illusions.

Mary is the mythic Helen of the Spanish Armada. It was hardly a thousand ships her face had launched, but it was sufficient. It wasn't beauty or love that set them off, but the aggression of a Catholic Spain against England was ignited by her death.

For Elizabeth, Mary just wouldn't go away. It was expedient to keep her penned.

One conspiracy led to another. The chopping blocks were always warm with the blood of traitors. Often they were guilty. It was a steady business. Mary was the center of many such plots over the years, and it is no surprise that at least one of them would end her life.

The Queen of Scots was, at last, implicated by her own handwriting in a plot that would have placed her on the English throne, and taken the life of Elizabeth. It was an old tale by then. But thanks to the Machiavellian talents of Francis Walsingham and William Cecil, the plot was not only found out, the two servants of Elizabeth suspended action long enough to let Mary incriminate herself through her own letters to the conspirators. Actually, the Babington Plot, as it was called, was the third of three such plots Mary was involved in.

No longer of any use to anyone in this world

Even Mary knew her "trial" to be a show only. It is the downside of knowing what only monarchs know. It is all theater. It is dangerous, the threats are real, and players lose their titles or their heads, but it is theater nonetheless. She knew she was doomed.

Shuffled about from one castle hold to the next in her eighteen-year confinement, Mary was under the "care" of the elderly Sir Ralph Sadler. While he was not gentle, Sir Ralph was older and not unkind. She was allowed her attendants, and all the usual perks of a royal inmate. In time, Sadler was replaced by a Walsingham appointee, Sir Amias Paulet. Paulet was every bit as harsh as Sadler had been pliant.

Mary said of Paulet that he was "one of the strangest and farouche [fiercest] men she had ever known."[11]

Like Walsingham, Paulet was Puritan. I might add "staunch," but that would be redundant. The word *Puritan* implied staunch. The Puritan was the religious extremist of their day. But Paulet had one quality that set him apart from the rest of the candidates for this important but delicate position, one that Sir Francis admired more than any other. It's an old song by now, but like Buchanan and a host of others, Paulet hated the Queen of Scots and everything about her.

> Thou art slave to
> Fate, Chance, kings,
> and desperate men.
>
> —JOHN DONNE, "HOLY SONNET X"

His first act was to remove the emblem of her station, the royal cloth of state. It was one of the few evidences she had left that told her she was a queen. Being a prisoner of England, Sir Amias said, it should never have been allowed in the first place.

Her confinement became increasingly arduous, constrictive. She was not even allowed to walk about in the fresh air. No exercise, nothing. She was to receive no correspondence, and her personal items were searched carefully and often. Walsingham may have thought to force some movement on her part, to aggravate some conspiracy. The world was watching.

Even her laundry was halted. Messages had been forwarded back and forth from her laundry ladies.

Mary was eventually arrested for treason by her complicity in the Babington Plot. Babington was a young zealot, wealthy, idle, full of dreams, surrounded by other headstrong youth, who, with his leadership, sought to replace Elizabeth with Mary. Babington had audience with the kings of France and Spain on this cause. But if he was zealous, he was also rather careless, which is not difficult once you have gotten the attention of one as detailed and as patient as Sir

Francis Walsingham, Elizabeth's spymaster. Walsingham was a cat. And here was another bevy of mice.

Loosening the reins only slightly, correspondence shuttled quietly between Babington and the queen through a pouch hidden in the hole of a beer barrel. Through the double agent Gilbert Gifford, a complicitous little mouse, Walsingham kept an interactive watch. The messages were written in code, one that Walsingham's decoder, Thomas Phelippes, spun out for his boss, in correspondence both coming and going.

Mary failed to suspect anything.

Just prior to these events, in 1585, the English Parliament passed a Bond of Association (not to be confused with the Association that would have made James and Mary corulers of Scotland). This bond, one that Walsingham and Cecil pushed forward, demanded the death of not only anyone who plotted against Elizabeth, but anyone who benefited by the attempt. In other words, if a plot was designed to eliminate Elizabeth and place Mary on the English throne, Mary could be tried for treason as any other plotter. This bond was, in essence, Mary's death warrant. It had a wide gaping mouth.

Mary even agreed to sign it.

To be fair, Elizabeth had cause for concern. There had been at least two such plots uncovered; both imagined a living Mary and a dead Elizabeth. Elizabeth was not safe as long as Mary Stuart was alive. Confining her for almost twenty years just wasn't enough. And yet taking Mary's life would bring about a whole different set of problems. It would rally a Catholic Spain to arms.

It would also prove queens and kings mortal after all. It would set an uncomfortable precedent, against which recovery would be difficult. To those begging her to proceed with the execution of the Queen of Scots, Elizabeth answered, "What will my enemies not say, that for the safety of her life a maiden queen could be content to spill the blood even of her own kinswoman?"

🙙🙙

Once Mary was fully aware of Babington's plan, in her last letter to him she said, "Orders must be given that when their design has been carried out I can be *quant et quant* got out of here."[12] It was an act of agreement, of consent. There was sufficient unused space beneath the text of her letter, so Walsingham, padding his bets, had Phelippes add a postscript to Mary's response, in the proper code, of course. The postscript asked for the names of the six gentlemen who would carry out the act. It had the appearance of deeper involvement. It would not only drive Mary's complicity with a bit more certainty, but it might give them the names of the conspirators, though it failed to do so.

One day, Sir Amias suggested a ride, an outing, maybe a rousing buck hunt. Mary was delighted. Anything. Her health had suffered irrecoverably from the conditions forced on her, and obviously her judgment had been impaired as well. She had no sense of the duplicity around her. Fresh air, movement in the limbs, a horse beneath her, and some company other than the sour Paulet would do her a world of good. The small kindness itself was a rare event.

As they rode along, horsemen approached. Sir Thomas Gorge, an emissary from Elizabeth, said to the unsuspecting Mary, "The Queen my mistress finds it very strange that you, contrary to the pact and engagement made between you that you should have conspired against her and her state, a thing which she could not have believed had she not seen proofs of it with her own eyes and known it for certain." She was dumbfounded. Gorge said her servants were to be taken away immediately, guilty as they also were.

Mary said she knew well she was no longer of any use to anyone in this world.[13]

You are now only a dead woman

Mary had no nose for the trap. Had she actually reigned somewhere, anywhere, other than in her own private cell and among her remaining servants, if she had somehow managed to rule her own heart or govern her passions more efficiently, she might have learned adequate queencraft, or at least the necessary art of survival. She had the brains. She had the backing. She just never had the luck, the corrected vision, or the simple knack for making good choices. By this time in her life, in ill health, in gloom, and in the tangles of a fading hope, her remaining thoughts turned to religion.

And what about James? Perhaps still under the influence of the impossibility of his mother's actual execution, he said she should "drink the ale she has brewed." Can we condemn him as many have for his lack of filial tenderness? One writer uses the phrase "sentimental nonsense"[14] to describe those who fault the king for his indifference to his mother. He never had a relationship with her.

When it came time for the trial, by merely showing up, Mary acknowledged its legality, the legality she challenged vehemently. She had no choice but to be there. All of her moves were anticipated and addressed. All the odds were against her. And no one on trial for treason was ever allowed counsel. Her only defense was herself.

The only catch in all of it was her existence as a sovereign queen. If she were a queen of a realm, she could not possibly be subject to another Crown. The loophole that negated this assumption turned out to be Walsingham's Bond of Association, the nifty piece of legislature that could try and condemn "anyone" committing an act of treason against Elizabeth. Against all this, and conceding nothing, Mary said,

> I am myself a Queen, the daughter of a king, a stranger, and the true kinswoman of the Queen of England. I came to England on my cousin's promise of assistance against my enemies and rebel subjects and was at once imprisoned.... As an absolute Queen, I cannot submit to orders, nor can I submit to the laws of the land without injury to myself, the King my son and all other sovereign princes.... For myself I do not recognize the laws of England nor do I know or understand them as I have often asserted. I am alone without counsel, or anyone to speak on my behalf. My papers and notes have been taken from me, so that I am destitute of all aid, taken at a disadvantage.[15]

In all her distress she remained calm. A royal chair was set for the absent English queen, and all Mary was allowed was a velvet chair with no token of her own state or queenship, and a pad for her feet. She was lame with rheumatism, and there was so much atrophy about her muscles, she had to be supported by two aides to walk to her place of judgment.

During her trial, in a moment of clarity, she said to her accusers, "Look to your conscience and remember that the theatre of the world is wider than the realm of England." She was aware that death itself was inevitable. She had been in its presence enough in the past. To her, of course it was a great injustice, but it was also a matter of faith. She had written to her cousin, the Duke of Guise, a month or so before her trial began: "For myself, I am resolute to die for my religion . . ."[16] Indeed, after a series of large speeches, the commission found Mary Queen of Scots guilty of "compassing and imagining since June 1 matters tending to the death and destruction of the Queen of England."[17]

Somewhere in the midst of it all, perhaps even before the trial, Mary had come to some quiet resolve to reconcile this whole tragedy to God. She sought only a martyr's death. Paulet, in a cruelty and a disregard that was somewhat unnecessary, told her, in response to her desire to die for her faith, that she would neither be regarded as a saint nor a martyr. In one last bit of scorn, he said, "You are now only a dead woman, without dignity or honours of a Queen."[18]

After Mary had been arrested, she began to fear for her life, and not necessarily by the executioner's block, but by a quieter, more diabolical method. She wasn't afraid so much of the death itself. By this time, she was disillusioned, broken, and somewhat welcomed the thought of death. Still, a secret death would rob her of a public martyrdom.

Elizabeth, as strange as it might sound, sought that very solution. A secret death for the Queen of Scots, a pillow to suffocate her, a bit of poison in her food might just let the English queen off the hook. For Mary to hang herself in her bedchamber, or to be the victim of some fatal accident would redirect blame. All of Europe, Spain, and Rome might just buy it. Though not directly, she hinted as much to Sir Amias. In a letter, Elizabeth said she regretted that no one has "found out some way to shorten the life of that Queen [Mary] considering the great peril she [Elizabeth] is subject to hourly, so long as the said Queen shall live."[19] Ironically, Paulet, perhaps the best of candidates for such a task, was put off by the idea. His response to Elizabeth's subtle suggestion?

> I am so unhappy to have lived to see this unhappy day, in which I am required by direction from my most gracious sovereign to do an act which God and the law forbiddeth . . . God forbid that I should make so foul a shipwreck of my conscience, or leave so great a blot on my poor posterity, to shed blood without law or warrant.[20]

Elizabeth, upon reading this letter from Paulet raged concerning his "daintiness" and the "niceness" of "those precise fellows" like

Paulet. *Puritans*. As Antonia Fraser put it, "unimaginative, bigoted, petty tyrant he might be, he was still no assassin."[21]

All this time, James was not convinced his mother was in any real danger. Surely, a sovereign queen (Elizabeth) who understands the sanctity of royal blood would think twice about taking the life of an anointed queen. It was one way royalty protected each other. They kept the illusion active, fertile. But, as we will see, there were exceptions. Even after Mary's death, James's so-called outrage was show only. It was expected of him. An obligation of state. An appearance he had to keep up for the sake of those around him who watched to see what he would do.

Of her own son, Mary used the painful word, *betrayed*.

CHAPTER NINE

Mum

In the circumstances, she must, with justice, be regarded as one of the most wronged women in history.

—ALISON WEIR, *Mary, Queen of Scots and the Murder of Lord Darnley*

"TOMORROW MORNING AT eight o'clock," was the answer to her next question. And in the great hall at Fotheringay Castle. She made a few personal requests, all of which were denied her. Papers, ink, account books, everything was refused. She sat "in sort of a dream." Transitioning—acceptance, submission. It is not difficult to imagine how perceptions might alter—some to clarify, some to elevate, as I suppose they must when one knows the hour of death.

When first told of her sentence, she said, "I thank you for such welcome news. You will do me great good in withdrawing me from this world out of which I am very glad to go."[1] She spoke again about her queenship, about royal blood, and to a somewhat indifferent and detached audience. It was expedient the execution be carried out quickly. She was given no interim.

8 February 1587. The execution was a private event. Elizabeth would have it no other way. But with three hundred people attending, in spite of the added guard and the locked castle gates, it was hardly private. Posterity has a way of seeing through walls.

Mary didn't sleep that night, or if she did, it couldn't have been much. She lay with her "eyes closed and a half smile on her face."[2] This is conjecture, even if you happened to be there. How can it be anything else? If her execution was a closed event, so was her suffering. Put on what face it may.

"In te Domino confido, non confundat in aeternum."[3] (In you, Lord, is my trust, let me never be confounded.) Mary's last words.

A pale emperor

Now that the mother had been so cautiously dispatched, all eyes turned toward the son. Truth is, no matter what detachment he may have felt, when he heard the details of her execution, it actually sickened him.* According to the memoirist Moysie, James was "very sad and pensive all that day and would not sup that night."[4]

For a time, and for the benefit of a Scots audience, James

---

*As Mary was led to the executioner's block, she removed her outer garment of black, revealing a red petticoat underneath. The blood-red color meant that Mary was no longer the queen of folly and misfortune, but a martyr for her Catholic faith. The execution was gruesome. It took the executioner three swings of the axe to sever her head. The first blow cut into the back of her skull. A servant, standing close by, thought she heard her say "sweet Jesus." Once the executioner's work was done, by custom he lifted the head of the queen. Unknown to Bull (the axe-man's name), Mary was wearing an auburn wig. Her actual hair was gray and cut very short. The severed head fell to the floor. It was said that her lips moved, as in prayer, for some minutes afterwards. There was also movement among her garments. It was her dog, a Sky Terrier, her one solace throughout years of captivity. The dog refused to be taken from her dead master. The creature panicked, and began shuttling back and forth between the head and the body of the Queen of Scots. For the sake of public opinion and possible sympathy, the dog was given to a French princess. In spite of the new royal surroundings, the dog died weeks later. It was said that the creature grieved to death.

maintained a silence toward England. Mum, indeed. All communications were off. Elizabeth's ambassador was not allowed to cross the border into Scotland. It was all very tactical. It was also histrionics, an act performed by one who was getting better and better at his trade.

James did not hear of the news until six days after the event. In March, the court received the official account of the execution. The king "would not abide to hear it read out."[5]

It was hardly grief for a dead mother. But his gloom was authentic. The accounts were conflicting, but the thought of death itself was a horror to him, especially a royal one. He feared death, and the very presence of death, above all things. This became even more pronounced later in life. The night before his son Henry died, James refused to go near his dying child even in his last hours. He went into another room and wept. His grief for the young prince was real, and indeed he suffered, but he was not about to enter into the confines of such a pale emperor as death—the deference one monarch might show for another.

From his earliest recollection, he feared personal harm. He eventually had extra padding fitted into his doublet and pants for defense against an assassin's blade. This addition made him appear heavier than he was.

Death seemed to always flip certain switches in his psychology. But if death is a thing he feared above all things, his own kingship is what he loved above all things. One writer says that James "shammed a false sorrow [at his mother's death] but could not conceal his joy."[6] As one witness notes, "The king moved never his countenance at the rehearsal [recounting] of his mother's execution, nor leaves his pastime and hunting more than before."[7]

"I am now sole king," was his response to it all.[8]

The Lords of the Congregation and the Lords Enterprisers still circled about the king, just as subtle, and with just as much teeth as ever, but it was a true monarch who now ruled. Savvy and streetwise.

Following the death of his mother, James had another sixteen years to occupy the Scottish throne, but those years proved him an effective king. A dissembling king, a player, a neurotic, canny, private, smutty, somewhat paranoid king, but a capable king, a king who had long learned to keep and attend his own counsel, who might nod *yes* and think *no*, but a king nonetheless. Remembering, too, that his young mind, in spite of the forceful schooling, was like a sponge, and he learned from all of them, if not more from Elizabeth, his southern master. Like her, he had learned to vacillate, to say one thing and mean or do another. Still, and for many reasons, he would never be an Elizabeth. Who cares? He was James. He, too, was one of a kind.

James had certain sensitive issues at stake, prickly issues that were exacerbated by a mere lack of clarity. One, he had to make a show of outrage for the Scots who actually were outraged (the same Scots who exiled Mary in the first place). It was expected of him. Mary was now convenient to them because it could be said of her that she was a victim of English oppression, an old issue of Scots pride. She was convenient to a truly astounded and outraged Catholic Europe because of her martyrdom. She was convenient to Philip II because he needed an excuse to set sail against England. *Convenient* is not the word to describe what Mary was to Elizabeth. Here, the thistle, the prickly little emblem of the Scottish state, provides the appropriate image.

It is a sad commentary, the way James was compelled to react to his own mother's death, but the English crown glittered with too much promise for him to abandon his course. After all, if England was the "promised land," as he was convinced it was, what did that make Scotland?

As time shall now try

He made all the moves Elizabeth and perhaps a few others expected of him. He protested, but not loudly, and with no real conviction.

Elizabeth, playing her own part, understood James more than the rest, and accepted his empty rant. He would not break the Anglo-Scottish alliance and had no intention to. He felt that by turning his head, so to speak, at the death of his mother, his possession of the throne of England was more certain. Elizabeth, however, was always herself—the calculating, well-counseled, far-seeing, hoarding queen. Still, she wrote, if she "did justice to the mother," there would be "nothing else but to advance the son."[9]

An argument could be made that Elizabeth thought of herself as a kind of mother to James, even from his birth, at least indirectly, if we can judge by her actions toward him. She was his *godsip*, or *gossip*,[10] that is, his godmother, but her attitude toward the foundling king was beyond that of a mere godmother. Not necessarily warm or maternal, but one who sustained a certain willingness toward him nonetheless, an oblique kind of maternity. It could be argued as well that this was her way of maintaining advantage, of keeping the reins safe within her hands. James, like his mother, hardly made a move or had a private thought without Elizabeth somehow knowing it, and, at times, inciting it.

Shortly following the death of Mary Queen of Scots came what history has called the Spanish Armada, an event that actually gave James even greater advantage in the eye of the English queen. Scotland was sore over Mary's death. They wanted revenge. The Armada could help them exact that revenge. James cried aloud with them, but his cry was all volume. It had no real heart in it. Elizabeth knew this, and understood. As much of a coward as history has pictured him to be, James held the leash firmly that kept Scotland at bay during this sensitive moment between the realms. There were border raids, a few ruined names and estates, but such efforts had no king behind them.

Though we can look back at the Armada by the omniscience that time allows, Elizabeth could not. England was small. Her navy was small and ill-equipped, especially compared to the Spanish. James, instead of taking advantage of her vulnerability, offered himself to Elizabeth as a son. He kept the Scots Catholics quiet, and would not allow Scotland to be a port of entry for the Spanish or anyone else.

But before getting all misty-eyed over his dedication to the English queen, in late July 1588, Walsingham sent a letter to William Ashby, the English ambassador to Scotland, with news that the Spanish Armada had entered the English Channel. Ashby told this to James, who was under obligation to his formal alliance with Elizabeth. Knowing James the way they did, Ashby was also authorized to offer him an English dukedom and to raise his annual stipend to £5,000. He was also to have money to maintain a bodyguard of fifty men and a force of one hundred horses. The following excerpt is from a letter James wrote to Elizabeth concerning this offer.[11]

> Madame and dearest sister,
>
> In times of straits true friends are best tried. . . . I hereby offer unto you my forces, my person, and all that I may command, to be employed against yon strangers in whatsomever fashion and by whatsomever mean as may best serve for the defense of your country. Wherein I promise to behave myself not as a stranger and foreign prince but as your natural son and compatriot of your country in all respects.

And James made good on his promise. But the letter doesn't end on that high note of fealty and devotion.

> I pray you to send presently down commissioners for the perfecting of the same, which I protest I desire not for that I would have the reward to precede the deserts, but only that I with honour, and all my good subjects with a fervent

goodwill, may embrace this your godly and honest cause, whereby your adversaries may have ado not with England but with the whole isle of Britain.

Thus praying you to dispatch all your matters with all possible speed, and wishing you a success convenient to those that are invaded by God's professed enemies, I commit, madame and dearest sister, your person, estate, and country to the blessed protection of the Almighty.

From Edinburgh the fourth of August, 1588.

Your most loving and affectionate

brother and cousin as

time shall now try,

James R.

In other words, I give you all my best, my resources, however limited they may be, my subjects to rule as your own in defense of your realm. I am your son. I am all good things to you and your safety. I even implore God on your behalf. Just make sure you send the cash first.

Elizabeth would have expected nothing less.

Following the Armada, whose victory James felt was as much his own as it was the English queen's, and never missing an opportunity to push his agenda, however subtle or well-scripted, he celebrated with a piece of text he called *Ane Meditation upon the 25, 26, 27, 28, and 29 Verses of the 15 Chapter of the First Buke of the Chronicles of the Kings*. In chapter 28, David, the man of war, has blood on his hands. God, therefore, does not allow him to build the temple, but confers it on his son, Solomon. James was Solomon to Elizabeth's David.

And of all my sonnes (for the Lord hath giuen me many sonnes) hee hath chosen Solomon my sonne, to sit vpon the throne of the kingdome of the Lord ouer Israel. And

he said vnto me, Solomon thy sonne, hee shall build my
house and my courts: for I haue chosen him to be my
sonne, and I will be his father. (1 Chronicles 28:5–6
King James Bible 1611)

Succession was the chief issue to James. It was always the prize
that suspended between him and Elizabeth. But in spite of his
nearness of blood, there were certain restrictions that could not
be ignored. Henry VIII had declared that descendants of his sister
Margaret Tudor, wife to James IV of Scotland, by something ugly
between the royal siblings, some old aggravation, should be excluded
from succession.

Margaret was James's great-grandmother (paternal and maternal). It was also law in England that anyone of royal blood tried
and convicted for treason must forfeit his or her rights to accession.
This included heirs. Not to mention that James was a Scot, not an
Englishman. He was an alien. These impediments were difficult, but
not impossible. Politics demands elasticity, that is, a good bit of stretch,
and perhaps the machinations of a tireless little man like Robert Cecil,
who succeeded his father as Elizabeth's first minister. It was through
Cecil that James would find his way to the English throne.

Requiem

One more thing. When James had been king of England for
about a decade or so, he ordered his mother's body exhumed from
Peterborough Cathedral, and reburied in Westminster Abbey. Mary's
new tomb was as elaborate and as grand as that of her cousin/nemesis
Elizabeth's. James built both of them. To this day, one faces the other.
I wonder if anyone can hear the small shrunken sound of the Virgin
Queen turning over?

 CHAPTER TEN

The Age Was Lousy with Poets

To love would be an awfully big adventure.

—J. M. Barrie, *Peter Pan*

Be warned. Some of the verse in this chapter is quite good. Much of it is not. This was an age when poems and letters were still written in longhand. Words were not merely scratched out, and ink was not just a useful metaphor. You have to imagine a slower, more even rhythm. You were writing with the feather of a bird, a winged creature—with a long slow hiss, and by a soft pulse of candlelight. There was romance in the very action. How could love not prosper under such conditions?

Love was often an epistolary tale. The age was lousy with poets.

This part of our story includes one Scandinavian princess, passage over a troubled sea, an obscene amount of alcohol, a witch or two, and one big fat dowry. It is not love at first sight. There are times when it is best that love be blind. Our king is, after all, an acquired taste. But he has all the bounce of a young man in love.

Her name was Anne, or Anna, as some called her. Anne was the younger of two daughters of Frederick II, King of Denmark. She was fourteen. The oldest daughter, Elizabeth, was first choice, as custom dictates, but she was already accounted for, betrothed as she was to someone quicker than James, and certainly better looking, with a bigger bankroll and perhaps more importantly *not* from Scotland. Before sending his ambassadors, one of them asked James what they should do if the oldest daughter was already spoken for. "Forfend the omen," the king said, "but if it happens, ask for the other."[1]

Elizabeth was the fairer of the two, but Anne was not unattractive. She was taller and more developed physically than her sister. "She was very blonde, with lovely white skin and golden hair, slender, graceful and of a good height." A contemporary of James describes her around the time of the wedding as "a princess, both godly and beautiful, as appeareth by all that know her. I trust she shall bring a blessing to the country, like as she giveth great contentment to his Majesty."

Time would prove Anne to be somewhat of an airhead, "incurably frivolous and empty-headed."[2] But, for the moment, she was in the king's sights for his bride-to-be. And airhead or not, she seemed to have the goods to make a compatible match with this complex young king.

France was in on the marriage negotiations as well, but they had neither the cash nor the patience with the King of Scots. Catherine de Bourbon—sister to King Henry of Navarre (the future Henry IV of France)—the maid in question, in spite of the intoxications of her name, was much older than James. He was twenty-three. Catherine was thirty-one. Plus, her miniature (her image painted on a small surface) was not much to look at. Not to mention the rumors that her dowry was already wasted.

So Denmark was it.

According to one account, James set aside a fortnight (two weeks) to pray and seek God for whom he was to marry. Catherine or Anne? Anne or Catherine? A Huguenot France or a Lutheran Denmark? A young and lovely Scandinavian princess or Catherine, rumored to be "old and crooked and somewhat worse if all were known"? *What to do?* After fifteen days, the king turned his eye and his hopes toward the younger, blonder, and more solvent of the two.

James did not particularly like the company of women, but then again, he did not dislike it either. James "was more interested in the ladies than is often supposed and found their immodesty attractive."[3] Remember, James is the conundrum king. We must also remember the misogyny of the times. His old teacher, Buchanan, maintained a negative attitude toward women even beyond his contempt for the Queen of Scots. And Knox's[4] *Blaste* was not revelation, as much as it was validation. In other words, the sixteenth century was not the twenty-first century.

Of course, against all the bias of the age, and whatever opinion one might have of women, Antonia Fraser suggests that having a wife was a different thing altogether. There was the state to consider, the perception of Europe and the world, not to mention the all-important production of an heir, the stability of any Crown. James told his Privy Council and the people of Scotland he was marrying for those very reasons.

James and Anne were to be married in Scotland. Arrangements were made and Anne set sail from Denmark to marry a man she had never met—a king, a young king, and doubtless a king she had not heard too much about. Not that she had much of a choice. Like statecraft, marriage, as Jane Austen would say, is a maneuvering business. It was refreshing to read David Willson's comments that the marriage to Anne was "the one romantic episode of his life," that it "forms a human and pleasant interlude in the turmoil and self-seeking of his reign in Scotland." He went on to say that James "was deeply in love with his new bride."[5]

For once, in spite of the tidy negotiations, and the old custom by which he was married, it was not a show. Well, it was always a show, but James allowed his heart to feel what it was disposed to feel. His heart had grown large and at times unwieldy in spite of the restrictions of his youth, and once again there was a genuine arousal of love within it. He turned to verse, to hyperbole and meter, excess and rhyming cadences to vent his ardor. Always the imaginative, literary, love-starved, and animated young king. Always our James.

Far from being an ordinary husband

Originally, James asked the Danes for £1,000,000 Scots in dowry. He asked also that Denmark form an anti-Catholic league with Scotland, and provide military assistance if he provoked Catholic states to anger with his proposals. The only one provoked to anger was Denmark. But a settlement was made, and the dowry came to about £150,000.

James was broke and embarrassed. But he was always broke. He was always much better at handling small amounts of money, say, a few thousand pounds (when he had it), than he ever was handling the large sums that kings are subject to. The one, he could understand. The other was a phantasm, as elusive as fairy dust. He was continually spending money he did not have. Adam Nicolson calls the English James "a money hose."

In her book *After Elizabeth*, Leanda de Lisle brings James right into the twenty-first century, saying that this particular malady is a "common problem in adults with ADHD."[6] Elizabeth used this to her advantage. She was always bailing him out (estimated at £58,000 from 1589–1603). Her allotments of three to five thousand pounds here and there were sufficient to keep James panting after her like one of his own dogs. A *Taming of the Shrew* in reverse. Against the pain of this current embarrassment before Denmark, Elizabeth sent him £1,000 in cash and a £2,000 advance to buy plate.*

When all the smoke cleared, the marriage was a go.

During this time and with the prospect of a *yes* on the lips of Denmark, James's heart became all warm and thumpy, romance bubbling about his brain. The only physic (medication) was verse, for his Anne was hundreds of sea miles away.

> What mortall man may live but hart [without heart]
> As I doe now suche is my cace,
> Devided eache in divers place.
> The seas are now the barr
> Which mak us distance farr
> That we may soone winn narr
> God graunte us grace.
> Full manie causes suire I have
> Which does augment my woe and caire
> But one more speciall nor the leave [than the rest]
> When I doe think what joye is thaire
> What gladness and what greeting
> At our long wished meeting
> I can not tell unwitting [without wetting]
> My chekis declare[7]

Granted, it is not a very good poem, and it is definitely not a sonnet, but it was sincere, and it was all James. The world he constructed with words was all that mattered.

Scotland would host a formal ceremony, but the marriage was celebrated by proxy in Copenhagen on 20 August 1589. There was

---

plate—"Gold or silver vessels and utensils. **b.** In extended use: vessels and utensils made of other materials; tableware." *Oxford English Dictionary* a bride and a bridegroom, but no James. As delicious as this image might be, it is unfair to read anything into it just yet.

Considering he was a king, and that he was a bit quirky, and that Anne was somewhat vacuous and shallow, that she was well proportioned and lithesome, and he was, well, James, that he was always broke and she was always spending, there was a kind of compatibility between them, a connubial justice which was rather amazing in itself considering the complicated psychology of the king.

Still, gazing into life beyond the royal wedding, William McElwee offers a summation.

> But she [Anne] had neither the character nor the intellect to deal with the special needs of James, who was very far from being an ordinary husband. She had not the wit to see where and how he needed buttressing against a mocking, hostile world, and she lacked the strength to do so if she had. She could not wrap him in the warmth of a great passion, and she could never become what he had dreamt of and needed so badly all his life, the one person with whom he could share his inmost secrets. On the other hand, in view of the mass of oddity which James landed on her, with his mixture of timidity and self-assertiveness, his physical awkwardness and his psychological twists, she did very well indeed to succeed in making him a good, ordinary wife.[8]

Ten days later, Anne—now queen—her retinue, and her goods embarked for Scotland. James, in the meantime, allowed his muse to labor.

> O cruel Cupid what a ruthless rage,
> What hateful wrath thou utterest upon me;

No medicine my sickness may assuage
Nor cataplasm cure my wound I see.
Through deadly shot alive I die,
I fry in flames of that envenomed dart
Which shot me sicker in at either eye
Then fastened fast into my hoalit heart.
The fever hath infected every part,
My bones are dried their marrow melts away,
My sinnows feebles through my smoking smart
And all by blood as in a pan doth play.
I only wish for ease of all my pain,
That she might wit [know] my sorrow I sustain.[9]

This my nakedness

It seemed to stick on everything. The drippy ooze of a love song, soft
as the pelt of a rose. And our sappy James. The lover-hunter. The
pacer. The poemsmith. The English ambassador Ashby noted that
the king played the role of "a true lover" who "thinketh every day a
year till he see his joy and love approach."[10]

Anne set sail, yet a strong west wind and storms made the journey impossible. After the third attempt, the Danish admiral turned
back toward Copenhagen. Anne, at the insistence of the Scottish
envoys, was taken to Oslo instead. They did not want her to return
to Denmark.

The young king, impatient and somewhat sorrowful at the delay,
playing Paris to his distant Helen, or the pining Leander to his Hero,
mounted up for the chase. His blood was up. His thoughts were alive
once again with conquest. With three hundred to accompany him,
James secretly resolved to fetch his bride, "to commit himself and
his hopes Leander-like to the waves of the ocean, all for his beloved
Hero's sake."[11]

Only to one who knows me as well as his own reflection in a glass could I express, my dearest love, the fears which I have experienced because of the contrary winds and the violent storms since you embarked, the more especially since the arrival here of some ships which put to sea after your own and came without word of you. My resultant anguish, and the fear which ceaselessly pierces my heart, has driven me to dispatch a messenger to seek for you, both to bring me news of you and to give you the same of me ... Praying you therefore to give credence to all that he will say to you on my behalf, I make an end praying the Creator (my only love) with all my heart to grant you a safe, swift and happy arrival in these parts so that you can make proof of the entire affection of him who has vowed to you alone all his love.[12]

This is not the dissembling king, the politic sovereign maneuvering about the affections of a young girl. He means what he is saying. Love was a powerful lord over the king, as it will be to the day of his death. *If history proves him a fool over anything.*

It is to the good fortune of our little history that the winds blew the way they did. All the proud images, all the old magic of chivalry, of a king in quest, and of the damsel in distress. I would suppose the marriage fared better because of this turn of events. It cost him something. The refusals of nature, and the fuss it made, evoked a challenge to the hunter-knight-king. She was suddenly a prize, spoil.

It made a great image in his mind, and that is what matters.

The Scots, who could care less about the bloom of love, demanded another response from its king. There were reasons for the marriage that had less to do with romance—succession, an heir, stability. And in the king's mind, his masculinity itself was in question. Taking a wife and bearing children would put certain whisperings to rest.

To "get" James, we have to imagine a creature who has no precedence, who is indeed an original, and mercifully unrepeatable. Like finding one's way through a labyrinth. Just when you are sure of one turn, a wall appears. You can never be quite certain.

With each letter to Anne he becomes more vulnerable, not only to his mystery bride, but to his own people. In the following letter he makes the somewhat famous assertion of his aloneness, "without father or mother . . ." The letter is addressed to the people of Scotland.

As to the causes, I doubt not it is manifestly known to all how far I was generally found fault with by all men for the delaying of so long of my marriage. The reasons were that I was alone, without father, or mother, brother or sister, King of this realm and heir apparent in England. This my nakedness made me to be weak and my enemies strong. One man was no man, and the want of hope of succession bred disdain. Yes, my long delay bred in the breasts of many a great jealousy [suspicion] of my inability, as if I were a barren stock. These reasons and innumerable other, hourly objected, move me to hasten the treaty of my marriage; for as to my own nature, God is my witness I could have abstained longer than the weal of my country could have permitted. I am known, God be praised, not to be intemperately rash nor flighty in my weightiest affairs, neither use I to be so carried away with passion as I refuse to hear reason.[13]

When he first heard of her delay, he couldn't sleep or rest, his agitation was so marked. He said, "Ay, upon the instant, yea very moment resolved to make possible on my part, that which was impossible on her."[14] In other words, *if she cannot make it here, I will go to her.* In less than a week's time, his ships were sighted off the coast of Norway (embarking from Scotland on 22 October and landing in Norway 25 October). Once disembarked, he made his way overland to Oslo where his bride awaited him.

Made good cheer and drank till springtime

James came bounding in, all confidence and odd manners. The Danes thought him "a tall, slim gentleman, thin under the eyes, wearing a red velvet coat appliquéd with pieces of gold so that there was a row of golden stars and another row where the velvet could be seen. He also wore a black velvet coat lined with sable."[15]

Anne wasn't all that impressed. It is not known what she may have expected, but it wasn't this.

Not breaking his stride, nor pausing to take off his boots, which was custom, he went right over to her and offered her a kiss "after the Scots fashion." She refused him (after the "fashion" of her own country). "Marry, after a few words privately spoken between His Majesty and her, there passed familiarity and kisses."[16] The little introduction took about thirty minutes, after which joy seemed liberal among them all.

Four days later they were formally married. James entered the ceremony and stood on the red cloth, his hands on his hips. Anne came and stood by his side. There was singing, a homily (in French), and the office of marriage. The marriage was blessed according to custom, and a bishop delivered an oration in Danish. One month of celebration followed, which included a bit of "deep drinking," sports, more drinking, and other events, after which the couple departed for Elsinore, and to the new Kronborg Castle.

Once at Elsinore, James met his new in-laws. Anne's brother, Christian IV, was only ten at the time. We will hear more about this notorious party animal later. James and Anne would remain at Elsinore until April. The "pervasive mood," according to Alan Stewart, was alcohol. Here, Hamlet, or rather Shakespeare, got it right. The Danes could put away the booze, and with a conviction that few could boast.

> This heavy-headed revel east and west
> Makes us traduced and tax'd of other nations:
> They clepe [call] us drunkards, and with swinish phrase
> Soil our addition.
>
> —William Shakespeare, *Hamlet*, I, iv, 19–22

Playwright Ben Jonson (1572–1637) wrote that the Danes sought to "drench their cares in wine." The Danish court doctor said it was more a sign of manliness to drink hard. Denmark was a manly state indeed if drink be the true measure. Anne's father, Frederick II, was famous for his bouts of drinking and the sport he made of it. In a drunken fistfight at Anne's sister's wedding, he fell from his horse into a river. Later, Christian IV would bring obscene behavior and riot to the English court that made the English blush, and they did not blush easily.

James fell into the rhythm himself with all the fellow inebriates of Anne's household. Sir James Melville remarked on James's "increasingly prodigious taste" for drink. "The king," he said, "made good cheer and drank till the springtime."[17]

My new rib

Once his head was clear and his eyes regained focus, it was time to go home. With the added, almost comic emphasis of "for God's sake," James wrote and asked to have the place cleaned up, and to make a good fuss over them when they got there. To have the people "tuned" to their finest pitch. In his own words, "Don't embarrass me."

> For God's sake, take all the pains ye can to toon our
> folks well, now against our homecoming; lest we be all
> shamed before strangers.... Thus recommending me and
> my new rib to your daily prayers, I commit you to the
> All-Sufficient.[18]

The fleet arrived at the Firth of Leith in May 1590. Scotland put on her best outfit for the arrival of her new queen. All was as tidy as the king had commanded.

Cannons were fired from the battlements and from the ships harbored near the town. Trumpets blasted. Five days later the couple arrived at Holyroodhouse. Scotland had no suitable conveyance for its queen, so Denmark sent a carriage fit for Her Majesty, a coach of silver, dressed with gold cloth and purple velvet, drawn with eight white horses. The carriage was for the queen alone. James and a few of his principals rode alongside on horseback. When they reached the palace, the king took her by the hand and escorted her to the Great Hall, and then to the chambers freshly decked with gold and silver cloth.

The mood back home among the gangs had not changed. The old bickering started up again. James and the Danes wanted the coronation to be held on a Sunday. The Kirk resisted, saying it was an abuse of the Sabbath. The Kirk objected to the ritual of anointing as well. Of course they did. They considered it popish. Tactically, James reminded them that it was biblical precedence that called for the anointing of a prince. After much "soul searching," the Kirk agreed to the Sunday coronation. After all, it was a minister's blessing, James suggested, and "a solemn oath passed mutually betwixt the prince and the subjects, and from both to God."[19] What other day would be as appropriate?

It was an incredibly smooth bit of kingcraft. As expected, and not to confound themselves, the Kirk found a loophole for the anointing of oil. On 17 May (Sunday), Anna was made queen of Scotland.

I, Anna, by the grace of God, Queen of Scotland, pro-
fess, and before God and his angels wholly promise, that
durning the whole course of my life, so far as I can, shall
sincerely worship that same eternal God according to
his will revealed unto us in the Holy Scriptures, and
according to those precepts which are in the same scriptures commanded and directed: That I shall defend the
true religion and worship God, and advance the same,
and shall withstand and despise all papistical supersti-
tions, and whatsoever ceremonies and rites contrary to
the word of God: And that I shall further and advance
justice and equity, and maintain the same, and shall pro-
cure peace to the Kirk of God within this kingdom, and
to the subjects thereof: so God, the father of all mercies,
have mercy upon me.[20]

The marriage would be a good one, and last until Anne died in
1619. It cannot be said that any romantic attachment survived those
first few years. Beyond that time they were warm and loving, in a
nurturing kind of way. They became good parents, doting parents.
James had a large heart in spite of his beginnings. Quirky, difficult,
unpredictable, but roomy and given much more to warmth than
coolness.

Whatever riddle the love life of James Stuart poses, the truth, for
the moment at least, is that James married a beautiful young Danish
princess, and for a time was in love. Even later, as the English king,
in his letters he addressed her as "my heart."

CHAPTER ELEVEN

Double, Double, Toil, and Trouble

Thou schalt not suffre witchis to lyue.

—Exodus 22:18, Wycliffe Bible, 1395

So far, the story of King James includes murder, regicide, attempted regicide, a lot of lying, conspiracies, betrayals, a mean schoolteacher, a terrified young boy, kidnapping, more lying, more kidnapping, a beheading or two, a confused Scotland, even more conspiracies, a new wife, a trail of dead bodies, and one dead bird.

His life is overpopulated with ghosts—mum, dad, maybe his own misbegotten childhood—all four of the regents, Esme, and the poor sparrow.

The procession creeps along, slowly, and with hardly an interruption, adding numbers as it passes, and we are not finished with them yet.

We now add witches to our tale.

Considering his childhood, it is little wonder that a fascination with witchcraft began to fester in him. James grew up in rooms lit with candles and slants of daylight through a window, large rooms peopled with life-sized statues, immense draperies you could sail a small ship with, and old staring portraits. As a young child his room was overlaid in black damask, his bed with black silks. And there were devils all around him.

Treachery and majestie have a powerful attraction one for the other.

Every sound had to be accounted for, processed by youthful imagination. Every snap and every hiss in the fireplace, every crack of tread on the wood floor. Candles moved at the mere suggestion of a wind, and the shadows they threw suddenly came alive, often with odd living forms. And there was always the threat of assassination (the young monarch's imaginary playmate). Against the restlessness of such a precocious child, one given so to fantasy, the boy who suffered terror at the hand of his keepers, we can assume his fascination with the dark arts or demonology had an early start. It was old in him by the time the trials were under way, around 1590.

James considered witchcraft a branch of theology. This, too, was not innovative. In such a world as sixteenth-century Scotland, mysticism infused all of life. It was an enchanted age. The plague was considered a judgment of God because of wickedness. The city was a wicked place, they reasoned, so there was more affliction in the city than in the country, and more affliction among the poor than among the rich because there is more wickedness among the poor. Wicked, wicked, wicked.

The word *plague* is a descendant of the Latin *plaga*, which means "stroke, or wound"—the avenging angel striking a city or an individual. The *Oxford English Dictionary* suggests divine affliction or divine punishment. It was a way of interpreting life. If God is real, James asserted, there is a "Devill" who is just as real, with servants, prophets, evangelists.

A scriptural precedent, the witch of Endor was a necromancer, that is, one who speaks to the dead, the one Saul tricked into raising the spirit of Samuel.

> Then said Saul vnto his seruants, Seeke me a woman that hath a familiar spirit, that I may goe to her, and enquire of her. And his seruant said to him, Beholde, there is a woman that hath a familiar spirit at Endor. (1 Samuel 28:7 King James Bible 1611)

In 1563, three years before James was born, legislation against witches and witchcraft was enacted in Scotland. It was a capital offense to practice witchcraft or even consult with a witch. England had initiated legislation the year before.

It was an imagination he was born into. An imagination infused into the times.

Elizabeth had her Doctor John Dee. *When was the appropriate time for a coronation? Do we go to war or do we wait? Who? When? And the Spanish?* God-fearing people, who could sit through two-hour sermons or longer, who could recite long passages of Scripture, who did their best to live according to those Scriptures, all did as James did, and accepted much of the superstition of the age.

Religion and culture, church and state, all lived by a type of symbiosis. There was no separation. It is just the way life was conducted, the only way they knew how to perceive. When the winds tipped the scale for England during the Armada, Elizabeth said it was a "Protestant wind" that blew. Clever as it was, it was not a light jest. *God spoke and his enemies were scattered.* She was convinced, and so was the world at large. Perceptions changed. Elizabeth's father, the homicidal Henry VIII, had the Maid of Kent executed for treason because she prophesied unwisely (that is, against him).

In 1583, in response to a complaining public, the Kirk demanded a tougher enforcement of the existing laws against witchcraft. For James, at that particular time in his Scottish reign, it was more a matter of toleration and distraction than it was active engagement, in spite of his love for the hunt. He had always dealt with snakes and slithering things, pack animals and hissing cats, trying to gain, strengthen, or regain what was by right his own, that is, Scotland. He hardly had time to notice the witches. He was too busy wrangling with the Kirk and the nobles.

 For that olde and craftie Serpent, being a spirite, hee easilie spyes our affections, and so conformes himselfe thereto, to deceaue vs to our wracke.

—James VI of Scotland, *Daemonologie, Book One*

Later, he would prove a real scourge to witches and the like, and even take some sadistic pleasure out of it, but it would take a kind of epiphany to make it happen.

Don't read anything into this, but his real fascination with witchcraft and demonology began, or at least was aggravated, during his acquisition of a wife. Once he retrieved his bride and set sail for Scotland after so long a time in Denmark, their ships were once again harassed by storms.

The witches of Berwick

He called them "extreme lyars." Witches were a hot item in Scotland, particularly in the late sixteenth century. This is not so difficult to imagine with arch-misogynists like Buchanan and Knox bleating so feverishly about women. James reasoned that there were more witches (women) than sorcerers (men), because women are more delicate than men. The Devil had seduced Eve, so he was "homelier with that sex,"[1] that is, more familiar.

In the town of North Berwick, on the eastern coast of Scotland, there were witches who claimed to raise the storms that threatened him and his new queen on their return from Denmark. Again, it was more irritating than anything else, a powerful distraction, but a distraction nonetheless.

It wasn't until a witch named Agnes Sampson whispered to James the exact words he and Anne had spoken privately on their wedding night that his opinion altered. He then "swore by the living God that he believed all the devils in hell could not have discovered the same."[2] She testified that she meant to raise storms while the king was on his way to Denmark. Of course, Agnes and others like her confessed to these weird rituals only after horrific torture. James was convinced nonetheless of their authenticity. The account reads:

> When His Majestie was in Denmarke, she took a cat and christened it, and afterwards bound to each part of that cat the cheefeste partes of a dead man, and severall joynts of his bodie, and that in the night following the saide cat was conveied into the midst of the sea by all these witches . . . this doone, there did arise such a tempest in the sea, as a greater hath not beene seene.
>
> Again it is confessed that the said christened cat was the cause that the Kinges Majesties Ship at his comming foorth of Denmarke, had a contrary winde to the rest of his ships, then being in his companye, which thing was most strange and true, as the Kings Majestie acknowledgeth, for when the rest of his ships had a faire and goode winde, then was the winde contrarye and altogither against His Majestie: and further the said witche declared, that his Majestie had never come safe-lye from the sea, if his faith had not prevailed above their ententions.[3]

The name (or the cash) behind it all was that of a Scottish earl employing the local coven to further his career—another tempestuous Hepburn, descendant of the Bothwell ruined by the Queen of Scots. One witch said the King of Scots was targeted for destruction, "that another might rule in his Majesty's place and the government might go to the Devil."[4]

At this point, it was no longer a matter of distraction, but of fascination and obsession. Another switch was flipped in the mind of the king. It was said "the King took great delight to be present at their examinations."[5] It also brought up something cruel and savage in him, reminiscent of the ruined sparrow, I suspect, or a felled beast on the hunt. He allowed brutal tortures of the accused, and executions. He questioned witches himself and did whatever he had to for a confession. Once a witch confessed, it was thought, she lost her powers. His finesse at interrogation was a source of pride.

"He [James] permitted gross indignities and horrible torture. He has been accused of sadistic pleasure in inflicting pain, but this is unjust. Fear is a potent cause of cruelty, and James was in great terror." All this action summoned up an uncivilized kind of hatred in the king. Then again, is there a civilized one? He considered it all a part of his royal commission. They were of the Devil, and he was king, the Lord's anointed, a child and servant of God. "For these witches, whatsoever hath been gotten from them hath been done by me myself, not because I was more wise than others, but because I believed that such a vice did reign and ought to be suppressed."

One witch, it was told, asked the Devil why their incantations or powers did not work on James. The Devil, speaking French, answered, "*Il est un homme de Dieu.*"[6] (He is a man of God.) A very political Devil.

As he always did when moved deeply, his passions turned literary.

The fearful aboundinge at this time in this countrie, of these detestable slaves of the Devill, the Witches

or enchanters, hath moved me (beloved reader) to dispatch in post, this following treatise of mine, not in any
way (as I protest) to serve for a shew of my learning
and ingine, but onely (moved of conscience) to preasse
thereby, so farre as I can, to resolve the doubting harts
of many. (James VI of Scotland, from the preface of
Daemonologie, 1597)

Now that he was convinced, he became annoyed at the skepti-
cism of others. To forward his thoughts on the matter—on witches,
witchcraft, necromancy,[7] and the Devil—James wrote *Daemonologie*.
Divided into three "books," it is written in the form of a dialogue.
The enlightened sage and his eager disciple.

Amplifying a pre-existing tension, the book provided fuel for
public hysteria against witches. We can look to the spirit of the initia-
tor, that is, James, and the love of the hunt. Always the hunt. Though
he is quite detailed, his writing added nothing new to the existing
beliefs, but it reinforced them nonetheless. It is, after all, the validation of a king. Here is an excerpt from book one on the forms the
Devil "oblishes" to take—a dog, a cat, an ape.

By formes, I meane in what shape or fashion he shall
come vnto them [the Magician, or sorcerer], when they
call vpon him. And by effectes, I vnderstand, in what
special sorts of seruices he bindes himselfe to be subject
vnto them. The qualitie of these formes and effectes,
is lesse or greater, according to the skil and art of the
Magician. For as to the formes, to some of the baser sorte
of them he oblishes him selfe to appeare at their calling
vpon him, by such a proper name which he shewes vnto
them, either in likenes of a dog, a Catte, an Ape, or such-
like other beast; or else to answere by a voyce onlie.[8]

And dog will have his day: a word about the chase

Having mentioned it, to pry into the psychology of James it is necessary to examine his obsession with the hunt. It was key to his perception of himself.

All his life he had been the hunted, the one stalked and cornered. His father, his mother, were both victims of the hunt and of the unfortunate kill. Being chief among his passions, and particularly once he became king of England, it is not unfair to say that James preferred the hunt above the tedium of running a kingdom. That, he left to his "beagle," as he called him, Robert Cecil. (Elizabeth called Cecil her "pygmy.")

The town of Royston, in Hertfordshire, was the king's favorite hunting site. He discovered the town on his way to London in 1603, still aglow with the news of his inherited kingdom. One year later, while hunting at Royston, James noticed one of his hounds was missing. The king loved his hounds. He had about thirty of them, and he knew all their names. The farms around Royston suffered by the chase—trampled crops, abuses by some of the king's minor officials, depletion of local stores for supply. But the king was aggravated at the loss of his dog.

The next day the dog returned and found his usual spot among the pack. A note was attached to the dog's neck. "Dear Mr. Jowler," it said, "we pray you speak to the king (for he hears you every day, and so doth he not us) that it will please his Majesty to go back to London, for else the country will be undone; all our provision is spent already and we are not able to entertain him long."[9]

James thought it was a joke and stayed two more weeks.

Not the only way to hunt, but one he particularly enjoyed, he called "running hounds." The dogs would get the scent of a specific stag, and the horsemen went full stride after the creature. Once the animal was felled and killed by the dogs, the king would dismount, slit the stag's throat, and open its belly. He would then thrust his hands—and sometimes his feet—into the goo and allow the dogs the satisfaction of the animal's blood. Not stopping there, the king often daubed the faces of his friends who hunted with him. To their smiling disgust.

The hunt was more than a pastime. A Venetian ambassador remarked, "He seems to have forgotten he is king, except in his kingly pursuit of stags, to which he is quite foolishly devoted."[10] It was up and out by eight, and in by four in the afternoon. His energies were always youthful, at times feverish. Here, there was no question who was king. Prerogative was unquestioned. And he was predator, not prey. The domain was simpler, more defined, in some ways more civilized. The rules actually meant something.

The hunt either raised or lowered his spirits, depending on the spoil. Some weighty matters of state may have suffered after a bad day at the chase. Either that, or by sheer neglect.

_____, or *The Scottish Play*

We are not there just yet, but *Macbeth* is worth sharing space with the king's *Daemonologie*. It was considered *lèse-majesté* (an offense against the sovereign authority) to portray the life of a living monarch from the stage—a treasonable offense. But there was no such law against meddling with the king's psychology, as long as you knew how to finesse around it, to tamper with the exposed nerve or the little filaments just below the surface. Shakespeare's *Macbeth*, or *The Scottish Play*, as it was eventually called, was written with James in mind.

By the way, it was called *The Scottish Play* because actors eventually refused to call it by its proper name. There was a lot of bad luck surrounding, well, _____. Even character names are suspect. Instead of saying Lady _____, an actor might just say "the

Queen." Many years later, one actress playing the role of "the Queen" thought the sleepwalking scene might be more realistic if she closed her eyes. This innovation was good for one night only. She walked off the stage and fell into the orchestra pit, injuring herself, forcing her to rethink the strategy.

Macbeth was performed at Hampton Court in 1606 (the birth-place of the *King James Bible*) and at the invitation of the king himself. At that time, James was entertaining the king of Denmark, Christian IV, the inebriate brother-in-law, who was by that time all grown-up. And who better to show off than your best? Shakespeare held nothing back.

Macbeth gave James everything. All the stuff he feared, that rattled him to the quick. The dramatist pushed every button—the naked blades, the regicide, witches, old Scotland, the dirty jokes, subtle topical references, prophecies, royal lineage, all of it.

> And oftentimes, to win us to our harm,
> The instruments of darkness tell us truths,
> Win us with honest trifles, to betray's
> In deepest consequence.
> —William Shakespeare, *Macbeth*, I, iii, 123–126

Harvard professor Marjorie Garber, in *Shakespeare After All*, compares Lady Macbeth to the two major female influences in James's life, his mother and Elizabeth I. Lady Macbeth is indeed a powerful, tactical, and dangerous character: "Somewhere behind the dominant figure of King James, whose image is everywhere in *Macbeth*, lie the shadows of these strong female figures, 'mothers' and queens, with their inescapable aura and their evident power over his life, his fate, and his future."[11]

James is also a descendant of Banquo, one of the characters in the play. Banquo and Macbeth are close friends, brothers in arms, until

Macbeth has him killed. The witches ("the weird sisters") prophesied that Banquo would sire a whole line of kings, a line that would
"stretch out to the crack of doom." James VI of Scotland is among
them. The following is an allusion to the baby king.

> [Third apparition: a child crowned with a tree in his hand]
> What is this that rises like the issue of a king,
> And wears upon his baby-brow the round
> And top of sovereignty?
> —*Macbeth*, IV, i, 87–88

The Scottish Play was written in the wake of the assassination attempt of 5 November 1605 that came to be known as the
Gunpowder Treason and Plot, when a crew of radical Catholics
placed thirty-six barrels of gunpowder underneath the floor of Parliament (House of Lords). The intent was to end both the reign and succession in "one fell swoop" (to borrow a line from *Macbeth*).

For that olde and craftie Serpent, being a spirite, hee easilie spyes our affections, and so conformes himselfe thereto, to deceaue vs to our wracke.

—JAMES VI OF SCOTLAND,
DAEMONOLOGIE, BOOK ONE (1597)

The entire royal family was scheduled to be at this particular opening
session—the king, the queen, and all
the little princelings. The plot was
discovered at the last minute. There
remains some mystery about just how it was discovered, but James
was convinced it was God's protection, and that is all that mattered.
He made November 5 a memorial.

> Remember, remember, the fifth of November,
> The Gunpowder Treason and Plot.

I know of no reason the Gunpowder Treason
    Should ever be forgot.[12]

Macbeth is about killing a king and the consequences of killing a king. Madness, paralyzing guilt, self-deception, murder, suicide, and a most ignominious end are the fruits of Macbeth's "vaulting ambition." He entraps himself, with the aid of his wife, the "weird sisters," and his own appetite. But more than all these considerations, behind it all, and germane to our task here, *Macbeth* is a study of how even the subtlest hint of sovereignty, the most delicate step toward majestie, can so infect the mind and corrupt the heart of an otherwise honorable man.

> The happiest marriage in all of Shakespeare is that of Macbeth and Lady Macbeth.[13]
>
> —HAROLD BLOOM

Macbeth is one of the shortest plays in the Shakespearean corpus. Suitable length for the ADHD king and his semiconscious brother-in-law.

CHAPTER TWELVE

The Supremest Thing on Earth

Not all the water in the rough rude sea
Can wash the balm off from an anointed king.

—WILLIAM SHAKESPEARE, *Richard II*, III, ii, 54–55

JAMES WAS CONVINCED that his lineage could be traced backward some "three hundred years before Christ,"[1] beginning with Fergus I of Scotland,[2] around 330 BC. George Walton Williams, in the May 1982 issue of *South Atlantic Review* says that "modern historians discount many of James's ancestors as being mythical figures, but James did not."[3]

The coronation of a king or a queen is much more than ceremony, or the changing of the reigns. "The coronation was the most solemn ritual known to church and state. Its symbolism was sacramental, and conferred religious as well as civil legitimacy." During the coronation ceremony an individual is "transformed," that is, he or she becomes "possessed of those sacred powers of majesty that God alone could bestow or call into account."[4] This is the faith James was born into, a belief system that had been sustained for centuries. Coronation was a type of baptism and epiphany all in one.

As a seasoned king, he recorded his thoughts, and for public consumption. In 1598, settled as he was on the Scottish throne, James set his thoughts on divine right in *The Trew Law of Free Monarchies* (*Or, The Reciprock and Mvtvall Dvetie [duty] Betwixt a free King, and his naturall Subiectes*).

A fine first sample of kingly spin, this document, along with its successor, *Basilikon Doron* (1598), expressed and amplified his beliefs in divine right and absolute monarchy. To James it was a matter of doctrine. It was an order established by God himself.

Divine right did not originate with James. There was nothing new about his beliefs. Indeed, for centuries dynastic rulers had been led by these precepts, acting and judging as "little gods" on earth. Nor was this notion just some idle fancy of monarchs, some device to monitor and control life beneath them. It was the "faith" of the commoner as well. In a culture that mingled religious faith and civil headship, it was unquestioned. There was as much spectacle about the throne of a king as there was at the altar of God.

The Jacobean age was *preliberal*, meaning that the rights of an individual, personal freedom, the right to question were not a consideration at the time. Today we demand a separate church and state. They did not. One did not exist

The *Stone of Scone*, also known as the *Stone of Destiny*, or the *Coronation Stone*, the stone James was crowned upon, was first brought to Scotland from Ireland by Fergus I (or so the tradition says). Taken as spoil by Edward I of England, kings and queens sat upon this stone during coronation. One legend says the stone was the very "pillow" upon which the biblical Jacob rested his head at Bethel.[5]

without the other. The claims of divine right were not a shock to the Jacobethan. It was not the hard sell we might imagine.

A troubled shadow

One of the spectacles of the Jacobean court was the *masque*, particularly those presented by Ben Jonson and Inigo Jones (friends of Queen Anne). The masque was not a stage production as much as it was a grand pageant that often included dancing, music, elaborate props, living statues. It became the fashion at the Jacobean court. So much so that between 1606 and 1611 an estimated £75,000 was spent on court entertainments featuring the masque. The *Oxford English Dictionary* says the masque became a "clearly defined genre during the reigns of James I and Charles I."

> Monarchie: which forme of government, as resembling the Divinitie, approcheth nearest to perfection, as all the learned and wise men from the beginning have agreed upon.
>
> —JAMES VI OF SCOTLAND, *THE TREW LAW OF FREE MONARCHIES*, 1598

Different than a play, the masque was often interactive. It engaged the audience and was highly symbolic. In the masque "a deep truth about the monarchy was realized and embodied in action."[6]

The masque often expressed "the strongest Renaissance beliefs about the nature of kingship, the obligations and perquisites of royalty." Anne, "enraptured by the possibilities of self-glorification presented by the masque,"[7] was represented as *Bel-Anna, Queen of the Ocean*. Young Prince Henry was represented as *Oberon, Prince of Faery*, or some warlike god.

James is presented, oddly enough, as *Pan, the universal God*. He was delighted, of course, and I'm not sure there is a better image to capture this king. But my brain thinks in English not in ancient Greek, so the Pan I have imagined is not necessarily the Pan Ben Jonson featured in his masque. Mine is a bit more puckish, and like our king, has a troubled shadow.

The Scribber King: a pardonable ambition

James Stuart has the distinction of being the only English king to ascend the throne as a published author. His works make an impressive list. His initial efforts, as we have seen, were lyrical. First love is a powerful muse. *The Phoenix* (or *Ane Metaphoricall Invention of a Tragedie Called Phœnix*) was written with Esme Stuart in mind. It traces the flight of an exotic mythical bird that comes to Scotland, is attacked by three other "birds," seeks safety in the poet (the king), who is also attacked. It takes flight and eventually its own life.

> Draw farr from heir, mount heigh vp through the air,
> To gar thy heat and beames be law and neir.
> That in this countrey, which is colde and bair,
> Thy glistring beames als ardent may appeir . . .
> —James VI of Scotland, excerpt from *Ane Metaphoricall Invention of a Tragedie Called Phœnix*, 1584

It was a way of processing grief, and other powerful emotions.

James was "in his own opinion a deeply religious Prince, well versed in the Scriptures and in theology, with a pardonable ambition to make these qualities more generally known." He was never shy to preach, to pontificate, or to write it down for the rest of us. "He was, he believed, the elect of heaven, chosen not only to rule the State and to be a nursing father of the Church, but also to publish, to elucidate and to defend the Scriptures."[8]

His major works include *Daemonologie* (1597), *The Trew Law of*

Free Monarchies (1598, revised in 1616), *Basilikon Doron* (1599), and *A Counterblaste to Tobacco* (1604). He wrote quite a few meditations on Scripture, including a meditation on the Lord's Prayer. He even translated many of the psalms. The following is his rendering of Psalm 100, the familiar "Make a joyful noise unto the Lord, all ye lands."

Make all ye Lands a joyful Noise, to Him that is the Lord
  of Might,
With Gladness ever serve the Lord, and come with Singing
  in His Sight.
Know that the Lord is our great God, He us, not we, our
  selves did make,
We are His People, and the Sheep that He as His own
  Flock did take.
With Thanksgiving come in His Gates, and in His Courts
  His Praise proclaim,
Be always thankful unto Him, and ever bless His holy Name.
For lo, the Lord is wholly good, His tender Mercy lasts
  for ever,
  And unto Generations all, His Truth doth constantly
  perservere.

He might have made a decent hymnwriter, but I, for one, am grateful that James exercised some restraint during the creation of his Bible a few years later. In spite of the misfortune of much of his poetry, he was prolific. He loved nothing more than the sound of his own voice. After the chase, of course.

That precious stinke

It is not difficult to see where James is going with a title like *A Counterblaste to Tobacco*. Tobacco was a novelty, and forgive the pun, but it was pretty hot in England at the time. All the gallants of Oxbridge* were in on the habit, and as they do, pushed it to extremes. Merchants caught on and offered expensive gold and silver contraptions for a deep satisfying draw—the posturing, the reckless puff of the libertine. For novices, there were actually teachers available, adept "in the art of whiffing." Ahead of his time, and with a kind of earthy charm, James says tobacco, that "precious stinke," is habit forming and expensive.

> And for the vanities committed in this filthie custome, is it not both great vanitie and vncleanenesse, that at the table, a place of respect, of cleanelinesse, of modestie, men should not be ashamed, to sit tossing of Tobacco pipes, and puffing of the smoke of Tobacco one to another, making the filthy smoke and stinke thereof, to exhale athwart the dishes, and infect the aire, when very often, men that abhorre it are at their repast? (*A Counterblaste to Tobacco*, 1604)

He really doesn't like the stuff, nor does he like the guy responsible for it. James accused Sir Walter Raleigh of bringing the disgusting weed into England in the first place—a plant imported from Raleigh's disenchanted colonials at Roanoke, Virginia. A visitor remarked that Londoners are "constantly smoking tobacco and in this manner; they have pipes on purpose made of clay, into the farther end of which they put the herb, so dry that may be rubbed into powder, and putting fire to it."[9] Raleigh made smoking fashionable at the Elizabethan court, and in London at large. He smoked with the queen herself. She liked a good smoke now and then, and particularly in the company of her favorite, her "oracle" the handsome dash, Raleigh.

---

* Oxbridge—a way of combining the two great universities (Oxford and Cambridge).

James said, "It [tobacco] was neither brought in by a king, great emperor, nor learned doctor of physic, but by a father generally hated." That is, Sir Walter. When the king and Sir Walter met for the first time, James attempted a pun with the great man's name: "On my soul, man, I have heard rawly of thee."[10] There is no record whether or not the pun worked. I would doubt it. The king's final word on tobacco?

Surely Smoke becomes a kitchin far better then a Dining chamber, and yet it makes a kitchin also oftentimes in the inward parts of men, soiling and infecting them, with an vnctuous and oily kinde of Soote, as hath bene found in some great Tobacco takers, that after their death were opened.

Haue you not reason then to bee ashamed, and to forbeare this filthie noueltie, so basely grounded, so foolishly receiued and so grossely mistaken in the right vse thereof? In your abuse thereof sinning against God, harming your selues both in persons and goods, and raking also thereby the markes and notes of vanitie vpon you: by the custome thereof making your selues to be wondered at by all forraine ciuil Nations, and by all strangers that come among you, to be scorned and contemned. A custome lothsome to the eye, hatefull to the Nose, harmefull to the braine, dangerous to the Lungs, and in the blacke stinking fume thereof, neerest resembling the horrible Stigian smoke of the pit that is bottomlesse. (A *Counterblaste to Tobacco*, 1604)

Trew law of free monarchies

It was basically a primer, a practical guide to teach his subjects their obligation to their sovereign and his obligation to them. Obedience to the king, that is, himself, was therefore a religious obligation, and any revolt was wickedness, a transgression against God. *Trew Law* is brief, and it is written in very plain speech, with few ambiguities. "My purpose is to instruct, not to irritate," the king said. Kingship is scriptural, and all the laws that determine kingship are written in the Scripture. Even bad kings are sent among us as a kind of judgment sent of God. The following excerpts serve to highlight James's thought on the matter. James is utterly sincere.

> Kings are called gods by the prophetical king David because they sit upon God his throne in earth and have the count of their administration to give unto him. (James VI of Scotland, *The Trewe Law of Free Monarchies*)

King, father, judge, lawmaker, minister of God, peacemaker, pastor, James leaves little room for any other interpretation of his office, nor will he suffer any. The king is *Dominus omnium bonorum* (the Lord of all good). He is *Dominus directus totius Dominij* (direct Lord of the entire dominion). And again, this is not an innovation, but a recapitulation, a clarification of an old order.

But there is more to it than that. His writing, much more than a display of erudition or craftsmanship, was a shepherd's staff. His whole intention is imperial. He sees himself "a louing [loving] nourish-Father."[11] The redefinition he sought, he could move along with words. He was king in a time when words were power, and he knew how to make them do his bidding.

> Let your owne life be a law-booke and a mirrour to your people, that therein they may reade the practise of their owne lawes; and therein they may see, by your image, what life they should leade. (*Basilikon Doron*)

A subject's service to the king is their service to God. Any resistance or opposition to the king is opposition to God himself. It is a very tight order. *The king is appointed by God. He is responsible only to God. And the king is accountable to no law but God.* This is the real key to understanding King James. This is heart central, the underpinning of all he believes. His belief is profound, incompatible with a world tending toward the individual, but if there is greatness to be discerned about him, it is on this wise. This is where he is most grounded.

In his speech to the English Parliament on 21 March 1610, James's words began:

> The state of monarchy is the supremest thing upon the earth; for kings are not only God's lieutenants upon earth, and sit upon God's throne, but even by God himself they are called gods. . . . they [monarchs] exercise a manner or resemblance of divine power on earth . . . power to create or destroy, make or unmake . . . to give life or send death, to judge all and to be accountable to none.

Basilikon Doron

Any search for James will bring you to the Solomon, the Abraham, and the Jacob in him—that is, the wise, the fatherly, the canny. In his book, *Basilikon Doron* (Greek for "a Kingly Gift"), he engages all of them.

Divided into three "bookes," the text is at once personal, then formal, but always instructing. It is difficult at times for modern tastes, and stalls in places. The Solomon is lucid and generous. The Abraham is warm and nurturing. The Jacob is the one doing the writing itself. Still, James is not selling as much as he is stating his belief. He is more Israel than Jacob. The text is translucent, bright with instruction and command.

But James, as clear and as wise and as fatherly as he expresses himself, simply does not live by what he preaches, at least not completely.

But being James, he believes what he is saying and he is utterly sincere. It was meant to be a private publication, a gift from father to son. Prince Henry was five.

> I onely permitted seaven of them to be printed, the
> printer being first sworn for secrecie: and these seaven
> I dispersed amongst some of my trustiest seruants, to
> be keeped closlie by them: least in case by the iniquitie,
> or wearing of time, any of them might have been lost . . .
> (*Basilikon Doron*)

By the time James was king of England, just four years later, it was a runaway bestseller. Is it shameless self-promotion? Did he plan it this way all along? Is it a message to the Kirk, to those who tried to hold him down or beat the monarch out of him? Is it a clever piece of princely propaganda? He is king. He is James.

Basilikon Doron is an amplification of *Trew Lawe*, in which James forwards the notion of divine right a bit further still. An opening sonnet acts as prologue to the body of the work, and a glimpse of its spirit:

> GOD giues not Kings the stile [style] of Gods in vaine,
> For on his throne his sceptre doe they swey:
> And as their subiects ought them to obey,
> So Kings should feare and serue their God againe.
> If then ye would enioy a happie raigne,
> Obserue the statutes of your heauenly King,
> And from his Law, make all your Lawes to spring:
> Since his Lieutenant here ye should remaine,
> Reward the iust, be steadfast, true, and plaine,
> Represse the proud, maintaining aye the right,
> Walk alwaies so, as euer in his sight,

Who guards the godly, plaguing the prophane:
And so ye shall in Princely vertue shine,
    Resembling right your mightie King Diuine.

Considered the best prose James ever wrote, *Basilikon Doron* is an instruction manual, a code of kingship. In a dream, James had a presentiment that his life would be cut short. He felt it necessary to write the book in response. Of course, he lived with that type of threat all his life. The specter was always present. It is difficult to imagine his dreams without some disturbing image.

By this time in his life, James VI of Scotland was no longer the frightened boy, but the seasoned king, with a wife and children. He saw an opportunity, and took it. Prince Henry was the oldest of the three surviving children of James and Anne: Henry, Elizabeth, and Charles. The others died within a year of childbirth.

Henry was a very different boy than his father had been. He would, as Fortinbras said of the dead prince Hamlet, "had he been put on, to have proved most royally." There was a great deal of hope for young Henry, and for the England that would have been his. He was interested in martial studies, in warlike games. He was also a friend to Walter Raleigh. When Raleigh was held prisoner in the Tower, Henry said, having a shrewd awareness of his father even at a young age, "No king but my father would keep such a bird in a cage."[12]

Basilikon Doron was "for his training up in all points of a king's office." William McElwee writes that "stressing the patriarchal nature of kingship, James sets forth a host of sanctimonious precepts for his son's guidance. Henry is told he must possess every virtue, eschew every vice, and stand before his people as a model of self-restraint, wisdom, and godliness."[13]

I am not sure just how harshly we should judge the king for his *Trew Lawe of Free Monarchie* or *Basilikon Doron*. He gives us something of himself. In particular, he lets us know just how deep his belief is.

 CHAPTER THIRTEEN

1603

Hark! Hark!

The dogs do bark,

The beggars have come to town.

Some in rags,

Some in tags,

And some in velvet gowns.

—ANONYMOUS (circulating during the inaugural days of James I)

SHE HAD LOST so many teeth it was difficult to understand her words. At sixty-nine, Elizabeth was ancient for the times. But the Privy Council had little choice but to press their queen, albeit gently, for a name. She said, "I told you my seat has been the seat of Kings, and I will have no rascal to succeed; who should succeed me but a King?"[1]

The dying queen had avoided naming a successor to her throne. Always the tactician, it was just smart to hoard the name of the prize-winner. Often, when a successor is named, the plots start rolling—the assassination attempts, the negotiating, the counter-negotiating, all the conspiracy mischief, the works. It was better to stay mute on the subject. Being shy of teeth had its advantages.

When she lost the powers of speech altogether, those with her asked if it was indeed the king of Scotland who was to succeed her. She reached and touched her crown, or so the legend goes. It was thought that she meant she would be succeeded by one who already wore a crown. It is a pitiful piece of theater, but it brought some assurance to those present.

In spite of the interpretation of the queen's dying remarks, arrangements had already been made in favor of the King of Scots. At the first sign of the queen's death, Robert Cecil began to shape the Scot's way to the throne, and had to use every bit of instinct and cunning to do it. If discovered, it would cost him his head.

But he would not be discovered. And it would cost him nothing.

Quasimodo

Much more than a mere strategist, the little Machiavel* was an artist. He was also magnificently corrupt. That must sound like a bad thing. The court of James I would itself become magnificently corrupt. James was too broke for it to be otherwise. Servants stole from the king, and from each other. The system of audits and inspections kept an imperfect math. The Woodyard officers charged for wood that never arrived. The officers of the Buttery sold the king's drink for their own profits. The officers of the Poultery sold "lamb, capon, and fowl intended for the use of the household."[2] And that is just the beginning. The royal head usually looked the other way. It was a kind of compensation, for there was very little cash.

Always dressed in black, always understated, Cecil was, like the rest of them, an actor, for they were all actors, with parts, speeches,

---

Machiavel—"A person who acts on principles recommended, or supposed to have been recommended," by Niccolo Machiavelli (1469–1527) "in his treatise on statecraft; an intriguer or schemer." *Oxford English Dictionary*.

and with exaggerated names. They all knew how it worked, and said nothing of it.

Small, not quite hunchbacked, but noticeably bowed nonetheless, "humped like a lute,"[3] Cecil made James, a man he had yet to meet, appear almost attractive. He had a deformity in one leg that added an arhythmical shuffle to his gait. James waddled into his new kingdom. He and Cecil made quite the image of power. A waddling, shuffling majestie.

Cecil used his lack of form and grace to his advantage. He was Quasimodo and he was Don Corleone. He could not help but be more than he appeared. He was part actor, yes, but he was also part magician—subtle, convincing, undetectable—manipulating thought and speech of those around him with a ventriloquist's art.

Possessing the conspirator's soul, Robert Cecil had to maneuver rather delicately, circumspectly, and in spite of the clamor around him or the drag in one of his shoes, there was never the slightest alarm in his steps. Like his father before him—William Cecil, Lord Burghley, Elizabeth's first minister and perhaps the greatest statesman England has ever had—Robert never made any move until he felt an almost mathematical certainty of its consequence. He always mapped out the possibilities, noting all the exits and entrances, all the plan *A*'s, plan *B*'s, right down the alphabet. For the nation's sake, this was fortunate indeed. Someone had to pay attention.

He was Shakespeare's Iago. Or if not, he should have been.

His steps were even softer of late. He had to circumnavigate the aging queen, who remained sharp-eyed and quick-witted until the end. That is, until one day she refused her bed, stuck her finger in her mouth (for some days), left it there, fell back as soft music played, and died some time in the hush of night, "mildly like a lamb, like a ripe apple from the tree."[4] A gold ring (the ring of state) was cut from her finger with a small saw, leaving a small track of gold dust.

It was that simple. It was that strange. *The queen is dead. Long live the king.*

For some time before the queen actually died, Cecil kept correspondence with James, using a simple code between them, appointing numbers for names. James was number 30. Cecil was number 10. Lord Henry Howard was number 3. It was a crude type of stratagem, and rather unconvincing, but it had the appearance of stealth, and it amused the king. Cecil instructed James how to behave toward the queen. Not to push. Not to ask, or worse, not to demand a clear acknowledgement of his succession, but simply treat her with "kindness and consideration."

James had come close to botching it a couple of times with his usual impatience. "In place of the petulant and jibing letters he had been writing to Elizabeth, his communications now breathed a beautiful spirit of love and affection."[5] He then laid it on rather thickly, and with a poet's sense of timing and balance. He was good at it. She bought it, and was much pleased with his renewed kindnesses toward her.

James had waited most of his life to come into the English possession. As the death of the old queen approached, James was, as Christopher Lee says, "tacitly waiting for the death of the second most famous virgin in history."[6]

Elizabeth was old. Her great city was young. The life expectancy in 1603 was thirty-two, and the legal age for marriage was fourteen for a male, twelve for a female. In his book *London: The Biography*, Peter Ackroyd writes that the "greatest proportion of the citizens were under the age of thirty, and it is this actuarial statistic which helps to explain the energy and restlessness of urban life in all its forms."[7]

As the dying time approached, anticipation rose. Everyone expected the King of Scots to be the next king of England. A Protestant king with a queen and children, heirs. Something England had gone without for many years.

Stability. Dynasty. Everyone began looking to the rising of the sun.

Elizabeth died just before three o'clock in the morning, Thursday, 24 March 1603. Within eight hours of her death, James Stuart was proclaimed King of England.

The promised land

Official word did not reach him for five days, but James was already aware. Robert Carey, Elizabeth's cousin, knowing all things would change under a new head, and hoping to gain favor he suspected would be lost under a new administration, was determined to be the first to bring James the news. The Privy Council had given orders to the contrary. No one was to leave or to enter the confines of Richmond Palace without a Council warrant. But Carey was thinking only of survival. Through a relative on the Council, he was able to bluff his way out of the gates.

Carey took with him a sapphire ring that belonged to his sister, Lady Scroope. James once sent her the ring and asked that it be returned to him only when Elizabeth was dead. The stories are blurred, like so much of the detail, but one of them says she threw the ring to her brother from a window at Richmond at the beginning of his journey. He left between eight and nine on Thursday morning and arrived in Edinburgh on Saturday, but not without being kicked in the head by a horse. Bloody, but undaunted, Carey persisted. Fortunate for us, he kept a diary.

> The king was newly gone to bed by the time I knocked at the gate. I knelt by him and saluted him by his title, "England, Scotland, France, and Ireland." He gave me his hand to kiss and bade me welcome.
>
> After he had long discoursed of the manner of the

Queen's sickness, and of her death, he asked, what letters I had from the Privy Council. I told him None and
acquainted him how I narrowly escaped from them. And
yet I brought him a blue ring from a Lady that I hoped
would give him assurance of the truth I reported. He took
it, and looked upon it and said, "It is enough. I know by
this you are a true messenger."[8]

Carey asked if he might be appointed to the King's Bedchamber.
It was not only an appointment of honor, it was a position of close-
ness with the king, to have your mouth close to the ear of England
itself. Perhaps in his state of mild to tottering euphoria, that bliss of
election, James granted him the request, saying, "I know you have
lost a near Kinswoman and a loving Mistress [Elizabeth]: but take
here my hand and I will be as good a Master to you and will require
you this service with honour and reward."

Carey, of course, was thoroughly contented, pleased with himself
and the new monarch. But outmaneuvering Cecil, if it was possible
at all, was never smart. Ever. Cecil told James that Carey should be
dismissed. And Carey was dismissed. He could only say, "Shortly
after coming to London [the King] deceived my expectation, and
adhered to those that sought my ruin."[9]

On the west side of High Cross in Cheapside, courtiers and
nobles listened as Cecil proclaimed:

James the sixt king of Scotland is now by the death of our
late Soveraigne, Queene of England of famous memorie,
become also our Onely, Lawfull, Lineall and Rightfull
Liege Lord, James the first, King of England, France,
and Ireland, defender of the faith.[10]

Cecil sent the king a draft of a proclamation announcing his succession, and asked for the king to examine it for any corrections. The king made no corrections whatsoever. The music "sounded so sweetly in his ears that he could alter no note in so agreeable an harmony."[11]

It would take him weeks to get to London, but his former impatience seemed softer, quieter. He was about to dismount the "wild, unruly colt" Scotland, for what he was convinced would be a smooth "towardly" ride. England, after all, knew how to appreciate monarchy, and the share of divinity that settles upon an anointed sovereign. England was rich. Scotland was poor. Elizabeth could command, where he could only "contrive and maneuver."[12]

Scotland had made him a fine king. Unfortunately, he left the lessons behind, and seems to have abandoned good kingcraft to play the little god he had always dreamed of. William McElwee says, "There is little evidence that James ever seriously considered or properly understood the complex problems of which his new inheritance was compounded. For him the English Succession had taken on all the qualities of fantasy."[13]

The Privy Council, curious to know how the king had taken the news of his accession, read the letter sent to them by Roger Aston, one of their eyes and ears in Scotland. He said James was "even, my Lords, like a poore man wandering about 40 years in a wildernesse and barren soyle, and now arrived at the Land of Promise."[14]

I have absolutely nothing to wear

Now this is where the real show begins, the one long day at the fayre. The first order of business, of course, was to get some traveling money. "The King wants present [immediate] money, and therefore you shall do well to provide to be sent forthwith, which he will take very thankfull."[15] James requested £5,000 from the Privy Council, money he thought was sure to be there. It was not. But the politic

Cecil did not want to dampen the festivities (or his position), so he raised the sum, and had it presented to the king in Berwick.

Since Queen Anne was going to be delayed in her progress to London, James suggested that Elizabeth's jewelry and her gowns would be just compensation for Anne's trouble. Clothes and jewelry would be the new queen's pacifier for the life to come. Whether there was money in the exchequer or not was no real concern of hers. Or her husband's for that matter. Before Elizabeth died, James had asked Cecil for an advance on his annuity.

Poor Quasimodo. Cecil would be dead in a little over eight years. The most powerful man in the kingdom outside the king, doubtless. But exhausted, beaten, squeezed. He was a genius and, like his father, among the greatest statesmen in English history, but the weight James heaped on him was just too much for his little bent frame. Cecil was made baron in 1603, viscount in 1604, earl in 1605, and dead in 1612.

Tuesday, 5 April 1603, Edinburgh. James kissed Anne goodbye before a crowd on the Royal Mile. He bent low and kissed her softly on the throat. Both king and queen were in tears, as were many in the crowd that day. He promised the people he would visit every three years. He returned to Scotland only once, seventeen years later.

A large train attended him as he made his way southward. He took his Scots favorites with him, including his old teacher, Peter Young. He took his old playmate, Jockie, and Ludovic Stuart, Duke of Lennox, the son of his beloved Esme. Ludovic was James's Mephibosheth.* The presence of his Scots would be a source of aggravation to the English, who would feel pushed aside.

Every town he passed in England shot off their cannons, if they

---

*2 Samuel 9:6–13. Mephibosheth was the son of Jonathan, David's beloved friend. Though he did not feel worthy, David assured the boy that because of his love for Jonathan, he would always eat at the king's table, and be considered as one of the king's sons.

had them. *Clamor, clamor, buzz, buzz.* Nothing was held back. No gift was too large or impractical for the royal guest. They fell to their knees shouting, *"Welcome!"* and, *"God save King James!"* In Berwick, he was given the keys to the city and a bag of gold.

Now Elizabeth might have known how to receive such adoration and give some portion of herself back, creating and nurturing that bond with her people that was so important to her. James did not. Nor did he really care to. Unlike his predecessor, he did not have the gift of banter with the drayman or the fishwife, the drover or the baker. Nor was he capable of the simple word of thanks to the local schoolmaster for the singing and dancing of his students.

But he did manage to be as light and *bonhomie* as possible. His thoughts and mood were too elevated to be otherwise. He also remained on his horse as much as possible. There was little, if any dignity in his "shambling" walk. His gait was a fair image of his ability to manage his new inheritance.

If there was a time to stick the hand out for a favor, this was it. James dispersed around £14,000 on his trip south, in "his careless, openhanded way."[16] Not to mention the £10,000 he spent on the journey alone. In 1603, this was an enormous amount of money. In some towns, he literally threw gold coins to the crowds in the street.

Rapt as he was at his new fortune, at the influence of either his English notables traveling with him, or his Scottish favorites, he dubbed more than three hundred knights on his way to London. For a little perspective: Elizabeth created fewer than three hundred knights her entire forty-four year reign, and each candidate had actually earned the honor. Even though Francis Bacon would be knighted four months later by the king, he wrote about "this almost prostituted title of knighthood." (In that same four-month period, more than nine hundred knights were dubbed.)

James was impatient to get to his new home, but not so much as to pass up a fat deer or two. Newcastle, Durham, Doncaster (where he stayed at the Bear Inn), then to Newark, hunting with every opportunity. Some of the locals brought their best dogs, and baskets of live hares.

Before his arrival at York, and taking inventory of his appearance, James commanded Cecil to send a state coach and with it some new clothes. Passing through Berwick and Newcastle, his appearance might have been tolerable, but as he approached the second largest city in the kingdom, he thought otherwise. "I have absolutely nothing to wear."[17] Annoyed, and yet ever obedient, Cecil suspended the machine of state to tend to the vanity of his new master.

The mayor of York, in anticipation of their royal guest, declared a major clean-up of the town. All the townspeople should "remove all clogs . . . dung hill and filth out of the streets, and shall paint the outside of their houses with some colours."[18] Vagrants were expelled, and the clean streets were to be strewn with "rushes, flower, and herbs."[19] The king was given a silver cup filled with gold coin. A fountain with a cast of a mermaid flowed with wine. As if that wasn't enough alcohol, a "conduit all the day long ran white and claret wine, every man to drinke as much as he listed [desired]."[20]

Celebration and excess of one sort or another met the new king in every city. It was a circus of fawning speeches and drool, of bad poetry and much feigning. This particular condition would follow James for quite some time, and long after he settled into his new digs in London.

The first mishap was at Newark-upon-Trent (Nottinghamshire). A young cutpurse had been following the king's train disguised as a gentleman. He was caught with a fairly large amount of coin on him. Once James heard about the young man, he had him executed without a trial.[21] "His Majestie hearing of this nimming gallant, directed a warrant, presently to the Recorder at New-warke, to have him hanged, which was accordingly executed."[22] The townsfolk were shocked. Though Scottish law did not require cutpurses to be tried before execution, with the exception of a few locations, English law did. This was bad form.

Sir John Harington remarked, "I hear our new King has hanged a man before he was tried, 'tis strangely done: now if the wind blows thus, why may not a man be tried before he has offended?"[23] Harington's comment has been used to validate claims of James's despotism. Then again, Harington's writing had gotten him in trouble with Elizabeth as well.

Writers.

Not all was lost, though. Harington was the man attributed for inventing the water-flush toilet, lovingly known as "the John." I suppose he had to have some way to dispose of his first drafts. The swirl and cough of unfortunate text. Harington did not prosper in James's court (nor in the former reign either). He started out well. Only months before the blessed event, Harington sent the king a gift, a lantern. On the lantern was an inscription: *Lord, remember me when Thou comest into Thy Kingdom.*

It didn't do Harington much good. For all he did for sanitation, his writing aggravated the king.

Anyway, other than the bad timing of a young cutpurse, a few foul opinions and some public spew hurled at the lynching king, a sermon or two, a lot of wine, a lot of liberal coin, a lot of fawning, hundreds of happy knights, the bad luck of an inventive writer and a few fat deer, the king's progress south was a complete success.

James arrived at Theobalds, the home of his first minister, Robert Cecil, the man he had yet to meet, on 3 May.

A few days later, 7 May 1603, James came into town, though not with the full retinue. He was mobbed. The sheer density of townspeople "in the highways, fields, meadows, closes, and on trees was so great that they covered the beauty of the fields; and so greedy were they to behold the King that they injured and hurt one another."[24] With some forty thousand attempting to get into court, and an extra one hundred thousand swarming about London, adding to the two hundred thousand or so population of the town, few had ever seen this kind of frenzy before. The last monarch had been crowned forty-five years earlier.

James was like a child visiting some monstrous theme park for the first time—giddy, wide-eyed, hardly knowing which ride to go on next, or which gift shop to plunder. From the Tower, he made his way to the palace at Whitehall. The Crown Imperial, that seven-pound marvel of gold, jewels, pearl, English antiquity, and glory, first cast by Henry VII and worn by all successive monarchs,[25] made a huge first impression. In an instant, he saw the image of his reign. All the blueness of his blood flushed warm with recognition. For the remainder of the summer and fall, he visited one royal dwelling after another.

To inventory our king upon first sight, as an Italian described him, "his colour blond, his hair somewhat the same, his beard square and lengthy, his mouth small, his eyes blue, his nose curved and clear-cut, a man happily formed, neither fat nor thin, of full vitality, neither too large or too small."[26] Historian of the reign, Arthur Wilson said the king "was rather tall than low, well set and somewhat plump, of a ruddy complexion . . . His beard was scattering on his chin and very thin; and though his clothes were seldom fashioned to the vulgar garb, yet in the whole man he was not uncomely."[27]

The clergy made over him as much or more than the others. David Willson notes that "astounded by his knowledge and grasp of theology, they declared that he spoke through the inspiration of the Holy Spirit and that God had bestowed upon him far more than upon ordinary mortals the power to interpret Scripture."[28]

But with these observations, Willson also says that one trait eclipsed all others, and that was the king's vanity. To the problems of the new kingdom, he says James "gave no serious study." Willson offers a summation saying, "His [James's] approach to government was personal . . . he did not love England though he professed to do so. He loved himself, and England must minister to that self-love."[29]

His book *Basilikon Doron* began to sell rapidly. Francis Bacon writes, "This book, falling into every man's hand, filled the whole realm as with a good perfume or incense before the king's coming in, for being excellently written and having nothing of affectation."[30]

Another bully in town

Once the king was in town, he was forced to turn around and leave again, and at the presence of yet another bully. It wasn't the Kirk this time, or a pack of growling nobles. It wasn't some raging pulpiteer, or another ambitious gamesman with his eye on the crown. It was a much bigger threat than any of these, and more deadly. It fed where it wanted, and did not discriminate between noble or commoner, royal or anyone else.

The early reign of James I of England was plagued with, well, the plague. It would come and go but not without leaving a trail of dead in its wake. Its feeding habits varied, but between 1563 and 1603 there were five major outbreaks,[31] the worst year being 1603, the year of our king. From April to December that same year there were more than thirty thousand deaths in London due to plague. The numbers were staggering, and its presence upset everything, all the wheels and pulleys that make a kingdom run.

And run they did. Nobles fled to country estates. Acting troupes went on tour. Even the preachers, the men of God who railed about the plague being the scourge of an angry God, who preached that the righteous need not fear; they, too, fled the city, or some did. For some good pastors stayed with their troubled flocks, and some died of the disease themselves. Their names were not recorded, nor were they given any just tribute.

If you had the means, you could flee. If you did not, you went nowhere. You took your chances. Of course *flee*, is an interesting choice of words. For the thing rode into town on the grizzly pelt of a rat, and there were lots of rats. Still, in spite of the whimsical mood of the Bubonic Plague (*Yersinia pestis)*, James and Anne were crowned 25 July 1603 in a "sadly empty"[32] Westminster Abbey. It was not unlike his first coronation in Scotland thirty-five years earlier, only this time he didn't sleep through it. The death toll was around twenty a day by that time, so the usual traffic was forbidden. It took almost another year for the plague to recede, but it did.

Elizabeth did have her funeral. It took place a little more than a month after she died. Custom dictated the delay.

> The coffin was taken at night, on a barge lit by torches, to Whitehall, where it lay in state in a withdrawing chamber, attended round the clock by many lords and ladies. It was then moved to Westminster Hall, where it lay "all hung with mourning; and so, in accordance with ancient custom, it will remain, until the King gives the order for her funeral."[33]

The king was upwind at the time, and did not care much for the business anyway, but he ordered the funeral, and Elizabeth had the sendoff she deserved. He did not attend. By now, I suppose we could not expect him to.

Pomp, flaunt, and James

On 15 March 1604, the royal couple made procession through the streets of London at last, from the Tower to Westminster. *Plague out, king in.* Seven large archways were built for the occasion, triumphal gates for the royal entourage to pass through. There were fountains, flames, and living statuaries.

Trailing behind the royal family were William Shakespeare, Richard Burbage, Augustine Philips, and other actors in their troupe. This is an odd sight to try to imagine. Posterity has given the name of Shakespeare a much larger girth than it has James Stuart, and yet here is the larger trailing behind the lesser. This brings up a curious little detail about the king's first days in office.

James arrived at his palace in Greenwich for the first time on 13 May 1603. Six days later, on 19 May, letters patent (official documents, warrants) were issued, making the "Lord Chamberlain's Men" the "King's Men." The Lord Chamberlain's Men was the theater troupe of William Shakespeare and Richard Burbage, the premiere troupe in London. The patent named "Laurentio Fletcher et Willielmo Shakespeare . . ." and the rest, and allowed them to perform as "well for the recreation of our loving subjects, as for our solace and pleasure when we shall think it good to see them . . . within their now usual house called The Globe," as well as all other towns and boroughs in the kingdom.[34] Solace, yes, but also a vehicle of propaganda. No one could give them kings like Shakespeare.

James was in town for less than a week, and in the heat of all his initial obligations, all the royal inspections and introductions, all the usual administration-changing duties, he made this odd and yet conspicuous appointment. Actors had enjoyed noble patronage before, but never royal. Not until now. Shakespeare and the King's Men were later appointed Grooms of the Chamber.

Will and his fellow actors were not only given the privilege, but were obligated to wear the royal livery—the red doublet, hose, and cloak. "Shakespeare was placed first in the list, by the Master of the Great Wardrobe, for receiving 4 1/2 yards of scarlet cloth for his uniform."[35]

Back to the royal procession: Edward (Ned) Alleyn, another fellow actor (Ben Affleck in Tom Stoppard's movie *Shakespeare in Love*), though not one of the King's Men, made a speech as the "genius" or guiding spirit of the city.[36]

It was the obligation of the new reign to flaunt itself. It was a confidence builder for the people. A new foundation was being laid over an old one. They wanted to see their new royal family, and the royal family wanted to be seen. At least the queen did, and all the little Stuart princelets—Henry, Elizabeth, and baby Charles. James was not all that interested. David Willson writes, "James had long since tired of playing the gracious sovereign. Large crowds, the normal precursors of trouble in Scotland, alarmed him, and he chafed at the petty tyranny of public ceremonies."[37]

Upon his London entry, he "sucked in their gilded oratory, though never so nauseous, but afterwards in his public appearances, especially in his sports, the access of the people made him so impatient that he often dispersed them with frowns, that we may not say curses."[38] When the king asked John Oglander what the people would like, he was told they would like to see their king. At this, the king replied in Broad Scots, "I will pull down my breeches and they will also see my arse!"[39]

And this is James Stuart, the first of a proud new dynasty.

The center and perfection of all things

Losing little time, in a gesture that was advanced for its time, James called three conferences in 1604. One would end a twenty-year war with Spain (the Somerset House Conference). Another called for the union of Scotland and England. A third was on the matter of religion.

His bid for union didn't take. It was an English parliament, and even without the xenophobia, the resistance was too strong and too old. When they denied his request for union, James did what he often did. He ignored them. He then proclaimed himself King

of Great Britain. Like the legendary Arthur, he was determined to
"embrace under one name the whole circuit of the island."[40]

But he is no Don Quixote. He is not tilting at windmills.

Union was one of the many things he brought with him from
the north. It was a kind of governing spirit with him. His divided
psychology seemed to demand it of him. Years into his English reign,
while on progress to Scotland, in a move that was typical James, he
stopped at the border that separated England and Scotland and lay
down with part of him in Scotland and part of him in England. He
did this to show those with him how two kingdoms could be found
in one person.

> Our princely care mon [must] be extended to see them
> [England and Scotland] join and coalesce together in a
> sincere and perfect union, and as two twins bred in one
> belly, love one another as no more two but one estate.
> (James I of England, excerpt from a letter to the Scottish
> Privy Council, 1604)

He had signets made with the rose and thistle intertwined, the
rose of England and the thistle of Scotland. He combined the flags of
Scotland and England, the St. Andrew with the St. George, to create
what is often called the Union Jack (named for himself), the flag of
Great Britain to this day. He had a twenty-shilling gold piece minted
that was to be called the Unite. Its motto: *Faciam eos in gentem unam*
(I shall make them into one nation).

He took as his own motto *beati pacifici*, that is, "blessed are the
peacemakers."

And his dream of unity did not end with Scotland and England.
It was much larger than that. He sought to bring about a unity
among all major divisions of Christianity—English, Calvinist,
Lutheran, Roman Catholic, Greek Orthodox—because they "shared

a common heritage." He even forwarded plans for an ecumenical council "to plucke up those roots of dangers and jealousies which arise for cause of Religion as well betweene Princes and Princes, as betweene them and their subjects."[41] In his first English parliament, 19 March 1604, he said he longed for a settlement that might end the divisions in his kingdom and on the continent. Speaking for himself, he said:

> I could wish from my heart that it would please God to make me one of the members of such a generall Christian union in Religion, as laying wilfulnesse aside on both hands, wee might meet in the middest, which is the Center and perfection of all things. (19 March 1604)

If there is greatness to be considered in King James, and there is, albeit unheralded, it was in his bid for unity among all Christians. Reconciliation means a world at peace. In his book, *King James VI and I and the Reunion of Christendom*, W. B. Patterson asserts that "James saw religious reconciliation as the key to a stable and peaceful Christendom at a time when religious disputes exacerbated the conflicts among the states."[42] James Stuart was "a shrewd, determined, flexible, and resourceful leader who had a coherent plan for religious pacification aimed at resolving urgent problems in the wake of the Reformation and Counter-Reformation."[43]

An old Welsh prophecy had said, "A babe crowned in his cradle; marked with a lion in his skin; shall recover again the cross; [and] make the isle of Brutus [Britain] whole . . . to grow henceforward better and better."[44] To James, to "recover again the cross" meant healing a divided Christendom. He had a birthmark on his arm shaped like a lion, which only strengthened his resolve.

The great *what if* dominated his global thinking. He thought in possibilities. This is the common cause of greatness in anyone, but it is magnificence in a king. Still, his bid for religious union failed, and with its own kind of magnificence.* It was perhaps one dream too big and too soon.

The third conference that year was the Hampton Court Conference. It is at this conference that the King James Bible was born, a piece of English history that changed the world.

---

*The walls were too massive, the hostilities too old and immovable. To "meet in the middest" was a distance too far, too deep of a death to ask. The pope himself played along at first hoping he might convert James to Catholicism. Four hundred years have passed and Christendom is no closer to unity than it was in 1604.

CHAPTER FOURTEEN

The Hampton Court Conference

I have often heard and read, that *Rex est mixta persona cum sacerdote* [a king is a mixture of a person and a priest], but I never saw the truth thereof, till this day.

—LORD CHANCELLOR ELLESMERE (THOMAS EGGERTON) 1540–1617, *statement made following first day of the Hampton Court Conference*

IT WAS CALLED the millenary petition. The name suggested at least a thousand petitioners, a thousand concerned and agitated Puritans seeking audience with the king on certain "abuses yet practiced and remaining in the Church of England."[1] The exact number of petitioners was a bit exaggerated, but it was a poetic age; everything was exaggerated—the clothes they wore, the ruffs, the doublets, the silk stockings, the silly pants, and the titles they gave things.

But it was a well-written document, conscious of its royal audience, making all the right verbal appeals to the king's vanity. It wasn't even that long of a petition, but the complaining voice made it unattractive. The use of the cross in baptism, for instance, or rings in the wedding ceremony, the rite of confirmation, these had to go, as well as the use of terms like "priest" and "absolution." They asked that clergy might be better educated, and not wear the cope or the surplice Elizabeth had allowed.* The "longsomeness" of the service should be abridged, and the amount of singing. And "no popish opinion to be any more taught or defended; no ministers charged to teach their people to bow at the name of Jesus."[2]

However serious the list of objections, or however trivial, the truth is, it could have ten thousand petitioners, or half the population of London for that matter. The Puritan complaint had little chance of success.

The Puritan was the radical Protestant, the zealous reformer. As mentioned earlier, he was the extremist of his day. The *Oxford English Dictionary* describes him as "a person who advocates or aspires to special purity or correctness in a field; a purist." To H. L. Mencken, Puritanism is "the haunting fear that someone, somewhere, may be happy."

The Puritan would not "get" someone like James (or his mother for that matter).

One of the oldest tensions in Elizabethan and Jacobean culture was the one that existed between the Puritans and, oddly, the playhouses. Long after the reign of James, into the reign of Charles I, the Puritans gained ascendancy. Once Charles was dispatched, and the kingdom gave way to a commonwealth, one of the first things the Puritans did was destroy the theaters, literally, brick by brick, board by board.

The Puritan hated the playhouse more than anything, with its idlers, and wastrels, those who might find a better use for their afternoons. They hated plays—the spectacle, the affected language, the

---

* *the cope or the surplice*—a *cope* is a long, loose cloak worn by a priest or bishop on ceremonial occasions. The *surplice* is a loose white linen vestment varying from hip-length to calf-length, worn over a cassock by clergy, acolytes, and choristers at Christian church services. (*Oxford American Dictionary*) Reference: David Starkey, *Monarchy*.

dark passions they exploited and aroused, the superstition, the counterfeiting of God's creation, the "ready emotionalism" that actors encouraged. It was, in essence, a condemning of a religious observance. It also provides us a way to understand the Puritan conscience.

Plays and playhouses were the "agents of the Devil."[3] They competed with the pulpits "in the matter of public instruction."[4] The Puritan hated them even more because they were immensely popular. In zenith, particularly at the changing of the reigns, the theater was unstoppable. With the rise of the theater in late Elizabethan London (1580s and upward), the Puritan movement itself rose in numbers, strength, and in fury. Another great tension of opposites (Newton's law of reciprocal action).

> Art is so wonderfully irrational, exuberantly pointless, but necessary all the same. Pointless and yet necessary, that's hard for a puritan to understand.
>
> —Nadine Gordimer, 1991 Nobel Prize winner (Literature)

The Puritan could not help himself. The magnetism to hate was too strong. After all, hate maintained a presence in religion, and would not go quietly away.

The petition was brought to the king as early as April 1603, while he was on progress to London. That bit of impatience didn't help their cause, if anything could. James was too busy being wonderful, being magnanimous—steeped as he was in his own fascination—to be bothered with nagging Puritans. But a conference was necessary for many reasons, so a conference was called. Then it was put off. Then called. Then put off again. The plague was no more a friend to the petitioners than James was. The conference was set for January 1604.

To the king, it was pure sport. Again, as it always is with James, it smacked of the hunt. Puritans were quarry—a few nervous rabbits, a quail or two. He did not like them very much. Actually, no one liked them that much. They were no fun. The Puritan was the original spoilsport. The name "Puritan" itself is derogatory. The following is a tavern scene from Shakespeare's *Twelfth Night* (II, iii, 151–158):

> MARIA. Marry, sir, sometimes he is a kind of puritan.
>
> SIR ANDREW. O, if I thought that I'ld beat him like a dog!
>
> SIR TOBY BELCH. What, for being a puritan? thy exquisite reason, dear knight?
>
> SIR ANDREW. I have no exquisite reason for't, but I have reason good enough.
>
> MARIA. The devil a puritan that he is, or any thing constantly, but a time-pleaser; an affectioned ass, that cons state without book and utters it by great swarths: the best persuaded of himself, so crammed, as he thinks, with excellencies, that it is his grounds of faith that all that look on him love him; and on that vice in him will my revenge find notable cause to work.

James associated Puritanism with antiroyal sentiment. That was "reason good enough."

Via media: the middle way

Since the reign of Henry VIII, England had been torn mercilessly, stretched and broken between Catholic and Protestant. Henry's son and successor, Edward VI, was a severe Protestant. Following Edward's brief reign was the reign of Edward's half-sister, the just-as-severe Catholic, Mary Tudor—the bitter, the vengeful. The deep wound in the kingdom was left without medication whatsoever.

Mary was responsible for more than three hundred Protestant deaths. For her efforts, she was given the charming name *Bloody Mary*.*

Elizabeth, observing the whole thing, had a different thought.

Elizabeth established her famous *via media* (the middle way). She would be the head of a church that was Roman Catholic[5] in appearance and Protestant in doctrine and belief. She was determined to end what she considered madness. One particular remark she made, as timeless and far-seeing as it was accurate, revealed her as a visionary queen. To her Privy Council, she said: *There is only one Jesus Christ. The rest is an argument over trifles.*

She had seen the result of religious extremism, and what it did to a nation. What it almost did to her. She thought it foolish in a monarch. Her *via media*, a church architecture that sought to appease a large middle swath of believers, offered the best of both worlds. Actually, it was far from being the best of anything, but it was certainly much better than what the nation had suffered under previous monarchs.

James saw no reason to change anything. He embraced Elizabeth's middle way. And other than a few extremists from either camp, Catholic or Puritan, it worked.

There is another way we might look at this religious settlement, this *via media*. According to Melvyn Bragg in *The Adventure of English*, the most consistent and the most powerful element of the English language, its "most subtle and ruthless characteristic," is *its ability to absorb others*, that is, to make foreign words English. To *absorb* is "to swallow up, to include or take a thing in to the loss of its separate existence; to incorporate." For example, in the sentence above, the word *ability* is borrowed from *abilite* (Anglo-Norman and

---

*With the legendary, albeit psychotic and homicidal, father—the lusty King Henry VIII and the deadly manner by which he managed his household—do we have any hope of expecting anything else from his children but a similar kind of bad behavior?

Middle French), *absorb* from *absorbe* (modern French), and *foreign* from *forain* (Old French).[6]

It serves a kind of justice that the English church, particularly under this complicated, multidimensional king, shares the same quality as its language, that is, its ability to absorb. The Anglican Church is an amalgam, a mingling, a "meet in the middest" kind of architecture, and yet it is autonomous, singular. The same could be said of the English language.

Bragg also suggests that nested within any language is a "unique way of knowing life."[7] The code of Englishness is bound in the language, its flexibility, its buoyancy, its power to absorb.* The United States, with its melting pot ideology, may be a good first example.

James had always been an admirer of the Church of England. To him it had a royal gloss, and seemed to stress the divinity of kings. A monarch sat at the head of its table. The sparkle of the liturgy itself is that of sovereignty. The Anglican Church is also bishop-friendly, and James likes his bishops. *Non episcopi, non Regis* (no bishop, no King). That was his summation.

This was no longer the snarling, antiroyal Presbyterian Kirk, who engaged their own type of absolutism, who claimed that the monarch was a mere participant in government, a church who would have no bishops and no archbishops, who governed by committees, or elders. This was England, a kingdom who knew how to appreciate its king.

Other than a few minor details, he saw no reason to change anything. Of course, at the beginning of the Hampton Court Conference, the bishops were not aware of this. What were they to think? James

---

*For this reason, and it is a subtle distinction, English (or rather, Englishness) will not sustain absolutism, the way other languages might, particularly Latin. Latin is a dead language. It is not flexible or pliant like English. It does not have the power or inclination to absorb. Therefore, it can sustain an absolute rule, like that of a pope. Whereas English cannot.

was the son of a Catholic queen raised by strict Presbyterian overlords. There was a touch of uncertainty about the new reign that made them apprehensive. Also, because of the nature of the Elizabethan religious settlement and its bulging middle, the English church had yet to clearly define itself. So a conference was in order. James wanted to settle accounts early.

How was the conference conducted? What was the tone, the climate? Like much of his life as we have witnessed it, it is at moments amusing, at times crude, but always entertaining. And, like the hunt, always at someone's expense.

Day one: like a good physician

Originally, Hampton Court was the home of Cardinal Wolsey, Henry VIII's version of Robert Cecil, the man who got things done. Like many such men who prospered under royal favor in and out of the king's eye, whose perceptions began to deceive them, who stepped too close and too often toward forbidden majestie or went at their art with a bit too much bandit enthusiasm, Wolsey's fall was a hard one. But he knew how to build a house. It was as fat and as rich and as well draped as he was.

Hampton Court was "a fairy palace, full of little towers and toy battlements."[8] Like the setting of a poem, there were a thousand rooms, stone gargoyles, mullioned windows, cloistered walks. Enchantment and gravity, the weight and feel of majestie. It was not difficult to be a prince in such a place. Not long after the coronation, James and Anne settled at Hampton Court as a safety precaution against the plague. It was about twelve miles from the heart of the city. Away from the rats.

The first day of the conference was Saturday, 14 January 1604. Just before eleven o'clock, all the attending conferees, or *almost* all, were led into the Presence Chamber by the Gentleman of the Royal Household. The large boding cloth of state displaying the royal arms hung on the wall. In front of it was a chair covered in velvet. The chair was empty for the moment.

The Puritans had initiated the conference more or less, and on this first day, they were quite conspicuously invited *not* to attend. The king had a few things to say to the leaders of the church first, those bishops and deans invited to attend the conference. The Puritans were anxious as well to hear what he had to say, and were denied the privilege of hearing him say it. They were commanded to wait outside the Presence Chamber. Was it an insult? Was it deliberate? They were Puritans. Was it anything else?

With true James Stuart élan, once his procession entered and all the obsequies were paid, he greeted the bishops and deans. There was never a compliment too high or hyperbole too over-the-top for James. He could be bought rather cheaply, in word or coin.

He removed his black beaver hat and told them how glad he was to be in "the promised land," that he was at last among "grave, learned, and reverend men." He was not in Scotland anymore, that chill remote lesser kingdom "without honor, without order, where beardless boys would brave us to our face." The more the king spoke, the more at ease the bishops and deans became. His words were medicine.

> I see yet no such cause to change as to confirm what I find settled already. . . . Yet because nothing can be so absolutely ordered, but something may be added thereunto, and corruption in any state (as in the body of man) will insensibly grow . . . our purpose therefore is, like a good physician, to examine and try the complaints, and fully to remove the occasions thereof, if scandalous; cure them, if dangerous; and take knowledge of them, if but

frivolous, thereby to cast a sop into Cerberus's* mouth
that he bark no more.[9]

(Once again we hear that deliciously royal "we" and "our" of the
majestic plural.)

The king spoke for five hours that afternoon. Another source
said three. All we know for certain is that he talked for hours, and
they listened attentively. He was the king. So very James-like, once he
prepped them, once they were warm with anticipation and renewed
hope for the reign, he then "criticized roundly" the corruptions of
the Church of England.

He cited certain theological "errors" of Anglican worship, particularly concerning certain orders of baptism, confirmation, and
absolution. These, he felt, were "popish," and therefore errant and
unnecessary. The king's attitude toward the bishops was more growl
and snap than was reported by some. It was the growl and snap of the
alpha male lording over his territory.

Lancelot Andrewes said, "The king did wonderfully play the
Puritan that day!"[10] Play, indeed. The king was having the time of
his life. Many of the bishops interpreted the king's meaning that he
himself was sympathetic with the Puritans. Andrewes knew better.
So did Cecil.

"Religion is the soul of a kingdom," he assured them, "and
unity, the life of religion."[11] They got the message. The king desired
to cleanse the church of its impurities. He would edit and emend,
compress and clarify. He would soothe the exposed nerve, and the
open wound. To their surprise, and discomfort, they were to show
more tolerance, to treat nonconformists "more gently than ever they
had done before."[12]

---

*In Greek mythology, Cerberus was the watchdog with three heads that guarded the
entrance to Hades.

This was the Solomon king, the self-styled *Rex Pacificus* (the peacemaker king), and though they chafed under his lecturing, they endured it, and literally at the end of the day, they were satisfied with the wisdom of their new sovereign.

Indeed, James acted wisely, and, rather like a king.

During the entire first day with the bishops, neither Robert Cecil nor Lancelot Andrewes said a word. But silence from men like this is anything but silent. Their intelligences were leagues beyond the others. And they both knew their king.

The following Monday, on day two of the conference, the king put to silence all doubt about his Puritan sympathies. He had none.

Brilliant lights among their kind

No one hurled anything at anyone. A few colorful words here and there, a few dirty looks, and only the occasional show of teeth. In spite of the king's foul language, there was much mutual respect among them. These men had grown up together, worshipped together, taught at university together, had all been swept up in the strong tide of the English Renaissance together, that late Elizabethan "efflorescence of male education."[13]

The Puritans attending the conference were handpicked by the Privy Council (by Robert Cecil, that is). A party of four. Four Puritan petitioners against close to twenty bishops, deans of the church, and Privy Councillors. Odds the king liked. Any truly radical or extreme Puritan was not invited. James did not want "brainsick and heady preachers," but only "the learned and grave men of each side."[14] The conference had the appearance of a meeting of opposites. And appearance is what mattered.

These four were substantial men, brilliant lights among their kind, each one steeped, as the Puritan soul was, in the Word of God. Samuel Hieron, not invited to the conference but one of the framers of the Millenary Petition, said once that the Bible gave the head of each household "direction for his apparel, his speech, his diet, his company, his disports, his labour, his buying and selling, yea and for his very sleep."

It is not difficult to see why they were despised in a liberal culture. London lawyer and diary keeper, John Manningham said, "A puritan is such a one as loves God with all his soul, but hates his neighbor with all his heart."[15]

The Puritans were at last led into the chamber. They wore customary black. One writer said they looked as if they wore "clokes and Nitecaps."[16] John Reynolds (or Rainolds) was the Master of Corpus Christi Oxford. Elizabeth had once criticized him, for even outside his own theology he was always the Puritan. She "schooled" Dr. Reynolds for his "obstinate preciseness, willing him to follow her laws and not run before them." Considered a "prodigy in reading, a living library and walking museum,"[17] Reynolds was the chief spokesman for the quartet. He also took most of the abuse.

Reynolds was joined by Laurence Chaderton, Master of Emmanuel College, Cambridge, the good friend and wrestling buddy of Richard Bancroft, Bishop of London (on the opposition). The remaining Puritans were Thomas Sparke, lecturer in divinity at Oxford, and John Knewstubs of St. John's College, Cambridge. These four made up the Puritan party. That was it. Two of them, Reynolds and Chaderton, would become Translators (always capitalized) of the king's Bible, so this was a fairly like-minded community of high churchmen on both sides, and all old friends.

On the bishop's side the principals were Lancelot Andrewes, Master of Pembroke College, Cambridge, Dean of Westminster Abbey, soon to be Bishop of Chichester; Robert Whitgift, Archbishop of Canterbury; and Richard Bancroft, Bishop of London. And of course, the quiet, understated, Robert Cecil, the puppetmaster himself.

Lancelot Andrewes is a volume in himself, and will be given a more complete profile presently. But among the grave and reverend, even against the higher title of Bancroft and Whitgift, Andrewes carried the most presence. He was the one man in the kingdom who could actually make the king nervous.

John Whitgift, a merchant's son, was the archbishop of Canterbury at the changing of the reigns, the highest office in the Anglican Church. He had once been bishop of Worcester, regius professor of divinity at Cambridge, and chaplain to Elizabeth. At age seventy-four the oldest of the divines who met at Hampton Court, he had been Elizabeth's faithful servant and manager of the Elizabethan church. She called him her "little black husband," because of his customary black chimere he wore (a loose upper robe worn by bishops). Whitgift was a militant watchman with a powerful bite who defended the Church of England against those who refused to conform to the Elizabethan settlement, the usual suspects of radicals—papists, Presbyterians, and Puritans. He died a month after the Hampton Court Conference.

Richard Bancroft's academic pedigree DD, BD, BA, MA, reads more like an Elizabethan rhyme scheme. Bishop of London during the Hampton Court Conference, he replaced Whitgift (who died in February) as archbishop of Canterbury shortly thereafter. Bancroft was "chief overseer" of the translation, the spiritual version of Robert Cecil, the man James charged with organizing, policing, and managing the enterprise of translation. He was a devout Anglican and spaniel to the king, or at least part spaniel, part bulldog. Like his predecessor, Whitgift, Bancroft had sufficient snap. Lancelot Andrewes may have the distinction of being the guiding spirit of the translation, but Bancroft was the busy little man who kept the house in order.

Whether it was a conference or a session of Parliament, it kept the king from his favorite pastime. But as we are about to see, in spite of this inconvenience to his leisure, day two of the conference had its compensations.

CHAPTER FIFTEEN

With All the Lightness of an Afterthought

Into this fierce, overheated atmosphere, where the mild divisions in the Church of England were being whipped into extremity by the quick, intellectual, joky, combative, slightly unsocialized banter, argument and bullying by the king, egged on by the exciteable Bancroft, the first suggestion, the seed of the King James Bible, dropped.

—ADAM NICOLSON, *God's Secretaries*

ACCORDING TO THE *Oxford English Dictionary*, to "pepper" someone is "to inflict severe suffering or punishment on; to hit repeatedly, beat severely. Also: to ruin, destroy (obs.). To pelt with small missiles; to bombard with shots, bullets, etc." Of course, that is the formal definition. The application is messier than that. The condiment can be applied with a kind of art, and if anyone was well schooled in the art, it was the king.

The bishops were more at ease, having been "tuned" by the king on opening day. The Puritans were not. They were outnumbered, and about to be "peppered." Perhaps suffer a bit of tenderizing as well, not so much by the bishops as by their master. By the way, the ten-year-old Henry, Prince of Wales, was at the king's side the entire conference, sitting on a stool.

The meeting on day two lasted for five hours. James had been "rude, challenging, and clever" with the bishops. But he upped his game with the Puritans, brought out a bigger club. I cannot help but think of the lone stag, the poor doomed beast marked by scent, and the dogs wild for the chase. And for blood.

William Barlow, Dean of Chester, called them "plaintiffs." James told the "plaintiffs" that he was "now ready to heare, at large, what they would object of, say; and so willed to beginne: whereupon the four kneeling downe, Dr. Reynolds the Foreman began."[1]

Reynolds was the "principall mouthe and speaker" for the Puritans. The others in his party had neither the tongue nor the stomach for it. Chaderton was "mute as any fishe." Sparke said little, if anything. Knewstubbes spoke up about his dislike, or loathing, of the cross in worship. To the Puritan, the use of the cross was superstition, an idolatry. It was symbol, and therefore toxic to genuine worship. That included making the sign of the cross as well. The bishops did not see it this way at all, nor did the king. Lancelot Andrewes answered Knewstubbes on that one. *Slam.* Knewstubbes had little to debate afterward. Other than the king, Andrewes swung the biggest club.

At some point, along with his dislike for infant baptism, the use of rings in the traditional marriage rites, Reynolds also took issue with the phrase "with my body I thee worship" as it is used in the Anglican wedding ceremony. "*With this Ring I thee wed, with my Body I thee worship, and with all my worldly Goods I thee endow . . .*" Only God should be worshipped, was the argument. But that wasn't all. Reynolds felt, as I suppose the Puritan would, that the vow was too overtly sensual. Knowing Reynolds was a confirmed bachelor, James responded, "Many a man speaks of Robin Hood who never shot his bow."[2] He said it with his odd geometrical grin, all eyes looking at Reynolds, the celibate, silenced. A few muted chuckles.

The king had open sport with the unfortunate petitioners, and particularly Reynolds, the first among them. James sent the following letter to the Earl of Northampton at the conclusion of the conference. His delight is conspicuous. Such effervescence in a text begs the original spelling.

> We have kept suche a revell with the puritanis heir [here] these two days as was never heard the like, where I have pepperid thaime [them] as soundlie, as ye have done the papists. They fledde me so from argument to argument, without ever ansouring me directlie, ut est eorum moris [as is their way], as I was forcid at last to saye unto thaime, that if any of thaime hadde bene in a colledge disputing with thair skollairs [their scholars], if any of thaire disciples hadde ansourid thaim in that sorte, thay wolde have fetched him up in place of a replye & so shoulde the rodde have plyed upon the poor boyes buttokis.[3]

This is quintessential James, the hunter Jack. He is playing his own Buchanan here, the merciless schoolmaster, maybe even the foul Solomon, the potty-mouthed Defender of the Faith. He could exercise pounce here in England, a strategy he could not indulge with as much verve in Scotland.

Richard Bancroft had his own go at the Puritans. Maintaining at least some decorum, it was pretty much shoot at will. Bancroft, always in hyperbole, fell to his knees to apply his indelicate text. He railed at them, calling them "schismatic scholars, you breakers of your laws."[4] Reynolds (for the others were mute) took the abuse as persecution, as most pious men might. He had to bend significantly, but he did not break. The Puritan dilemma was that of spiritual elitism, their reluctance to fit in, being, as they arrogated, the elect of God.

Reynolds, perhaps made bold under his perceived bloodless

martyrdom, continued to cite certain repressive Church policies. Hardly at midpoint, Bancroft fell to his knees again and implored Reynolds to say no more. "For it was an ancient canon," the bishop whined, "that schismatics must not be heard against their bishops." With a slight tug on the leash the king replied, "My Lord, you ought not to interrupt the Doctor. Either let him proceed or answer his objections." Bancroft complied and then began to rant on certain nonconformist doctrines, particularly predestination, calling it "a desperate conceit" that encouraged debauchery and license. Bancroft compared Puritans to infidels, at which point Reynolds interrupted him and implored the king not to allow this slander against him and his fellows. The king ignored him.

Reynolds then turned attention to church government. There was little he could do to salvage his cause, but he persevered, and in doing so touched a most sensitive nerve. Should bishops have all authority in their jurisdiction, or should they surround them-selves with administrative counsel? Had he actually used the words *administrative counsel* or something like it, he might have been able to continue, but he used the word *presbytery* instead. A large howl went up from the bishops. Reynolds knew he had blundered, but there was little he could do to take it back. The king became openly hostile at the awful and seditious word. The word itself was a direct challenge to his authority as "Supreme Governour in all causes, and over all persons, (as well Ecclesiasticall as Civill)."[5] Again, presbytery challenged kingship. Episcopacy validated it.

Day two ended. The only thing Reynolds and his deflated fellow Puritans came away with was contempt.

Day three the bishops and deans were called in to the king, but not the Puritans. Once again, they had to wait it out. After some time, the Puritans were allowed back in to hear the summation of the king. It was all over. John Harington, the unforgettable name behind the royal flush, wrote:

James talked much Latin and bid the petitioners away with sniveling. The Bishops seemed much pleased and said his Majesty spoke by power of inspiration! I wist [know] not what they meant, but the Spirit was rather foul-mouthed.[6]

In the end, other than the small concession to the Book of Common Prayer, which James intended to revise anyway, he dismissed *all* of the Puritan objections. He gave them nothing. Well, that is not entirely true. On Day Two of the conference, the good Dr. Reynolds did make one suggestion, one, and with all the lightness of an afterthought. "May your Majesty be pleased that the Bible be new translated?"[7]

It brought out the best that was in the king

For all the abuse he suffered, Reynolds was the big winner. He suggested that there be "one only translation of ye byble to be authenticall and read in ye churches." David Norton, in *A Textual History of the King James Bible*, says that Reynolds's suggestion "appears almost as a casual interjection."[8] It was not even listed on the Puritan's original list of grievances.

However he might have said it, the resonance was powerful and immediate.

Reynolds expressed his reasons for a new translation, or at least some of his reasons, though by this time it was doubtful the king was even listening. Richard Bancroft, good servant and snappy little dog that he was, at the mention of a new translation, began to growl. Confident he had the support of his master, he fell to his knees once again and shouted at Reynolds, "If every man's humor was followed there would be no end of translating!" Bancroft had not noticed the king was duly rapt, having taken flight into some private reverie.

The king, breaking his own spell, abruptly disagreed with Bancroft, and embraced the proposal "with a fervor that caught the prelates off guard."[9]

It is no stretch whatsoever to say that Reynolds's suggestion pleased the king decidedly. The royal mind was suddenly alive with possibility. If you were close enough you might have heard the synapses firing, the spark and sizzle of enterprise.

The conference was over.

James admitted he had "never yet seen a Bible well translated into English." And he longed for "one uniform translation." The unity he sought for Scotland and England might just live in a new Bible, a unity that might heal the breach that divided all Christendom. This was his *Irenicon.*[*]

The moment and the possibilities that existed for him in the moment brought out the best that was in the king. His mind began to work with its usual swiftness and acuity.

For all the "other," James had actual moments when majestie was no longer a mere posture, the cut of his clothes, an endowment, the warrant in the blood, or an act. For all the mess that such kings might make, all the blemish to his crown and character, the waste of idleness and privilege, there are times when a sudden greatness out-voices all other considerations. And majestie is most itself.

This is not difficult to believe of James. When greatness pressed upon him, all his folly went silent against a task that only *he* could accomplish, a commission that not only a king, but only *this* king could realize.

Hardly any time passed before James had the process already outlined in his head. It was reasonable. All the checks fell logically in place, the balances and counterbalances. It was all there. The rules of translation were safely itemized in his head. What he needed now

---

* A message of peace, meant to reconcile differences. (lit.—image of peace).

were the players. And money, too, but that wasn't an issue at present. He had servants around him, men like Cecil and Bancroft who could make it magically appear somehow.

> His Highnesse wished, that some especiall pains should be taken in that behalf for one uniforme translation . . . and this to be done by the best learned of both universities, after them to be reviewed by the Bishops, and the chiefe learned of the Church, from them to be presented to the Privy Councell; and lastly to bee ratified by his Royall Authority; to be read in the whole church and no other.[10]

Bancroft, as quickly as he had attacked Reynolds for the suggestion, just as quickly became the king's good servant in the work of translation. The king and Bancroft were the prime "moovers" behind the ambitious work, with of course, Robert Cecil, in the busy margins. It was, by nature, and by express delight of the king, to be a community effort.

Though he was the chief executive, James kept himself at a slight remove. This took courage, particularly from a capable, hands-on sovereign, one who meddles with as much spirit as James did. He, Bancroft, and Cecil would engage the finest of Greek and Hebrew scholars, whoever had brains and spirit for the task.

James wrote Bancroft a letter at the beginning of summer pressing him to push forward. It was not haste as much as it was a kind of excitement seasoned with a sense of higher calling. Whatever excuses the individual Translator may have were to be "sett aside."[11]

According to Bancroft, the architecture, the rules, and the detailed operations originated with the king. He was truly the "author" of the great work, that is, the one who authorizes. Bancroft wrote, "I am persuaded his Royall mynde reioyceth with good hope, which he hathe for the happy successe of that worke [the Bible], then [than] of his peace concluded with Spain." The Bible was to be "part of the new ideology," what Adam Nicolson calls the "large-scale redefinition of England."[12]

Companies, rules, and operation

Having been swept up in the king's excitement, Richard Bancroft wrote to a colleague in June 1604, saying, "You will scarcely conceive how earnest his majesty is to have this work begun."[13] Industry was humming. The king himself provided the animation. By the end of the next month he had approved the list of Translators. The work before them was immense, but the king was confident that the right men were chosen.

Majestie was awake. Alive and scintillate.

There were six "companies"—two from Westminster, two from Cambridge University, and two from Oxford University. Each company was assigned nine Translators, one of whom was the director of the company. The math should add up to a tidy fifty-four, but the actual number was closer to fifty. Only fifty names are recorded. This was perhaps due to death or other inconveniences. At least one source allowed only forty-seven Translators. This number may not have included the directors of each company.

English translations of the Bible up to 1604 had been the work of either a small group or that of a single individual. David Norton suggests that the king and Bancroft may have used the Septuagint as their model. The Septuagint, or "the Seventy" (LXX), is a Greek translation of the Hebrew Scriptures (Old Testament) assembled about 130 BC. Also on the order of a king, seventy translators (more like seventy-two) labored over the ancient Hebrew texts to produce the Scriptures that were quoted by Jesus and Paul. The LXX translators did not work in groups or companies, but individually, each producing an entire translation of their own. Tradition says that when all seventy manuscripts were compared publicly, each man's translation was identical to the others'.

Adam Nicolson suggests that there may have been metaphysical considerations concerning the number of Translators. Six (the number of companies) is the number of the Trinity (three) multiplied by the number of testaments (two). Forty-eight (the number of Translators, not counting the six directors over them) is the number of apostles (twelve) multiplied by the number of Gospels (four).

Then again, fifty-four may just mean fifty-four. It may have had no thought behind it.

It is not unlikely that the king and others may have considered these things. The mystical interfused with the ordinary with relative ease. Robert Cecil was fascinated with mechanical toys and the mathematical wonder of interlocking numbers.

Each company was assigned a different set of Scriptures to work on. The assignments were as follows (in biblical sequence).

COMPANY NAME	NAME OF DIRECTOR	ASSIGNED SCRIPTURES
First Westminster Company	Lancelot Andrewes	Genesis through 2 Kings
First Cambridge Company	Edward Lively	Chronicles through Song of Solomon
First Oxford Company	John Harding	Isaiah through Malachi
Second Cambridge Company	John Duport	Apocrypha
Second Oxford Company	Thomas Ravis	Gospels, Acts of the Apostles, Revelation
Second Westminster Company	William Barlow	New Testament Epistles

The king appointed Richard Bancroft to draft the "Rules to Be Observed in the Translation of the Bible." There were fifteen rules, which explained the operation and set guidelines for the Translators to follow.* According to Bancroft, his own task was more secretarial in the drafting of the rules. Each article of the rules was carefully thought out by the king, "sanctioned, if they were not indeed drawn up by James himself."[14] It is in the subtext of the rules where we get a closer glimpse of the royal mind.

> Rule 1. The ordinary Bible read in the Church, commonly called the Bishop's Bible, to be followed, and as little altered as the Truth of the original will permit.

This basically meant that if an alteration by a Translator could improve a line—make it sound with a clearer, more refined music—whether the change be but a word or an entire restructuring of a line, or if a better line from the other existing English translations is agreed upon, then the substitution is preferable. (Rule 14 lists these: *Tindall's* [William Tyndale], *Matthews, Coverdale's, Whitchurch's* [Great Bible 1539], and, oddly, the *Geneva*.)[15] "Truth of the original" refers to the reliable Hebrew and Greek manuscripts.

Samuel Ward (Second Cambridge Company), at the Synod of Dort in 1618, explained the translation, saying, "Caution was given that an entirely new version was not to be furnished, but an old version, long received by the Church, to be purged from all blasphemies and faults."[16]

In truth, the new Bible was not a translation at all, but a revision. It was a patchwork quilt, with the finest elements of its former voices stitched together. The whole intent was summed up in the preface to the 1611 version of the King James Bible (original spelling).

> Truly (good Christian Reader) wee neuer thought from

---

* Appendix C.

the beginning, that we should neede to make a new Translation, nor yet to make of a bad one a good one … but to make a good one better, or out of many good ones, one prinicipall good one, not iustly to be excepted against; that hath bene our indeauour, that our marke.

It was, in essence, a revision of the Bishop's Bible. But such an aged and dense translation gave the Translators a wide berth. Out of the existing English translations they would draw the "one principall good one."

The Bishop's Bible was the default translation. If it could not be bettered, it was to be left alone. The Bishop's was not as good as the Geneva, and nowhere near as popular. The language was lumpy, dense, and difficult to navigate, even to the Elizabethan and Jacobean ear.

Jacobethan culture was a culture of the word, a *listening* culture. The Jacobethan was saturated in sound. Poetry was an aural fascination, an auricular art. Just like the Jacobean love of excess, this was incorporate in the language as well. The Jacobean had an ear for it. This was a time in which an individual could sit or stand for the two or three, and sometimes four hours it took to enjoy a play. Unless it was a real dog, they remained fixed. Whether it be the "two hours' traffic of our stage,"[17] the three-hour sermon, the four-hour *Hamlet*, or James's five-hour delivery on the first day of the conference, there was a high tolerance for such prolixity.

There were exceptions. Dr. Miles Smith, who wrote the "Translator to the Reader" in the front matter of the King James Bible, who was one of those two or three chosen to supply "the finishing touches" to the translation, once left church in the middle of a particularly bad sermon and went straight to a local pub. Many in the congregation followed him. In fairness to Smith, he wrote, "A man may be counted a vertuous man, though hee have made many slips in his life."[18]

The plays of William Shakespeare were never written to be read, or worse, studied. He did not publish his plays in his own lifetime. The difference may be subtle, and though it is beyond my science to explain, there is a difference between listening and reading. A poor example, but an immediate one, might be the difference between listening to a song by your favorite singer as opposed to merely reading the lyrics. Certain intimacies are denied in the reading that are alive and resonant in the hearing.

In any culture, listening and speaking preceded the written word. One asks things of us the other does not ask. Jaroslav Pelikan in his book *Whose Bible Is It?* says:

> The language of the plays [Shakespeare's] has to be heard in order to be read. Unlike most readers of antiquity who read their books aloud, we have developed the convention of reading silently. This lets us read more widely but often less well, especially when what we are reading—such as the plays of Shakespeare and Holy Scripture—is a body of oral material that has been, almost but not quite accidentally, captured in a book like a fly in amber.[19]

The King James Bible was appointed to be "read in churches." Preferring sound as often above accuracy, the king demanded that the words be "sett forth gorgeouslie."[20] One of the last steps of the translation was a "hearing," an aural review. The following is an example of what might have been heard at this review. The difference between the two translations of Ecclesiastes 11:1 is conspicuous. More often the differences varied by a rhythmical movement in a line, the placement of a comma, an inflection, or an ambiguity that remained without resolve altogether.

Cast thy bread upon the waters (King James Bible).

Lay thy bread upon wette faces (Bishop's Bible).

I am almost positive it wasn't translated this way to amuse us four hundred years later. It is literal, cumbersome, and meaningless. Of course, the Miles Coverdale Bible doesn't do much better with "*Send thy victuals over the waters . . .*" William Tyndale was martyred before he could publish a translation of the entire Old Testament. That means you and I were robbed of something precious. How does the "trayterous" Geneva Bible translate the above Scripture?

Cast thy bread upon the waters (Geneva Bible 1560).

In spite of being the default text, the Bishop's Bible comprises only 8 percent of the King James Bible. That means the work before them was immense. Their job was to sift this massive press of words that they might not just speak, but sing, rhapsodize, lament, weep, and exult with the best in the English language.

This afternoon is our translation time

Robert Barker, printer for the king, provided forty folio-sized copies of the Bishop's Bible for the Translators' use. Only one exists today. They were not bound, but were delivered in quires, or signatures (basically sheets held together loosely), "so they could pass easily from hand to hand."[21] This made it easy for making the necessary edits to the text.

Concentrating only on his company's assigned Scriptures, each individual Translator read each line of text, each verse, and altered it as he saw fit or he left it alone. Was it a task for the intellect? Or did it obligate the imagination for a response? It was ultimately a cooperation between the two.

The imagination is the general port through which God speaks to the world. Augustine said that God is a poet and speaks in metaphors, symbols, and parables, just shy of intellect and reason. And a translation like the King James Bible is not exempt from a bit of meddling by the Spirit of God. This is how they perceived the work.

Once the individual Translator was satisfied with his own work, it was reviewed by each Translator within the company to decide which changes should remain and which needed further thought. It was not necessarily a free-for-all, but dispute was part of the charm of being a Translator.

Once the individual Translator's work passed through each hand, and the company was satisfied with their work, a single revised manuscript went to the other companies for perusal, suggestion, more alteration if necessary, and approval. In other words, everyone checked everyone else's work. Every word passed through every Translator.

When this part of the work was done, three bodies of work, one from each of the three institutions (Westminster, Cambridge, and Oxford) went to a review committee of select individuals for a hearing. From there, a single copy of the work was passed to three men appointed by the Crown for the "finishing touches."

Doubtless, the work of translation, the fine sifting of text, was a long, slow enterprise, and the king was eager for the work to get under way. If his passion for union and majestie was imposed on the translation, so was his usual impatience. By August, according to Sir Thomas Bodley, the Translators were "at it hard in Cambridge." So hard, it was thought, that it hastened the death in May 1605 of Edward Lively, Director of the First Cambridge Company, because of "too earnest study and pains about the translation."

According to Bodley, the work at Oxford had a slower start but it became so intense that one of the Translators, John Peryn, Regius Professor of Greek, resigned his post to work solely on the King James translation. Richard Bancroft sent a letter to the vice-chancellor of Cambridge on 30 June 1604.

> His Majesty being made acquainted with the choice
> of all them to be employed in the translating of the
> Bible . . . doth greatly approve of the said choice. And
> as for as much as his Highness is very anxious that the
> same so religious a work should admit no delay, he has
> commanded me to signify unto you in his name that his
> pleasure is, you should with all possible speed meet
> together in your University and begin the same.[22]

Such was the measure of resolve that moved the work forward
and held it together. But to say it was mere impatience or even obligation to the Crown that propelled the work is insufficient. For all
his indelicacy, for all his Broad Scots manners, and the sheer impossibility he posed at times, he had the power to inspire those around
him, and not just because of a crown. For all his oddness, he seemed
to know how to choose, how to recognize a kind of royalty in those
around him, a kind of *otherness* possessed in men close to him,
whether it be a Cecil, an Andrewes, a Bacon, or a Shakespeare.

James Stuart was never more of a true king than he was over the
translation.

CHAPTER SIXTEEN

The Elizabethan Aesthetic

The King James Bible is a flower that grows from the deep
mulch of sixteenth-century England.

—ADAM NICOLSON, *God's Secretaries*

SHE WAS ELIZABETH R. Gloriana. The Virgin Queen. She was
Bess. She was Spencer's *Fairye Queen*. She was Raleigh's *Cynthia*. She
was Cate Blanchett, twice. She was Helen Mirren and Bette Davis.
She was perhaps the greatest monarch England ever had. And she
was everything James is not.

She was the heroine of the Armada, the most feared name in
Christendom, the English Deborah, the true warrior poet. Her
speech at Tilbury on the eve of the Armada was no act. I mean it
was great theater, but it was pure Elizabeth. The threat was real. The
troops she addressed were real. She was a real queen, with real armor
on her breast, and her own words in her mouth. She was perhaps
the real spirit and voice behind Shakespeare's *Henry V* Agincourt (St.
Crispin's Day) speech (the model for Mel Gibson's "Sons of Scotland"
rant in *Braveheart*). On the back of a horse she said:

But being resolved, in the midst and heat of the battle, to live and die amongst you all; to lay down for my God, and for my kingdom, and my people, my honour and my blood, even in the dust. I know I have the body of a weak and feeble woman, but I have the heart and stomach of a king, and of a king of England too.[1] (Elizabeth I, *from a speech before her troops at Tilbury*)

Elizabeth provided the best of theater in a profoundly theatrical age. All of it was rather slippery and uncertain, yet she had a grasp of her own time. Her theatrics were not a vent for some artistic passion, but a survival tactic to circumnavigate the treachery around her. Tricks she learned as a wary princess, as Lady Elizabeth.

Elizabeth understood the balance between the theatrical and the political, between necessity and charm. The rise of the theater began in her reign and prospered along with it. There were reasons for its popularity and with dimensions much greater than that of a mere drama queen.

A big gaping hole in culture

The demise of the Roman Catholic Church in England—outlawed as it was from the days of Henry VIII, confiscated as all its properties were, abbeys, castles, lands—left a hole in culture, a big gaping hole. For centuries it had been a Catholic England. At its dismantling there was a void of large dimensions. As fluid as culture was, as teeming and as eager as early modern England was, there were strong currents that could not long be ignored.

The Roman Catholic Mass was, and still is, a grand spectacle. Mysteries were celebrated and with a language (Latin) just as mysterious to most of the faithful. The liturgy engaged all the senses. It was magnificent. And it was suddenly absent.

In 1576, James Burbage built the first theater in London. There had not been a theater in town for more than a thousand years, since the Roman occupation. He named his theater the Theatre. Burbage was a carpenter-actor-impresario, not a poet. His son, Richard, would become the greatest star of the Elizabethan stage—the first Hamlet, the first Othello, the first Lear, and Macbeth, the first to say, *"To be or not to be, that is the question,"* and *"We few, we happy few, we band of brothers."*

What was lost to the people with the pageantry of the Roman Catholic Church was returned to them with the rise of the theater. This great gaping hole in culture gave them a new champion, indeed, a new kind of church, a new priesthood. And it was so very English.

> It [theater] fulfilled the audience's appetite for significant action and iconic form.
>
> —PETER ACKROYD,
> *SHAKESPEARE: THE BIOGRAPHY*

The pulpit was exchanged for a stage, and the language of plays was reminiscent of the high tone of the Mass.* It was, after all, a listening culture, a culture of the word, a peculiarly English occupation. Other forms of art—sculpting, painting, music, even architecture—with only a few exceptions were to be found elsewhere, outside the little island, in Italy, Holland, Germany, France. English captures its reflection in words, in the subtleties of the human voice. It is a direct exchange, immediate, intimate. Majestie has no better home.

It should be little wonder that English has become the *lingua*

---

*To this day, the works of William Shakespeare provide a kind of secular scripture. He is quoted with a similar gravity we apply to the Bible. Sigmund Freud, for instance, when the subject of judgment or punishment came up in conversation, was known to reply, *"Use every man after his desert, and who should 'scape whipping"* (from *Hamlet*). I have dispersed quotes from Shakespeare throughout the main body of this text to illustrate this phenomenon.

franca[2] of the civilized world, or that English dominates music, film, literature, the dramatic arts.

There is empire indeed.

The English imagination was, and remains, aural. It expressed itself in sound, and the culture was tuned for it. An Elizabethan audience was capable of "picking up the intricacies of the rhetoric as well as the harmonies of the verse."[3] They would be quick, as well, to appreciate the topical allusions, however subtle. Shakespeare, and others, would not have written the way they did had the audience not been able to understand.

It was all very much alive. The Elizabethan audience was "eager, alert, and excited by this new form of entertainment."[4] Touching Englishness to the quick, the play was the very soul of the English Renaissance. It is a key to understanding the age itself. And its queen.

> The experience of the play has in fact been described as that of a ritual, in which the stage represents a heightened reality not unlike the gestures and movements of a Catholic priest at the altar.
>
> —PETER ACKROYD,
> *SHAKESPEARE: THE BIOGRAPHY*

The Catholic adoration of Mary—not Tudor, nor the Queen of Scots, but the Virgin Mary—since it was outlawed, left another conspicuous void. In a flourish of inspired stage/statecraft, Elizabeth gave them the Virgin Queen, with all the alabaster whiteness of a sculpture, something to be reverenced, admired, and possibly even loved. She understood her job, and the grand illusion that validated it, that gave it sparkle.

The film *Elizabeth* (Polygram, 1998), with Cate Blanchett, for all its make-believe, makes this very point at the end. Elizabeth ponders a statue of the Virgin Mother and Child, and muses, *"She had such power over men's hearts. They died for her."* Geoffrey Rush, who plays her spymaster, Sir Francis Walsingham, makes a powerful response. *"They have found nothing to replace her."*

It is Hollywood, and not to be trusted on the whole, but it makes a very real point. The Virgin Queen was a role Elizabeth played, and she played it convincingly well. A master of artifice, she had a prophet's sense of her own times, as well as her place in it. Like the husbands she enticed but never took, or the childlessness that agonized a nation, she used the role of the virgin strategically.

She was *Rosalind*. She was *Portia*. She was *Cleopatra*. But she was always Elizabeth.

To ignore the development of the theater is to ignore the spirit of the age, the powerful linguistic tide that swept everyone up, that saturated a culture. In the years between 1584 and 1623, hardly more than a single generation, more than fifty million people passed through theater doors. Considering the population of London at the time, which was around two hundred thousand, this was significant. The buzz was infective. And like any good church, nobles and commoners alike were welcomed. The theater was egalitarian.

Among those theater attendees were many of the King James Translators.

Plays and playgoing, in spite of an immense and accelerating popularity of the 1590s, had, since its inception, been considered beneath the educated or refined, even though the educated and refined were often found at the playhouses.

Again, perceptions change.

Thomas Bodley, of the Bodleain Library at Oxford, thought plays without value, base, vulgar, "not one in forty" worthy of his time, or space in his library. Bodley may have been right about the odds, but Shakespeare changed all that. *Hamlet* (1601) was the first play to be performed at both the Universities of Oxford and Cambridge. This was unprecedented. To quote the prince himself, and with an accurate assessment of the times, "buzz, buzz."[5]

The abstract and brief chronicles of the time

Any treatment of the Elizabethan aesthetic is impossible without featuring its first light, the dramatist, William Shakespeare. Peter Ackroyd uses the word *phenomenon* to describe him by the changing of the reigns. Shakespeare was the fashion.

Poet T. S. Eliot considered *Hamlet* "the literary Mona Lisa."[6] According to literary critic Harold Bloom, *Hamlet* is "the central work of Western literature."[7] Not only in the poet's own artistic evolution, but in English literature as well, *Hamlet* was a leap forward. Or as the poet would say, "a sea change."

There are reasons why *Hamlet* was so popular with the Elizabethan audience.

Robert Devereaux, the second Earl of Essex, was beheaded in 1601 for treason, the year of *Hamlet*. Essex was one of Elizabeth's lost boys.* He had been her favorite, perhaps as favored as one can be favored by a queen.

He was immensely popular with the people as well. They looked to Essex with promise. He was, as I suspect, and as Ophelia lamented of Prince Hamlet, *"the expectancy and fair rose of the state, the glass of fashion and the mould of form, the observed of all observers . . ."*[8] The Elizabethan audience would not miss the reference. His execution was fresh and immediate in everyone's mind.

The earl's plan was to overthrow the queen, and replace her with the King of Scots, that is, James, or maybe himself. Favoring his own suspicions, James eventually backed away from the earl.

Essex went quite mad at the end, the spoilage somewhat complete. *"What a noble mind is here o'erthrown. The courtier's, soldier's,*

---

*According to *Peter Pan* by J. M. Barrie, the lost boy is one who never quite grows up. Indeed, growing up is against the rules. The lost boy also lives in a suspended state somewhere between fantasy and adventure.

scholar's, eye, tongue, sword . . ." Essex even paid Shakespeare's troupe
(the Lord Chamberlain's Men) 40 shillings to stage a production of
Richard II at the Globe on the eve of the uprising. His hope was that
the old play might "tune" the public (*Richard II* is a play about depos-
ing a monarch). The public, however, did not wish to be tuned. They
did nothing. As might be expected, following the botched uprising,
the Lord Chamberlain's Men got into a bit of trouble. Francis Bacon
may have interceded in their behalf, or possibly a friend in the Privy
Council. Either way, the players were absolved.

James Shapiro, in his book *A Year in the Life of William Shakespeare*
argues convincingly that the age of chivalry died with Essex. He was
young and beautiful, the star of a generation. But Essex, as lost boys
do at times, came perilously close to Leviathan, to earthly majestie,
was corrupted by it, and consumed. Essex was Elizabeth's Absalom.

It is not an easy thing to love a queen. It would corrupt
the soul of any man. (Joseph Fiennes, as the fallen Robert
Dudley in *Elizabeth*, Polygram, 1998)

Prince Hamlet was an avatar, a mimic, some revived image of
the Earl of Essex—a fictitious prince with the dash, the charisma,
and the carriage of the young and once promising earl. Somewhat
of a pirate himself, this is how Shakespeare did things, appropriating
the image, the panache, and the carriage of the earl for his own uses.
Hamlet was the Earl of Essex liberated of all the "other" qualities, the
spoiled boy qualities that made him do dumb things, and that got
him executed.

If there was a big fat gaping hole in culture at the want of a
Catholic Church, in like manner the death of Essex left a gaping hole
of its own. Ever conscious of his audience, Shakespeare, who was
close to Essex and his entourage (the cream of London youth), simply filled the gap. He gave them back their favorite earl in the Danish

prince. But only in form and carriage. Intelligence and expression was something else. Essex himself was no Hamlet.

To move this forward, Hamlet had the physical carriage of the earl—the flaunt, the shine, the lift in his stride, the presence—and yet he had the sharp trenchant wit of perhaps Francis Bacon, doubtless the greatest mind of the age. Essex, for all his admirable qualities, did not have the intellectual heft Bacon did. Actually, none of them did. Shakespeare's own intelligence was of another kind.

Bacon had that grand Elizabethan quality of rhetorical magnificence as well. In a court of law, once he concluded his speech, he was often begged to continue. *More Bacon, please.*

Shakespeare was first and above all, an artist. A gregarious loner, he was an acute and tireless observer, as true poets are. He was not limited to the Essexness or Baconness of his models. They were merely raw materials. And he knew how to make the most out of a moment in time, how to sift it of all its sweetness. If not cash. As Brutus says in *Julius Caesar*:

> There is a tide in the affairs of men,
> when taken at the flood leads to fortune.
> Omitted, all the voyage of his life
> is bound in shallows and in miseries.
> On such a full sea are we now afloat,
> And we must take the current when it serves
> Or lose our ventures.
> —William Shakespeare, *Julius Caesar*, IV, iii, 243–249

Shakespeare was good with tides. And if it is true, as Samuel Johnson asserts, that an author will turn over half of a library to make one book, a playmaker might turn over at least a town, or a few of its greater lights, to create one character. We can at least assume.

Hamlet was the arch-Elizabethan. He was lyrical, melancholic, inward (Hamlet was the first to bring inner monologue to the stage). He possessed a dangerous cunning. He was savvy and sea-wise, and could dissemble with the best of them. He could *outJacob* Jacob.

In Hamlet lived the truest representation of the Elizabethan aesthetic, embodied both in character and in speech. That he was fictitious makes it somehow more appropriate. Hamlet threw a shadow over the great city.

In the mingling of these two cultural giants, Essex and Bacon, and perhaps others, Shakespeare not only gave the crowd what it wanted, he had a character that was as animated and

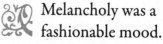 Melancholy was a fashionable mood. It was the other face of the Renaissance.

—ROBERT LACEY, *SIR WALTER RALEIGH*

as large or larger than the times, larger than Shakespeare himself. Hamlet quickly outgrew his maker.

Like James, Hamlet is wonderfully and outrageously sane.

There are two points to consider. One, the King James Translators were steeped in this Elizabethan aesthetic, this powerful linguistic vitality, this Hamletized soul of the age that was characterized by a penetrating, high-velocity wit and melancholy that spun forth the finest lines ever written in any language.

The poet's so-called rival, Ben Jonson,[9] quite famously said of Shakespeare that "he was not for an age but for all time." Jonson also referred to Shakespeare as the "soul of the age." Hyperbole aside, or hero worship—which Jonson was guilty of in spite of the fuss he put up—it is an accurate assessment.

This might even beg the question: *Did William Shakespeare have anything to do with the making of the King James Bible?* The reasonable answer is *no*, he did not. Influence, however, is another issue. Remember, the circles in late Elizabethan and early Jacobean London were quite small. And all of this somewhat amazingly took place within the same few square miles of earth, and at the same moment in time.

The perfect storm

What it *doesn't* mean is that the Translators attempted to make the Scripture sound Shakespearean. I'm not sure they consciously wanted the Scripture to sound like anything but itself. But what does that mean?

The King James Translators did not attempt to impose a voice or any sense of style upon the translation. They felt that beauty lay nested in the original Hebrew and Greek texts, and they submitted themselves accordingly. Their task, as they saw it, was to coax it forward, to draw it out. And yet, as any miner or archaeologist understands, to do this kind of precision work, to finesse this kind of detail, you need the right tools. The Translators had the right tools, but more than that, the tools they had were well calibrated. Also, the Rules of Translation included nothing about sonority or style. The Translators were left to their own instincts as to the sound it made.

Overlooking the obvious perhaps, more than one source used the word *miracle* to describe the singularity of the voice, the grand harmony and splendor that stretches from first to last in the King James Bible. The same word *miracle* was applied to the notion of art by committee, that beauty of this magnitude and weight could be rendered by a company of scholars and clerics—that somehow it all just happened. One modern scholar goes so far as to say "the achievement of prosaic and poetic elegance that resulted was, so to speak, *a most happy accident of history*"[10] (emphasis mine).

Beauty, grace, stateliness, pith, charm, deep primal movement, none of this comes by accident, or by committee. It never does. Other than the intrinsic beauty of the original text—and the source from which it springs—there is no miracle here. There is no accident, any more than *Hamlet* is an accident, or a sermon by Lancelot Andrewes is an accident, or *Sonnet X* by John Donne.

No, in the Elizabethan aesthetic is the perfect storm, the collision of powerful and unrepeatable elements, among them a language coming into its own, a spirit disposed to the word, and one ridiculously fine poet.

An entire culture was swept up in a powerful linguistic current that included not only Shakespeare, but Ben Jonson and John Donne, as well as their predecessors, Edmund Spenser and Christopher Marlowe. We could include Francis Bacon and his brother Anthony in with this lot, and Sir Walter Raleigh. Even Elizabeth herself. And James. All literary. All empowered by the poetic ideal of the age.

> What a piece of work is a man! how noble in reason!
> how infinite in faculty! in form and moving how
> express and admirable! in action how like an angel!
> in apprehension how like a god! the beauty of the
> world! the paragon of animals! And yet, to me,
> what is this quintessence of dust?
> —William Shakespeare, *Hamlet*, II, ii, 315–320

> What is man, that thou art mindfull of him?
> and the sonne of man, that thou visitest him?
> For thou hast made him a little lower then the Angels:
> and hast crowned him with glory and honour.
> —Psalm 8:4–5 King James Bible 1611

Does this consideration somehow diminish the King James Bible? No, it does not. On the contrary, the times were alive, effervescent. English was in the throes of discovering itself. The late Elizabethan age was an age of linguistic sizzle. Its echo has been long and powerful. The Translators were all Elizabethans, all passionately literate.

This aesthetic could only enhance the beauty and magnificence that was already there in the folds of Scripture. It had the ability to make beautiful even more beautiful. The way God himself is beautiful. It is still and always a matter of divine election. The men, the times, the king.

The math works.

Point two. After 1603, once James came to town, Shakespeare's gift seemed to enter another, grander stage of artistic evolution. As if majestie had liberated something, lit some deeper fuse. For the poet's new king was not only a real king, but there was something *other* about him, a presence only someone with Shakespeare's sensors could distinguish. He wrote a series of his finest plays. Deep and groaning rhapsodies—*King Lear, Othello, Anthony and Cleopatra, Macbeth*—all written after 1603, and each one with links to James. And strangely, all tragedies.

Both the king and the poet had their best years between 1604 and 1611. After that, something just cooled with both of them.

The Elizabethan aesthetic was the filter through which the King James Translators tested every word. Was it a conscious effort? No, it was not. It was a literary spirit that governed culture, a *spirit of the word*, a profoundly English spirit that had risen to its zenith in the age of Elizabeth. The well-defined Golden Age was an age of prosperity, of educational florescence, of unprecedented greatness for the island. The lion's share was in the language itself.

> The quality of mercy is not strain'd,
> It droppeth as the gentle rain from heaven
> Upon the place beneath: it is twice blest;
> It blesseth him that gives and him that takes:
> 'Tis mightiest in the mightiest: it becomes
> The throned monarch better than his crown;
> His sceptre shows the force of temporal power,

The attribute to awe and majesty,
Wherein doth sit the dread and fear of kings;
But mercy is above this sceptred sway;
It is enthroned in the hearts of kings,
It is an attribute to God himself;
And earthly power doth then show likest God's
When mercy seasons justice.

—William Shakespeare, *The Merchant of Venice*, IV, i, 184–197

CHAPTER SEVENTEEN

All the King's Men

A man may be counted a vertuous man, though hee haue
made many slips in his life.

—KING JAMES BIBLE, *Preface to the Reader (from the Translators)*

THEY WERE ALL weaned on the Elizabethan sonnet, even as they
were Cranmer's *Book of Common Prayer*, and the Scriptures. In spite
of the king's distaste for the Geneva Bible, it was the translation they
fed on the most. They all grew up, lived, and studied within that
Elizabethan linguistic miracle, the lyricism that seemed to permeate
every element of culture. Preachers, playmakers, poets, the ooze stuck
on everything. They were all, including the king and his humorless
"beagle" Robert Cecil, under the same bright sorcery.

These are men who spent time with Sir Walter Raleigh at his
Mermaid Tavern (Cheapside) in that moveable feast of intellect and
debate—men like Ben Jonson, Thomas Dekker, Shakespeare, Francis
Beaumont, and other eminent Jacobethan lights.

With the exception of Reynolds and Chaderton, our good
Puritans, they had all seen *Hamlet*.

By the way, it is not difficult to love these people. I am not sure it can be helped. Their lives are somehow large and irresistible, dateless, timeless. They seem to open things up. Magnificently alive, like the times they inhabit, they somehow allow you to come close. The bad spelling helps.

James is a world in himself, and he established an elite community around him, men of wit and color, men not unlike himself—bright, analytical, translucent, literary, flawed, steeped in the enchantments of the age. When you look closely at their lives, they tend to raise a mirror. The following anecdotes and bio fragments make the period breathe again and give you a more intimate look at the variance and the large personhood that went into the making of the King James Bible. Some of it is crude. Again, rather like its king. It is this amalgam of light and shadow, of crudeness and high gloss that gives us the Jacobean portraiture. The occasional shadow gives an image its necessary depth.

Not enough is known about many of the Translators other than education and pedigree, but this cross-section will provide clear enough image of the general population.

Light and shadow

Lancelot Andrewes. Other than the king, Cecil, and possibly Bancroft, Lancelot Andrewes proved a kind of guiding spirit of the new translation. Though I have already applied the word to Reynolds, Adam Nicolson uses the word *hero* to describe Andrewes. In a kind of rhapsody, he says Andrewes was

> as broad as the great bible itself, scholarly, political, passionate, agonized, in love with the English language, endlessly investigating its possibilities, worldly, saintly, serene, sensuous, courageous, craven, if not corrupt then

at least compromised, deeply engaged in pastoral care, loving, in public bewitched by ceremony, in private troubled by persistent guilt and self-abasement.[1]

A responsible treatment of this period in English history often asks this kind of application from a writer, from the scholar, the biographer, the historian. The rhapsody is inescapable. It is interesting that many of these same writers are also novelists, in particular Peter Ackroyd and Alison Weir.

Lancelot Andrewes prayed five hours every morning, and often with tears. He once said that if anyone knocked on his door before noon they clearly did not believe in God. I am almost certain he was not joking. He wept "abundant tears" in his prayers. The original manuscript of his *Preces Privatae* (Private Prayers), a collection of prayers published after his death, was "slubbered with his pious hands and watered with his penitential tears."

Fluent in fifteen modern languages, and six ancient, it was said of Andrewes that he "might have been interpreter general at Babel."[2] Considered the greatest preacher of the age, an "angell in the pulpitt," he was also the greatest prose writer of the age. Against the many brilliant men who trafficked the age, he rightfully earned these superlatives. Twentieth-century poet and Andrewes zealot, T. S. Eliot, said the preacher had a way of "taking a word and deriving a world from it." Eliot would not be an Anglican churchgoer, he said, had it not been for the sermons of Lancelot Andrewes.

Like his contemporary, Shakespeare, and indicative of the age, Andrewes loved word play, and wielded it with finesse and charm. He toyed with his words, one Scot said, "as a Jack-an-ape does, who takes up a thing, tosses and plays with it, then takes another, and plays a little with that too."[3] The following is an excerpt from a sermon (on the three wise men) Andrewes preached before the king on Christmas Day at Whitehall, 1622.

Just the worst time of year to take a journey, and especially a long journey in. The ways deep, the weather sharp, the days short, the sun farthest off, in solstitio brumali, the very dead of winter.

An example of the Elizabethan aesthetic in play.

Like his new king, and again, like the age itself, Andrewes was not without contradictions. Under Elizabeth, he had been twice offered a bishopric. He turned down the honor, but not because he felt unworthy; the pay just wasn't that good. He also spoke loudly against such things as nepotism, only to make sure his insanely unpopular and corrupt brother Roger had all the best appointments, including that of Translator for the King James Bible (the First Cambridge Company). Wherever Lancelot went, Roger went. And prospered.

Among his many obligations, Andrewes was also vicar of St. Giles Cripplegate, north of the city, outside the old walls. Cripplegate was a poor section of town. It was the site of bowling alleys, dicing houses, and the Fortune Theater. There were seventy breweries in the parish. Disease was rampant. Early in 1603 there were four thousand people in the parish. By the end of the year, nearly three thousand were dead of the plague.

James and Elizabeth both revered Andrewes "beyond all other divines." Due to Andrewes's "gravity of manner," James would restrain his usual crudeness around him. He also slept with sermons of Lancelot Andrewes under his pillow.

James was most impressed with Andrewes's support of divine right.

On a providential note, Andrewes was consecrated as Bishop of Chichester on 3 November 1605. The ceremony delayed the king's attendance at Parliament for one day, and that one day may have saved the king's life. He was scheduled to be assassinated on

5 November along with his family at that session of Parliament. *Remember, remember, the 5th of November* . . .

In August of that awful plague year 1603, Andrewes preached: "The Razor is hired for us that sweeps away a great number of hairs at once." As the spiritual wisdom of the age (and Lancelot Andrewes) dictated, plague was the result of wickedness. It was the manifestation of God's wrath. It was also the common spin of most pulpiteers. Andrewes even blamed Puritan preachers for the calamity with their "new tricks, opinions and fashions, fresh and newly taken up, which their fathers never knew of."[4]

> And hovering between a vision of overwhelming divine authority and a more practical understanding of worldly realities, in some way fudging the boundaries between those two attitudes, reveals the man.[5]
>
> —ADAM NICOLSON, *GOD'S SECRETARIES*

Andrewes preached heavily that the righteous would be kept safe in time of plague, that the dread disease was punishment for sin. To believe otherwise, he continued, was a sin. But when 2,878 of his parishioners suffered and died of the plague that year, their vicar (pastor) Lancelot Andrewes was nowhere to be found. We are left perhaps with the only conclusion we can make, one that leaves a stain.

To understand Lancelot Andrewes, again, is to understand the ambivalence of the age, and that of its new king. It is theater. It is great theater. Is it sincere? Absolutely. But it is also, as Shakespeare phrased it, "the sweet smoke of rhetoric."[6]

This duplicity did not go unnoticed. One man, Henoch Clapham, wrote a pamphlet on the issue. Pamphlets were always a bit of fun. The long titles, the short pithy bursts of venom. In Clapham's pamphlet, *Epistle Discoursing upon the Present Pestilence*, he turns up the volume and accuses Andrewes of hypocrisy, of preaching one thing and doing the opposite, of hiding beneath an elm tree, very Jonah-like, and saving his own skin.

Clapham asserted that Londoners should behave as though the plague were not contagious, that there was no need to flee, that it was a disease caused by sin. "If death came because of sin and not contagion," he reasoned, "why would the innocent have to flee the city?"[7]

The outcome? Clapham served almost two years in jail. "To suggest that the Dean of Westminster was a self-serving cheat was insubordinate and unacceptable."[8] He was forced to sign a retraction, one that was written by Andrewes, of course. Clapham refused, but did agree to a compromise (after spending much time behind bars). The compromise said there were actually *two* plagues. Only one was contagious. The other was a reaction to sin. *Ah, the sweet smoke.*

⁂

John Overall, like many of the Translators, is not a name you would associate with the word *scandal*. A devout, dedicated man, Overall was Dean of St. Paul's (1601), Bishop of Coventry and Lichfield (1614), Bishop of Norwich. A friend of Lancelot Andrewes, he was among the First Westminster Company of Translators. Overall got the attention of courtier poet Fulke Greville, who helped him with the St. Paul's appointment. Greville was also a friend of William Shakespeare's (his father had been a Warwickshire patron of the schoolmaster in Stratford where Shakespeare was educated). Again, the circles were small.

Brilliant to a kind of absentmindedness, Overall was fluent in Greek and Latin, so much so in Latin he admitted he had trouble speaking English. Latin was the language of the classroom and the teacher's lounge, the *lingua franca* of the academic world. His committee discussions were in Latin. While this was an advantage in a life of books, it was a disadvantage on a pure personal level.

While all that is fascinating, John Overall had the distinction of falling in love with the most beautiful girl in London. Anne Orwell was reputed to be "the greatest English beauty of her time." But the match was not ultimately an even one, and there was trouble at home. She was "wondrous wanton, and so tender-hearted that she could scarce deny any one." As you do with legends, particularly Elizabethan ones, someone wrote a poem.[9]

Face she had of Filberd hue
and bosom'd like a Swan
Back she had of bended Ewe,
and wasted by a span.
Her Haire she had as black as Crowe
from her head unto her toe
Downe downe all over her,
hye nonny nonny noe.

"Hye nonny nonny noe" is Elizabethan and Jacobean parlance for a bit of naughty. Shakespeare uses the tag in *Much Ado About Nothing*. In spite of his wife's little problem, Overall "loved her infinitely," though he could ultimately keep her neither contented nor contained. The Latin was too much for her.

I have tried to imagine breakfast together, the husband with his Horace and his Virgil; the wife with her eggs and butter, a blank stare, and some distraction in her gaze. She ran off with a man named John Selby, a Yorkshire squire, who I am sure was much more interesting than Overall, and who I suppose spoke fine English.

There was a colorful little poem written on this subject as well, that I have purposely omitted. Undaunted, loving her beyond her crimes, to his credit, and ever as in love, Overall sent a posse to find her. Husband and wife reconciled, and, learning his own lesson perhaps, the dean became more attentive. He learned a better, higher English.

I would have her learn, my fair cousin, how
perfectly I love her; and that is good English.

—William Shakespeare, *Henry V*, V, ii, 309–310

❦

Richard "Dutch" Thomson, also in the First Westminster Company of
Translators, was rector of Upwell in Norfolk, and a Hebrew Scholar.
Born of English parents in Holland, Thomson was "a debosh'd drunken
English Dutcheman."[10] True to the duality of the times, he was bril-
liant but worldly, an ordained minister, a theologian, but somewhat of
a party hound, a cosmopolitan man who "seldom went to bed sober."
He also translated Martial's obscene epigrams on the side.

❦

Laurence Chaderton, of the First Westminster Company, was one of
the four Puritans invited to the Hampton Court Conference. He
was appointed Dean of Christ's College, Cambridge, and Master of
Emmanuel College, a Puritan institution founded to "train up godly
ministers." Chaderton was disowned by his father for becoming a
Calvinist while a student at Cambridge. His father wrote him, saying he would cut him off completely, that he would have nothing to
fall back on, "if you do not renounce the new sect which you have
joined." He enclosed one shilling for his son to buy a wallet, then
said, "Go and beg."[11] Laurence bought the wallet, and got himself a
full university scholarship. He became a superb linguist, proficient in
Hebrew, Latin, Greek, Spanish, and French.

Chaderton was said to be one of the great preachers of his day.
He had a "clear and pleasing" voice, "of wonderful flexibility, accom-
panied by a great dignity of manner." He was apparently so good that

those who heard him could not get enough. On one occasion, he had preached for two hours. He stopped only out of courtesy, not to try anyone's patience. The entire congregation cried out, "For God's sake, go on! Go on! We beg you!"[12] He did just that, and for another hour.

❦

George Abbot, member of the Second Oxford Company (responsible for the entire New Testament), in 1604 was at the threshold of a brilliant career. He went on to become Dean of Winchester Cathedral, Bishop of Lichfield and Coventry (1609), Bishop of London (1610), and Archbishop of Canterbury (1611). Described by one source as a "terrifying man" and a "severe Calvinist," on one occasion Abbot arrested 140 undergraduates for not taking their hats off in his presence at St. Mary's Church.

Once, as an archbishop, Abbot shot a gamekeeper while hunting. It happened on a Thursday, so for the rest of his life, he only ate meat pies on Thursday. Kind of a memorial I suppose, or a kind of self-imposed Lent. He was cleared by the authorities, and pardoned by the king, but many prelates refused to be consecrated by his hands. Once when his coach was blocked in a London street he entreated the crowd to let him pass. One woman cried out, "Ye had best shoot an arrow at us, too!"[13]

A gifted writer and lover of Scripture, Abbot once told King James that "Scripture doth directly or by consequence contain in it sufficient matter to decide all controversies."[14] The king thought the notion absurd.

❦

Sir Henry Savile, one of the brightest intellectual lights, also of the Second Oxford Company, was the only one of all the Translators not ordained. Savile was born in Yorkshire, educated at Oxford, Fellow of Merton (1565), Warden of Merton (1585), Provost of Eton (1596—against the statutes of the school that said the seat could only be occupied by an ordained minister), founder of Savile professorships of geometry and astronomy at Oxford. His cousins owned the land that would become Savile Row.

He was tutor of Greek to Elizabeth. He was scholar, courtier, politician, mathematician, astronomer, and from the looks of his portrait, a wannabe pirate. Adam Nicolson describes Savile as the "totally corrupt, extraordinarily venal [susceptible to bribes], cheating, and lying Warden of Merton College and Oxford."[15]

In an age of superlatives, Savile takes the honors as the greatest scholar of the age. He changed the academic landscape in mathematics particularly, arguing that the study of mathematics turned a man into "an educated, civilized human being."[16] Undergraduates at the time could not understand the importance of this discipline.

One of the more notable achievements of Henry Savile was an eight-volume folio edition of the complete works of John Chrysostom, fourth-century patriarch of Constantinople, the great theologian, liturgist, and preacher. Over the course of twenty years, Savile collected all known manuscript editions of the patriarch's work. His work on this translation overlapped the King James Bible translation, and was finally published in 1610, a year before the publication of the KJB.

As a marginal note, the liturgy of John Chrysostom is celebrated weekly in the Eastern Orthodox Christian Church to this day. Not only that, it retains the sonority of the King James Bible, the rhythms, the gravity, the vocabulary. All that's missing is the odd spelling.

Savile's publication of Chrysostom has been called "the one great work of Renaissance scholarship carried out in England."[17] Savile's passion for Chrysostom says volumes about Savile himself. John Chrysostom was both thunder and lightning, power and volume. His name *chrysostom* means "the golden-mouthed," which is an interesting choice of name only because his "elegant, conversational, witty and morally fierce"[18] sermons made Byzantine nobility a bit nervous, suspended as they were between laughter and dread at his rant against wealth and its pretensions.

One of the more endearing stories about Henry Savile has to do with his bookishness. He was all about books, totally in love with them. So much so that his wife, Lady Margaret, once commented she wished she were a book so he might pay more attention to her.

"I would I were a book too," she said.

"Then it would be better that you be an almanac, then I could change you every year."[19]

Samuel Ward, a Puritan diarist, was a member of the Second Cambridge Company (the Apocrypha). Educated at Christ's College Cambridge, he was a Fellow of Emmanuel under Laurence Chaderton (1595), Master of Sidney Sussex College, Cambridge (1610), King's Chaplain (1611), Prebendary of Wells (1615), Archdeacon of Taunton (1615), Prebendary of York (1618), Lady Margaret Professor of Divinity at Cambridge (1623).

Ward's diary is one of the most famous of all Puritan documents. This small, bound paper book of ninety-five leaves, pages measuring five inches by six, is "devoted to an agonized conversation between the diarist and his conscience."[20] This diary, written a decade before the Hampton Court Conference when Ward was in his twenties, is a glimpse into the Puritan soul.

Ward was "an introspective and uncertain soul."[21] He was compared to Moses "not only for slowness of speech, but otherwise for meekness of nature."[22] Self-critical and self-punishing, he entered all his self-judgments in this diary he began at eighteen years of age. He verbally castigated himself for such things as eating too many raisins

and plums, and pride, of course, or for an excessive "desire of preferment." He agonized over the following (original spelling):

> Prid, Desire of vainglory, yea, in little things. Wea-
> risomnes in Godes [God's] service. Non affection. No
> delite in Godes service. No care of exhorting my breth-
> ren. Non boldness in the confessing of Godes name. No
> delite in hearing Godes word, or in prayer, or in receiv-
> ing of the Sacramentes. Shame in serving God.[23]

He is bored by one of Mr. Chaderton's sermons, gets angry
with a Mr. Newhouse for praying too long, and he punishes himself
in horror for these transgressions against God. He has "adulterous
thoughts." He has a verbal altercation with his roommate and writes
shamefully on his "excandescentia," that is, his violent anger against
him in words.

"I must learne to desire more after Sundays than the Mondayes,"
he says, and to restrain his "overmuch delite in these transitory pleasures of the world." Then there is "My overmuch quipping and desire
of praise thereby."

Diary entry 14 June 1595. (Ward was twenty-three.) It was a
Sunday, a day he began by not wanting to go to church, and being
distracted when he got there. He didn't pray. He didn't talk about
holy things at mealtime.

He slept through the first afternoon sermon and through the
second. He failed to go to evening prayers, and drank too much
afterward. He did not take leftovers to the poor. He prided himself on how good he was at Greek. He laughed at other's mistakes
when they could not keep up with him. He wrote that he "magnified
myself inwardly," and was a dullard at prayer. A single day of ruin
and perdition, recorded in his diary, his private confessional. "Thus
sin I dayly against thee, O Lord."

He longed to go after God the way he lusted after plums in the orchard. "Oh that I could so long after God's graces." Here is the portrait of yet another tortured Puritan soul. But it reveals something to us of the times, of the severity of belief, and just how deeply it is infused in the daily hum of life. Not all the Translators kept diaries, but this type of conviction was more common than we can imagine today. It provides evidence of the tremendous humility present among the Translators.

CHAPTER EIGHTEEN

The Lost Bois

Seest thou a man diligent in his businesse? hee shall stand
before kings.

—PROVERBS 22:29, KING JAMES BIBLE 1611

OF THE ACTUAL work of translation little is known. There remain
only shreds and patches. Records of the Translators' original work
were destroyed by fire, thrown away, or lost. Considered unimportant, whatever white paper there may have been was recycled in some
manner of the times—a to-do list, a grocery list, a sonnet scribbled
to a wife or a girlfriend. However they may have been disposed of,
they have receded into oblivion. What pieces we do have allow us
to reconstruct a basic image of the general enterprise of translation.

Other than fragments from the few letters that passed between
the king, Bancroft, and Cecil, and select others involved with the
translation, are three manuscripts that lay undiscovered for more
than three hundred years.

A single copy of the Bishop's Bible (provided at the beginning of the enterprise by the king's printer, Robert Barker) was found in 1955 by California scholar, E. E. Willoughby at the Bodleian Library at Oxford. Like something from a Dan Brown novel, lying dormant for centuries, it was catalogued in the Bodleian as "a large Bible wherein is written down all the Alterations of the last translation."[1] It was one of the forty copies of the Bishop's Bible dispersed among the companies. Heavy with the altered text and Translator notes, this manuscript and its siblings were the heart of the enterprise for seven years.

Around the same time, Dr. Willoughby discovered another manuscript called *An English Translation of the Epistles of Paule the Apostle*. This manuscript, known as Lambeth MS. 98, was found in the London palace of the archbishop of Canterbury at Lambeth. Richard Bancroft established the residence as a library in 1610. MS. 98 is another busy hands-on document upon which the Translators of the Second Westminster Company (New Testament Epistles) made their alterations, those little touches of history.

The third manuscript is the diary of John Bois, found in the library of Corpus Christi College in Oxford by Ward Allen, an American scholar. Until its discovery in 1964, this diary was little more than a probable fiction. In it, Bois records the final stage of the translation, at least part of it, the review at Stationer's Hall. We get to look over his shoulder into the mechanics of the translation.

A man of the book

He was no puritan, but John Bois was deeply devout, almost to distraction. A "man of the book," he was an exceptional individual who left us an exceptional piece of history. Without his diary much of the latter process of the translation would remain opaque.

Not unlike his king, the little prodigy was able to read the Bible cover to cover before he was five years old. He spoke Greek by the time he was six, and was able to read the Old Testament in Hebrew. He walked four miles to school as a boy and walked back at night. One of his grammar school friends was another Translator, John Overall. They were friends for life.

Bois was accepted at St. John's, Cambridge, at fourteen. He knew more Greek than anyone at the college. It took Bois one week to advance from the first level Greek to the second, a task that normally takes a full year. In summers, he prowled the university library from four in the morning until eight o'clock at night. He was elected fellow of St. John's and took his final exams wrapped in a blanket (he was suffering smallpox at the time).

He eventually married the daughter of a vicar in Boxworth, whose vicarage Bois succeeded. "His darling," though, was not the little wife, but his immense personal library, which included almost everything ever written in Greek. The poor girl's name is not even recorded.

Taking the vicarage at Boxworth, he left university life. When he was invited to be a Translator for the Second Cambridge Company, some of the other members actually scoffed, saying they "needed no help from the country."[2] The meaning was clear enough. (Similar taunts were made about William Shakespeare.) But Bois finished his work long before the others did. He helped another company with their work, probably the other Cambridge Company, and was appointed to the General Committee of Review.

"[Bois], with his finicky precision, the awe-inspiring hours he devoted to his work, his monklike removal from the world, was as great a scholar as England could provide."[3] He rode often on horseback to listen to a lecture or to attend some other academic business, always reading, his eyes and his attention fixed in a book, not the road. It could be raining. The sun could be shining. Children could be pelting him with stones, rotten fruit, or snowballs. Not looking up, he let the horse find its own way.

He walked after each meal and fasted once a week. He ate twice a day, with nothing in between, and carefully picked and rubbed his teeth afterward. It was said that he "carried to his grave almost an Hebrew alphabet of them [teeth]."[4] England was still infatuated with sugar from its new slave-operated plantations in the Caribbean, and yet Bois's teeth survived to chew and sparkle another day.

When he was old, he did not suffer the usual complaints others did. He always studied standing up. And when he preached, instead of preaching lofty sermons with the usual pyrotechnics or the complicated math of scriptural exegesis, Bois preached with simplicity. He did not wish to alienate the young or the simple to the truth of the gospel. Any other approach to his text would, he thought, "like to slay than to feed their souls." It is little wonder that Bois is one of the more memorable lights among the Translators.

Once all the Translators had reviewed and emended each other's work; once they had discussed, revised, argued, revised again, and settled on a course; once the entire effort was condensed to three manuscripts, one single copy from each institution, a select committee of Translators met together at the Stationer's Hall in London for a hearing.

The first stage of translation began in 1604 and though much of it was completed by 1609, some of the work may have been completed as late as 1610. This next step took nine months.

Twelve men were appointed to this final review committee, two from each company, or so it is thought. It might have been as few as six on the committee, one from each company. The general consensus is twelve.

What we do know about this final review is that the fastidious John Bois took notes, and was the only one who did. "Whilst they were imployed in this last businesse, he, and he only, took notes of their proceedings: which notes he kept till his dying day."[5] The entire process was oral. "One read the translation, the rest holding in their hands some Bible . . . If they found any fault, they spoke up; if not, he read on."[6]

In this final step, one man read from the translation and the others sat around and listened. Each Translator had in his lap a copy of the original Greek or Hebrew texts. Only the reader had a copy of the translation. The original texts were necessary only when discussion demanded it.

It was an auditory review. It was an auditory enterprise.

There was no fidgeting, no note taking (Bois excepted). When anyone objected, a discussion followed, which meant suggestions, revision, more discussion, and at last a bit of head bobbing, the sweet nod of approval. This is, after all, "the Kingdom of the spoken." The ear is "the governing organ of this prose; if it sounds right, it is right. The spoken word is the heard word, and what governs acceptability of a particular verse is not only accuracy but euphony."[7] *Euphony* is "the quality of being pleasing to the ear, esp. through a harmonious combination of words."[8] Fluid and easy, as conversation can be.

Also, listening is direct human intercourse, a person to person exchange. It involves the sound of the human voice and all the nuance that goes with it. Peter Ackroyd, writing about the English creative spirit says, "The spoken word is always a more conservative form than the written language; one of the secrets of the King James Bible's success, and of its continuity, lies in its employment of this natural power."[9]

At most, only a few verses per chapter were addressed. Some complete chapters were left alone. It was still a formidable amount of work, but the coarse sifting had already taken place. This stage was polish and finesse, the purification, the silty detail.

The twelve, whoever they were, other than Bois, were the first to listen to the King James Bible, its first audience. The diary only hints at some identification. "A. D." suggests Andrew Downes, of the Second Cambridge Company. Downes had been Bois's brilliant but somewhat jealous teacher (Bois ultimately outshone him). In his diary, Bois noted a "C," a "B," a "D H," a "Harmar" (John Harmar, of the Second Oxford Company), and a "Hutch." Ralph Hutchison of the Second Westminster was dead by 1610 so "Hutch" was someone else. The image is too faded to be exact. Other than Bois, Harmar is the only name we can be sure of, and possibly Downes, these three. The rest is silence.

Forthshining and flagitious fact

As to procedure, the diary is more generous. Each page reads like an itemized list. The notes are terse yet articulate. The writing is meticulous—the spacing, the handscript—Bois mixes Latin, Greek, and English in each note.

The diary covers the reviewers' work from Romans to Revelation. A few samples, a fragment or two, will allow you and me access to a moment at Stationer's Hall. Andrew Downes, for instance, thought Hebrews 13:8 should read:

Jesus Christ, yesterday, and to day the same, and for ever.

"If the words be arranged in this way the statement will be more majestic [A. D.]."

Being, as he was described, "a most subtle weigher of words," Downes was probably right. In the final rendering (below) only the arrangement of the words differ, and yet the line is somehow more immediate, meaning is pushed forward.

Jesus Christ, the same yesterday, and to day, and for ever.

The first sample lacks the smooth cadent rhythm of the second, as if the surface has been smoothed. The first sample stalls. The second does not. It drifts into an "even-flowing tempo" an "ease and naturalness and harmony."[10] It is a subtle distinction, but you can hear it. And though the message appears to be the same in both samples, it is not.

By making majestie accessible, as they have done, by placing majestie within reach, though, as a listener, I may not be aware of it at the time, I am given more information about God, a God who is now one degree closer, and by a subtlety of speech.

The word *majestic* in Downes's argument reveals something as well. Majestie is on everyone's mind. The reviewers in Stationer's Hall are after the majestic, the *aural majestic*. Majestie is the ultimate context in which each utterance is to be framed.

> The members of the meeting [final review] engaged in arguments, which were sometimes violent, consulted dictionaries, pored over and discussed current and antique theologians, traced textual variations, studied classical authors to settle questions of diction, thought about style, composed in places original readings. We know that the meeting deliberated over questions which were so difficult that the translators themselves had reached a deadlock over correct answers. In the light of this, thirty-two discussions provided a full day's work.[11]

Single words and sentence fragments were sorted and weighed, literally swirled about the mouth as if considering a fine wine, the subtle distinctions only a master would know. The disputes here, unlike the former work of the companies, were over language and style. They brooded over ambiguities and uncertainties, things that would have no ultimate resolve.

Surprisingly, many alternatives were discussed. The following familiar passages demonstrate the reviewers' task. The variance between the reviewers' draft and the final rendering of Scripture is at times small, hardly detectable, and at times conspicuous. Listen and judge for yourself. In the following samples, the reviewers' draft is in the left column, the final rendering of the Scripture (KJB) is in the right.

Hebrews 11:1

Faith is a most sure warrant of things, is a being of things hoped for, a discovery, a demonstration of things that are not seen.	Now faith is the substance of things hoped for, the evidence of things not seen.

1 Corinthians 13:11

I understood, I cared as a child, I had a childs mind,	When I was a childe, I spake as a childe, I vnderstood as a childe, I thought as a childe: but when I became a man, I put away childish things. I imagined as a child, I was affected as a child.

1 Thessalonians 5:23

. . . that your spirit may be kept perfect.	. . . your whole spirit, and soule, and body be preserved blameless.

Philippians 1:21

. . . life unto me is Christ, and death an advantage.	For me to live is Christ, and to die is gain.

In all the above, the traffic flows much smoother on the right than the left. All are stately. Majestie is liberal between them, in spite of the occasional hurdle. And yet some are endowed with a fluency the others do not have. The movement is graceful, liquid. There is no rush. Nothing halts or stutters, and the resonance is that of a viola, or an alto flute.

"Evil communications corrupt *good manners*" might have been "Evil communications corrupt *good natures*" (Galatians 3:24).

"The law was our *schoolmaster*" won out over *leader* or *pettymaster* (1 Corinthians 15:33).

Glory was chosen over *forthshining* (Hebrews 1:3).

Fiery indignation over *vehement wrath*.

Pernicious ways beat out *lascivious ways, impure ways, flagitious facts, an outrage*, and *a sin worthy of lashes*.

Apparently the Translators actually used words like *flagitious* and *forthshining*, and as odd as it might seem to you and me, the verdict was both close and intense.

We may conclude from Bois's notes that literary considerations were subordinate to accuracy. That is, soundness over sound. According to David Norton, "Whatever one considers the positive literary qualities of the KJB to be, they do not exist through a deliberate attempt on the part of either the KJB translators or their predecessors to write good English."[12]

The following are typical of the entries in Bois's notebook from 1 Peter. His notes will seem a bit cryptic to you and me, and I include them just for a sampling of Bois's note taking at the review. Still, the evolution of a single passage of Scripture can be rather fascinating.

1 PETER 1:7

Tyndale	*. . . that youre fayth . . . myghtbe founde unto lawde, glory, and honoure, at the apperynge of Jesus Christ . . .*
Geneva Bible	*That the triall of your faith . . . might be founde unto (your) praise, and honour and glorie at the appearing of Jesus Christ.*
Bishop's Bible	*That the triall of your faith . . . might be found to*

> *be unto you unto laud, honor, and glory, at the appearing of Jesus Christ . . .*

King James Bible *. . . that the trial of your faith . . . might be found unto praise and honour and glory at the appearing of Jesus Christ . . .*

Bois's note: ". . . that is to say, praise of God or your praise. We have not thought that the indefinite sense ought to be defined."

1 PETER 1:23

Tyndale *. . . by the worde of god which lyveth and lasteth for ever.*

Geneva Bible *. . . by the worde of God, who liveth and endureth for ever.*

Rheims Bible *. . . by the word of God who liveth and remaineth for ever.*

King James Bible *. . . by the word of God, which liveth and abideth for ever.*

Bois's note: "The participles 'living' and 'abiding' seem to be referred rather to 'word' than to 'God,' because of that which follows in the last verse."

1 PETER 2:5

Tyndale NT *. . . and ye as lyvynge stones, are made a spretually housse . . .*

Geneva Bible *And ye as livelie stones, be made a spirituall house . . .*

Bishop's Bible *And ye as lively stones, be you mad a spirituall house . . .*

Rheims Bible *. . . be ye also your selves superedified as it were living stones . . .*

King James Bible	... *ye also, as lively stones, are built up a spiritual house* ...

Bois's note: "Be built up, or, ye are built up"; Beza and Andrew Downes accept "imperatively"; others "infinitely."

1 PETER 2:13

Tyndale	... *unto the kynge as unto the chefe heed* ...
Geneva Bible	... *unto the King, as unto the superiour* ...
Bishop's Bible	... *unto the king, as having preeminence.*
Rheims Bible	... *unto the king, as excelling.*
King James Bible	... *to the king, as supreme.*

Bois's note: "as to the highest, to the sovereigne. Sovereigne, i.e. the French word for *summus, supremus.*"

In this last entry, there was concern about the word *supreme* in that it was unclear if the "king" was the reigning English sovereign or God himself. It is difficult to imagine any argument from James.

CHAPTER NINETEEN

To the Chief Musician

Scripture is a light, and showeth us the true way, both what to do and what to hope for, and a defense from all error, and a comfort in adversity that we despair not, and feareth us in prosperity that we sin not ... Suck out the pith of Scripture and arm thyself against all assaults.

—WILLIAM TYNDALE, *Doctrinal Treatises*

THEIR COMMISSION WAS to render a sparkling jewel, and with an English voice. They were to transmit, not innovate. They were to submit to the original text. They did not create. They did not assume. They invented nothing. They were not authors. The role of the King James Translators was more of a secretarial role. And they understood.

It was not an elitist agenda, as Christianity had once been. Unity doesn't work that way.

Majestie was to be dispersed, by means of the Scriptures. It was to be the connective tissue that held a people together. Or so was the desire of the dreamer/priest king. If the Scriptures were hoarded in days past, and they were, the effort was now to open what was sealed shut, and allow all people access, and at all levels of culture. The Scriptures were to be prepared for the poorly or noneducated, tuned to the pitch of the general listener, to set their sights, as William Tyndale said originally, as low as "the ploughboy." And yet they never intended it to sound like London streetspeak.

For simplicity and majestie to come together as thoroughly as it did in the final approved text is perhaps the greater miracle of the enterprise. In aiming for this simplicity, they did not think to bring God down, but to raise the English up, and specifically as that same English submitted to the original text (Greek and Hebrew manuscripts). It opened things up.

Suddenly God was accessible. Majestie was not so distant. No longer hidden or obscured, he seemed to genuinely care. Worship was no longer the remote procession of mystical events. The ploughboy was now the participant in the liturgy, no longer a mere spectator, or worse, an alien. The English translations that preceded the King James Bible tuned the people, made them susceptible to a verbal God.

The Translators' task then was to make English godly, to make it richer, to enhance its deep basses, to bring them forward and without losing the immediacy and simplicity. This was a poet's dominion perhaps, and yet there was not a poet among them. The text before them demanded things that academic text or popular literature could not demand.

> I wish the farm worker might sing parts of them [the Gospel and St Paul's Epistles] at the plough and the weaver might hum them at the shuttle, and the traveller might beguile the weariness of the way by reciting them.
>
> —DESIDERIUS ERASMUS, *PREFACE TO 1516 GREEK NEW TESTAMENT*

When God first spoke with an English voice

The Translators worked in the presence of great spirits. And I am not just referring to the king, Lancelot Andrewes, and others like them—great spirits as they are—but to the pioneers, those daring men of faith like John Wycliffe and the martyred poet, preacher, and holy man William Tyndale who were the first to give God an English voice.

> According to the *Oxford English Dictionary*, Sir Thomas More was the first to use the word *paradox*.
>
> —IN A PIECE CALLED *THE CONFUTACYON OF TINDALES ANSWERE*

It is difficult to imagine a time when an English Bible was outlawed. But there was no hatred so vile as the hatred toward upstart English translators, men like Wycliffe and Tyndale. Thomas More, the Catholic saint, the *man for all seasons*,[1] hated William Tyndale with a rare passion. His language went completely foul at the mere mention of the man, or the moonfaced monk, Martin Luther.

John Wycliffe (1320?–1384) is the forerunner of all English translators. He was the first to offer the entire Bible in the vernacular, the common tongue.* He has been justly called the *John the Baptist of the Reformation*, its *Morning Star*. That is, its first light. It was Wycliffe who first challenged the authority of the pope and made argument for the authority of the Scriptures. He was the English Luther before there *was* a Luther. To some, he was just plain annoying.

> That wretched and pestilent fellow, son of the serpent, herald and child of Antichrist, filled up the measure of his malice by devising the expedient of a new translation of

---

*While Wycliffe is attributed as the first to offer the complete Bible in English, his translation was taken directly from the Latin Vulgate (a Bible translated by one man, Jerome, in the fourth century). Wycliffe's translation was awkward, and often a too literal translation of the Latin, which made it difficult, if not impossible, at times to understand. The Latin Vulgate is riddled with mistakes and is not considered a reliable translation. It was William Tyndale, however, who first translated the Bible into English using the original Hebrew and Greek manuscripts.

Scripture into the mother tongue. (Arundel, Archbishop of Canterbury (Roman Catholic), his opinion of John Wycliffe)

To Wycliffe, the Bible was the "sole authority for religious faith and practice and everyone had the right to read and interpret scripture for himself."[2] He even dared to ask where in the Bible was such a thing as a pope anyway? His ideas eventually migrated to the German monk, but it was Wycliffe who made the fuss in the first place. By the time Martin Luther came along, more than a hundred years later, the world was prepared for the thunder he made. But even children know that before thunder there is a lightning that precedes it, that brief flash of power and dazzle that must by nature be brief. That honor goes to the Englishman.

John Wycliffe was the lightning to Luther's thunder.

Nature is beautiful in its raw and naked expression, as was Wycliffe's Middle English. The beauty lies in the lack of restraints, in its wildness. Reading Wycliffe, I cannot help but be aware of some faint resonance, like the movement of deep memory. The recognition is faint and yet familiar, the irrepressible English of my origins. Here are the first lines of the Bible in our common tongue:

In the bigynnyng God made of nouyt heuene and erthe. Forsothe the erthe was idel and voide, and derknessis weren on the face of depthe; and the Spiryt of the Lord was borun on the watris. And God seide, Liyt be maad, and liyt was maad. (Genesis 1:1–3, The Wycliffe Bible, 1395)

(In the beginning God made of naught heaven and earth, Forsooth the earth was idle and void, and darkness were on the face of depth; and the Spirit of the Lord was borne on the waters. And God said, Light be made, and light was made.)

Light be made, indeed. It is raw. It is undomesticated. It was "rude, coarse, but clear, emphatic, brief, vehement, with short stinging sentences."[3] And it is magnificent. It is Middle English, the English of Chaucer, *Piers the Plowman*, John of Gaunt, Richard II, and of six centuries past. It is glorious in its freshness, its vitality. I have tried to imagine what it might have been like to hear the Scriptures in my own tongue for the very first time. How it must have suddenly stepped forth in a sublime and immediate light.

Wycliffe believed that "a flowery, captivating style of address is of little value compared to right substance."[4] Flower or not, as only boldness and innovation can, John Wycliffe put into currency hundreds of words and constructions that first entered the stream of English in his Bible. The phrases *an eye for an eye, salt of the earth* (often attributed to William Tyndale), both make their first appearance in Wycliffe. *Canopy, child-bearing, communication, crime, envy, frying-pan, godly, humanity, injury, jubilee, madness, menstruation, middleman, novelty, pollute, puberty, unfaithful,* and *zeal,* all make their English debut in Wycliffe. The word *glory,* referring to the glory of God, was first introduced into English by Wycliffe.[5] Conviction and daring at this level have little choice but to arouse genius, or at least what we call genius. I think at this level "genius" is something else altogether, something closer to our origins, something deeply and satisfyingly human.

It is not difficult to see why the church at the time, the Roman Catholic Church, hated Wycliffe so much. Hate was a preoccupation of the medieval and the early modern church. Reading the sources you almost feel as if they could do no better than to hurl something at him.

In 1382, a synod of bishops met at Blackfriars in London to discuss Wycliffe's literary achievements. It was theater, and not very good theater at that. Their minds were made up before the meeting began. Wycliffe's translation was declared heretical, and simply because it was English. His followers, known as Lollards (a term of abuse that literally meant "mutterers"), many of whom were itinerant preachers, were captured, tortured, and put to death. This eventually led to a parliamentary ban on all English Bibles. Wycliffe and his Bible were outlawed. He died of a stroke two years after this verdict (1384).

And burning his books just wasn't enough. It took a few years, and one huge conclave that included a pope, an emperor, and thousands of priests and bishops, but in 1414, thirty years after his death, Wycliffe was finally declared a heretic, and not just for his English Bible but for his other efforts as well, all that he taught and spread about. Still, in no real hurry, a few years after that (1428) they carried out the sentence.

The remains of John Wycliffe, resting quietly in consecrated ground for forty-four years, were disinterred and borne along in solemn procession through the streets of Lutterworth, until they came to a hillside next to the River Swift.

Blackfriars, where the first English bible was declared heretical by a sham trial, was eventually bought by Richard Burbage, Will Shakespeare, and other players in the King's Men around 1608, during the time of translation. It became the Blackfriars Playhouse.

As a heretic, he was to be punished severely and condemned to an eternity in hell. I would guess, having been a priest, he was defrocked as a part of this ritual. Because the Church could not shed blood (*Ecclesisa non novit sanguinem*), they called in the locals for the sentencing and execution of the condemned man. "After cursing the remains, Bishop Fleming therefore delivered them up to the high sheriff of the county."[6] The Sherriff then turned Wycliffe over to the executioner.

Offering the executioner no resistance whatsoever, the condemned man was bound to a stake with chains, and then torched. As an added precaution, to make sure the skull and bones were burned to ashes, the executioner broke them up with a mattock.

At last, the ashes were carefully swept into a barrow and taken to the little arched bridge and cast into the Swift, a tributary of the Avon (Shakespeare's Avon).

The vexation was deep. And old. The Catholic Church understood exactly what Wycliffe's presence meant, that there was something insidious and unstoppable about this troublemaking little man. A poem remains that implies an influence that is deathless.

> The Avon to the Severn runs,
> The Severn to the sea,
> And Wycliffe's dust shall spread abroad,
> Wide as the waters be.[7]

Dispersing his ashes in the stream is a sufficient metaphor for Wycliffe's contribution to our English.

The following excerpt is taken from 1 Kings 19:12 as rendered in earlier English translations, starting with Wycliffe. I have listed them in chronological order that you might observe the evolution of a single line of text. The Wycliffe translation was not listed in Rule 14 of the King James translation, but I have included it here. There is an effervescence about the Wycliffe English that is too engaging to pass over. It reads like a sanitized Chaucer.

And aftir the stiryng is fier; not in the fier is the Lord. And aftir the fier is the issyng of thinne wynd; there is the Lord. (John Wycliffe Bible, 1395)

And after the earth quake there came a fyre, but the Lorde was not in the fyre. And after the fyre came there a styll softe hyssinge. (Miles Coverdale Bible, 1535)

And after the earthquake came fire: but the Lorde was not in the fire: and after the fire came a still and soft voyce. (The Geneva Bible, 1560) *And after the earthquake came fire, but the Lorde was not in the fire: And after the fire, came a small still voyce.* (The Bishop's Bible, 1568) *And after the earthquake, a fire: but the Lord is not in the fire. And after the fire, a whistling of a gentle air.* (Douay Rheims Bible, 1582) *And after the earthquake, a fire, but the Lord was not in the fire: and after the fire, a still small voice.* (The King James Bible, 1611)

We will ultimately make our own judgments concerning the sonority of the Scriptures, that delicious sound with its long echo, but in the above samples we open the window into the Translator's thoughts, and into his dilemma. In a transposition of two words the lyric comes forth full-bodied, as if liberated somehow. What is that distance between *"a small still voyce"* of the Bishop's Bible* and *"a still small voice"* the Translators settled upon? I do not have an answer. I am not sure *they* did. But I can hear it, as I suppose they did too. Did the Translators argue over this as I assume they must have? We don't know. But the alteration, this leapfrogging of one word over another, made all the difference, and taught us what to listen for.

When the Scripture came out from hiding, that is, from the Latin, or out of the dense thickets of archaic syntax and voicing, it was a wonder to its hearers. It liberated God.

To be fair, Wycliffe did little translating himself. He left the majority of the task to his followers.** But he set it in motion. He was their captain. It originated in him. He was the great spirit, the prime "moover" of the translation that bears his name.

---

* *"a small still voyce,"* was the translation of William Tyndale. In the 1530s, Tyndale translated the first fourteen books of the Old Testament and the book of Jonah. He completed his translation of the New Testament (1534) but was martyred before he could complete the entire Old Testament. All English bibles that came after Tyndale, including the King James, depended heavily on his translation.
** Nicholas Hereford and John Purvey.

To the chief musician

Though he never sought any such title, William Tyndale is nonetheless the quintessential English poet, the true forerunner of others in the pantheon—Wordsworth, Milton, Keats, Shelley. The others have the larger names, names that we love to repeat, and with a reflective sigh, but they don't have near the distance or reach that Tyndale does, which is the true measure of literary greatness. Every day in the English-speaking world, someone somewhere is speaking the words of William Tyndale.

We have all memorized his words. *"Our Father which art in heaven . . ."*

It is the master wordsmith who leaves behind a mint of phrases, who introduces whole volumes into the general stream of language. Not only that, but he gives shape to the English thought life as well, which language does. He provides the props and rigging by which we think and speak. That makes Tyndale immediate, current.

> More of our English is ultimately learned from Tyndale than from any other writer of English prose, and many erstwhile illiterates did indeed "go to school with Tyndale" and his successors. (David Norton, *The History of the English Bible as Literature*)

Only Shakespeare compares with Tyndale at this level. We use Shakespeare's verbal constructions and his peculiar linguistic geometries every time we tap out another blog or microblog, having coined more than two thousand "fire-new" words and phrases himself. Like Tyndale, he, too, is rather invisible.

It is the stamp of linguistic genius that your words remain in circulation. This profluence exists as a common denominator between the two Williams. But this may be where the comparison ends. One can move swiftly over the playwright's words. Hamlet instructs the players, "Speak the speech, I pray you, as I pronounced it to you, trippingly on the tongue . . ." Not all of Shakespeare speeds along at high velocity, nor should it. But much of it can be spoken that way and it loses nothing. Of course, *Hamlet* is a four-hour play. It must be moved along rather quickly so people can go home at a decent hour.

The same cannot be said of Tyndale, or the text of the King James Bible. Tyndale must be taken at another pace. It cannot be rushed.

William Tyndale was endowed with a profound lyrical gift, and yet he worked within a more confined space than Shakespeare. Shakespeare was limited only by his imagination. That, and the pentameter. Tyndale had restrictions of an altogether different kind. And what is remarkable about his work is that he remained true to "the rhythm of the original Hebrew," to its "balance, imagery and conciseness of expression,"[8] and produced a work of astounding beauty and clarity, one that joins majestie and simplicity.

The two Williams also had different objectives. Like his predecessor, Wycliffe, Tyndale had a dispute with the *powers that be* (a Tyndale innovation). A priest acquaintance, weary with Tyndale's persistent rant about the authority of the Scriptures said, "We were better without God's law than the Pope's." Tyndale's reply? "I defy the Pope and all his laws, and if God spare my life, ere many years I will cause a boy that driveth the plough [plow] shall know more of the Scriptures than thou doest." Of course, this got him in trouble. Branded a heretic, Tyndale said of the confrontation, "He thretened me grevously, and revyled me, and rated me as though I had bene a dogge."[9] It was at that moment he knew what his life's work was about:

> I perceived that it was impossible to establish the lay-people in any truth, except the Scripture were plainly laid before their eyes in their mother tongue, that they might see the process, order, and meaning of the text.[10]

Henry VIII hated Martin Luther with a Henry VIII kind of passion, kind of large and lusty. Luther once called Henry "a swine of hell." Thomas More hated Luther, as well, and with a similar passion. Tyndale was not a part of this meltdown, but he was associated with the growing sweep of Lutheranism and was in ill favor with the king and particularly the saintly More. Luther and Tyndale seemed to bring out the real trash in the man. Tyndale and More were both idealists, but at opposite ends. More was devoted to the authority of the Church, and Tyndale to the authority of the Scriptures. There was very little elasticity or bend in either man.

The Tyndale New Testament was smuggled into England from Antwerp, Cologne, and Worms, and could be purchased on Honey Lane or Coleman Street. Thomas More ranted against those who read Tyndale before attending worship service. One person described the men in his town who "did sit reading in lower end of church, and many would flock about to hear them reading."[11]

The appetite for an English Bible was present and unstoppable.

The bishop of London (Cuthbert Tunstall) once paid for an entire inventory of Tyndale New Testaments, thousands of copies. He then made a huge bonfire and burned them all. "I am the gladder," Tyndale said in response, "for I shall get money of hym for these bokes, to bring myself out of debt, and the whole worlde shall cry out upon the burning of Goddes worde."[12] Tyndale used the money he got for the condemned books to prepare a new and improved edition of his work. And the church paid for it.

> William Tyndale gave us our English Bible.
>
> —DAVID DANIELL, *WILLIAM TYNDALE: A BIOGRAPHY*

William Tyndale was as fertile in wordcraft as the other English William. And if there is music in the New Testament, and there is, it is the music of William Tyndale. Estimates vary, some as low as 76 percent and as high as 94 percent, but the general consensus among historians, Bible scholars, and biographers is that William Tyndale is responsible for at least 90 percent of the King James New Testament. And since he translated the first fourteen books of the Old Testament and the book of Jonah, we have much to thank him for. *"Let there be light"* is a William Tyndale translation. How is that for a start?

Remember, his words had the power of first love upon them in the sense that no one had ever heard them before. Like the sweet Englishing of a benediction:

> The lorde blesse thee and kepe thee.
> The lorde make his face shyne apon thee
> and be mercyfull vnto thee.
> The lorde lifte vpp his countenaunce apo thee
> and geue thee peace.

Alister McGrath writes, "Tyndale was a master of the pithy phrase, near to conversational English, but distinct enough to be used like a proverb."[13]

> For thine is the kingdom and the power and the glory
> fight the good fight
> my brother's keeper
> the apple of his eye
> the spirit is willing but the flesh is weak
> sign of the times
> in the cool of the day
> ye of little faith
> a law unto themselves
> peace-maker
> long-suffering
> The Lord's anointed

There are hundreds more. And the single-word wonders, like *Passover, Jehovah, scapegoat, atonement,* irrepressibly English, thoroughly Tyndale, and so infused in our language, so natural, at times it is easy to forget that each individual contribution had its start somewhere. Words like *landlady, seashore, fisherman, stumbling block, taskmaster, two-edged, viper, zealous,* and *beautiful* (a word that meant human beauty only—until Tyndale. He applied it to creation). The Hebraic superlatives like *holy of holies* and *song of songs* and all such *noun + of + nouns* constructions.

William Tyndale was the first to translate the word *caritas* in 1 Corinthians 13 as *love.* Like the other William, we speak Tyndalese every day of our lives and are hardly aware of it. Not a church service goes by, a wedding, a funeral, that we do not hear a strain from his lyrical ghost, albeit friendly, fatherly, and generous. David Daniell in *The Bible in English* says, "Behind the statistics is that unmeasurable feeling that the KJV's rhythm, vocabulary and cadence, which can be so exquisite and so direct, has a root in an essence of the English language. The cause of that is Tyndale's genius."

William Tyndale understood something about Scripture that could only be released in a lyric. The clarity and purity, even the accuracy he sought, he found in rhapsody.

Aural imagination

In spite of the greatness of his gifts, Tyndale was still sifted and refined by the Translators. And yet far from obscuring Tyndale or consigning him to the background, the Translators gave him a greater clarity, a higher, smoother gloss. They removed some of the heavy footing—that was all. Adam Nicolson summarizes the Translators' obligation to the text: "Tyndale's words become, very slightly but very significantly, musically enriched."[14]

In the Tyndale New Testament, Matthew 11:28 reads, *"Come unto me all ye that labor and are laden and I will ease you."* The King James translation, with a slight alteration: *"Come unto me all ye that labor and are heavy laden and I will give you rest."* The effort is taken out of it. It can be spoken in a single breath, unbroken. This was the medication the Translators brought to the text. Adding the single modifier *heavy* softens the alliteration and improves the fluency of the line. The iamb *"and-I* will-*give* you-*rest"* improves the footing at the end.[15] Here once again is a perfect example of the Elizabethan aesthetic.

John 15:12–13 in Tyndale reads (spelling modernized): *"This is my commandment that ye love together as I have loved you. Greater love than this hath no man than that a man bestow his life for his friends."*

The King James Bible: *"This is my Commandment, that ye love one another, as I have loved you. Greater love hath no man than this, that a man lay down his life for his friends."*

Tyndale supplies the framing, the original blueprint for the line. The Translators simply do the finishing. And the introduction of the comma, little thing that it is, allows the necessary hesitation, that slight suspension that intensifies the payoff. It teaches us how to sing. In the second sentence, Tyndale trips and stumbles. The King James Translators simply remove the obstacles. The entire process is a work of aural imagination.

William Tyndale maintains a presence in all English Bible translations that came after him. There is no way to circumnavigate him. He is everywhere. And the King James Translators did right by submitting to such a large and inevitable spirit. If the assertion is true that the King James Bible helped to shape not only the English language, but also Englishness itself, then William Tyndale must be placed in the foreground as the chief musician and architect.

 CHAPTER TWENTY

Finishing Touches

TO THE MOST
HIGH AND MIGHTIE
Prince, Iames by the grace of God
King of Great Britaine, France and Ireland
Defender of the Faith, &c.

TOWARD THE END of 1608, the king ordered that the work be "finished and printed as soon as may be."[1] The Translators thought they had more time. Some of them were still negotiating places "of special obscurity" seeking brain and counsel from sources outside the companies in compliance with Rule 11.* Though another year went by, royal impatience is royal impatience. It was time to make an end, to "put the finishing touches to the whole."

Appointed to the task were Thomas Bilson, the bishop of Winchester, and Dr. Miles Smith (or Smyth), a Translator in the

---

*Rule #11 (Rules of Translation) *When any Place of special Obscurity is doubted of Letters to be directed, by Authority, to send to any Learned Man in the Land, for his Judgment of the Place.*

Second Oxford Company (later bishop of Gloucester). Smith was a sincere and humble man, well respected among all the Translators. It is a subtle justice that he, the son of a butcher, was appointed to this last stage of the translation. Speaking for the Translators, in the preface of the King James Bible he wrote of his peers, "There were many chosen, that were greater in other men's eyes than in their own, and that sought truth rather than their own praise."

Thomas Bilson had no part in translation whatsoever, but carried impressive weight in the ecclesiastical community. "As reverent and learned a Prelate as England ever afforded, a deep and profound scholar, and a principal sustainer [of the Anglican church]." It was said of him that he was so "complete in divinity, so well skilled in languages, so read in the Fathers and Schoolmen, so judicious is making use of his readings, that at length he was found to be no longer a soldier, but a commander in chief in the spiritual warfare, especially when he became a bishop!"[2]

The king liked him. That was credential enough.

"With frowning concentration and spluttering pen [Bilson] underlined, crossed out, accepted, or rejected"[3] the Translators' work. *Spluttering?* When I first read this, knowing that each of the Translators had committed four, possibly five to six years to the enterprise—after all the argument, debate, the long hours, the emotional investments, the reiteration, to have an outsider come in at the last minute seemed odd in spite of his credits. A pinch hitter who had no feel for the game, who had not been swept up on the same currents the others had. One source suggested that Smith and Bilson's "finishing touches" might have been only the Dedication and the Preface to the Readers.

There was no such title, but Miles Smith was the man with the commas, the copy editor, albeit inspired and overqualified. He was the flourish. He brought to the page a sense of space, and a feel for rhythm. It was said that he must have inserted the commas while on horseback because of the conspicuous canter many of the rhythms make. Among other details, Smith was responsible for the page and chapter headings.

As Bilson and Smith, Misters Piety and Humility, the pinch-hitting prelate and the butcher's boy, were about to wrap it up as a present for the king, in charges Richard Bancroft, the heady little archbishop, in a slight steam, demanding the last word as if it were Rule 16.* Bancroft died November of that same year (1610), so his impatience is forgivable. Robert Cecil, the king's best dog, died two years later, simply worn out, suggesting that those who were closest to the king, who undertook him or did his close bidding, could not bear up under the demand.

Bancroft claimed to make fourteen changes to the translation, though only one is certain. "For it is written in the booke of Psalmes, Let his habitation be desolate, and let no man dwell therein: And his *Bishopricke* [italics mine] let another take" (Acts 1:20). Because an argument followed between Smith and Bancroft, the Translators' draft obviously read "And his *charge*" (Geneva Bible) and not *bishopricke* (though *bishopricke* was found in both the Bishop's and Tyndale Bibles).

Ever the spaniel, Bancroft knew the king would appreciate the switch. James had seen to it that the word *tyrant* was absent from his Bible, and here Bancroft indulged him one of his favorite words. The other thirteen changes the archbishop may or may not have made, no one really knows. Smith's argument went nowhere. Bancroft "is so potent," Smith said, "there is no contradicting him."[4]

Wonder of the world

Bilson wrote the dedicatory Epistle to the King. It was lavish, High Church, full of high-stepping pomp. It sounded like the reign. It

---

*There were only *fifteen* Rules of Translation. See Appendix C.

sounded like the carving on the throne or the royal mantelpiece, the gilt, the profundity, the hyperbole, the excess, all the dense ornament and luster of the age, all that was Jacobean. I imagine to Bilson's ear it sounded like favor and advancement, or the clink of coin. But there is more to be read in it than that.

Men can be what they are, be led how their passions lead them, however their inner Hamlet drives them, but the Bible these men labored over is above merit and credentials. Pinch hitter that he was, Bilson was fresh. The king had not wearied him. Bilson's epistle, like the King James Bible itself, is about kingdom, glory, and majestie. In what amounts to two pages of text, the two realms—temporal and spiritual—lose their distinctions and seem to be caught up together. His attention is on king and kingdom. The translation itself recedes to midstage.

One of the differences between the Jacobethan age and our own is that we no longer know or understand how to address a king. It is too distant and too old-world for our perceptions, a relic of deep cultural memory. Any such awareness was lost in the gradual disenchanting of the past two hundred years. Bilson's dedication allows us to hear once again how it is done. His words seem fawning or obsequious to our twenty-first-century ear, but it is a king he is addressing. "To the Most High and Mightie Prince, Iames . . . ."

The actual type in the dedication is larger than the type anywhere else in the 1611 Bible.

Bilson is well tuned. Adam Nicolson refers to him as an "archetype of the Jacobean courtier-politician-bishop."[5] Instead of allowing the glory of the realm left behind by the former queen, the "Occidental [western] Starre," to fade or droop, the new "Sunne" will take his subjects to an even greater glory, by observing in their prince his duty to God, the "zeale of your Maiestie towards the house of God . . . manifesting itself abroad in the furthest parts of Christendom, by writing in defence of the truth,"[6] which will give the "man of Sinne" a blow he will not recover from. The image of the king at home, the king at the House of God, the king hearing the Word preached, the king "cherishing" the teachers of the Word, the king caring for the church as "a most tender and loving nourcing [nursing, nourishing] Father." The surface both panders and glorifies the king. The subtext admonishes him, imposes a subtle rule.

Bilson dedicates the great work . . .

> which now with all humilitie we present unto your MAIESTIE . . . For when your Highnesse had once out of deepe iudgment apprehended, how convenient it was, That out of the Originall sacred tongues, together with comparing of the labours, both in our owne and other for-reigne Languages, of many worthy men who went before us, there should be one more exact Translation of the holy Scriptures in to the *English tongue*; your MAIESTIE did never desist, to urge and to excite those to whom it was commended, that the work might be hastened, and that the businesse might be expedited in so decent a maner, as a matter of such importance might justly require.

James is noted as the "principall mover and Author of the Worke." The word *author* here implies authority, dominion, authentication, according to the *Oxford English Dictionary*, "he who *authorizes* [italics mine] or instigates; the prompter or mover. *Obs.*" Bilson cites the king as the protector, the defender of the faith. He then ends with a blessing:

> The Lord of Heauen and earth blesse your Maiestie with many and happy days, that as his Heavenly hand hath enriched your Highnesse with many singular, and extraor-dinary Graces; so you may be the wonder of the world in this later age, for happinesse and true felicitie, to the honour

of that Great God, and the good of his Church, through Jesus Christ our Lord and onely Saviour.

That we may love it to the end: preface to the readers

"But now what pietie without truth? What trueth without the word of God? What word of God (whereof we may be sure) without the Scripture?" *The Translator to the Reader* (preface), the other piece of front matter, written by Miles Smith teaches, explains, warns, and blesses. It is in this long bit of lovely excess that we are given something about the translation. He reveals the soul of the translation, and, in essence, the soul of the Translator.

The preface is all about the obligation of the Translators to the enterprise of translation, what they sought, where they sought it, what they plundered, what they left alone. Bilson pays homage to visible majestie, and does so with eloquence befitting his host. Smith reveals and pays tribute to the veiled majestie the Translators obligated themselves to, the great presence they sought among the ancients. We are bereft of the *hows*, but Smith gives us the more critical *whys*. He writes,

> Happy is the man that delights in Scripture, and thrice happy that meditates in it day and night. But how can men meditate in that which he cannot understand? How shall he understand that which is kept close in an unknown tongue?

Like its king, the truth was born in a mask. The Translator's obligation is to remove the mask, for he is convinced there is no need for one.

> Translation it is that openeth the window, to let in the light; that breaketh the shell, that we may eat the kernel;

that putteth aside the curtain, that we may look into the most Holy place; that removeth the cover of the well, that we may come by the water, even as Jacob rolled away the stone from the mouth of the well, by which means the flocks of Laban were watered. Indeed without translation into the vulgar tongue, the unlearned are but like children at Jacobs well (which was deep) without a bucket or some thing to draw with.

Smith writes with a rare mix of warmth and erudition. His sincerity is as refreshing as it is conspicuous. And his reference to Jacob will not go unnoticed by the king either. At more than eleven thousand words the preface is exhaustive and for the general reader it may seem dense, with the heavy tread of the academic. He speaks with less pomp than Bilson, but nonetheless majestie does not abandon him. Indeed, it lies in the plainness, in the transparency of his text, providing even another level of rightness and providence.

Smith makes no apology for the longevity of the Translator's task, nor from "going over it againe, having once done it." The image Smith uses is that of rubbing a surface until it shines. In the following he clarifies the Translator's duty:

But let us rather bless God from the ground of our heart, for working this religious care in him, to have the translations of the Bible maturely considered of and examined. For by this means it cometh to pass, that whatsoever is sound already . . . the same will shine as gold more brightly, being rubbed and polished; also, if anything be halting, or superfluous, or not so agreeable to the original, the same may be corrected, and the truth set in place. And what can the King command to be done, that will bring him more true honour than this?

In the end, speaking for the Translators, Smith commends the reader to God. And only as a prayer can be, it is immediate, dateless.

It remaineth, that we commend thee to God, and to the Spirit of his grace, which is able to build further than we can ask or think. He removeth the scales from our eyes, the vail from our hearts, opening our wits that we may understand his word, enlarging our hearts, yea correcting our affections, that we may love it to the end.

I do groan under the burden of this book

It is uncertain just what was delivered into the hands of Robert Barker, "The Printer to the King's most excellent Maiestie," as it reads on the title page. Like so much of the documentation surrounding the enterprise, whatever came into his possession no longer exists. It may have been an annotated copy of the Bishop's Bible. It might have been a single manuscript stitched together from the three institutions. Either way, Barker paid £3,500 to underwrite the costs of the printing. Considering that a perfectly good house in London might cost £120, Barker put up a fortune.

The first run of the King James Bible was riddled with printer errors. It was known as the "He" Bible. Not because of its manliness, or its weight, but because there is a typographical error in Ruth 3:15. The last few words should have read, ". . . and *she* went into the city." She never made it. *He* did. *"Also he [Boaz] said, Bring the vaile that thou hast vpon thee, and holde it. And when she [Ruth] helde it, he measured sixe measures of barley, and laide it on her: and* he *went into the citie."* In this edition, there was a typo for every ten pages of text.

Printing was still a primitive enterprise. The press was a monolith flatbed with a huge screw mechanism. The content of each page was placed into a wooden form by a compositor, letter by tiny letter, verse by verse. To conserve time, once the first sheet was pulled from the press, a "reading boy" read the copy to the compositor to check his work. Homophones were particularly slippery. A homophone is a word that sounds identical to another word, but differs both in spelling and meaning. *Hour* and *our* is a good example, or *flee* and *flea*, the little pest from chapter 13.

It was too expensive to keep vast numbers of individual letters, so once a sufficient number of page one was printed, the form was emptied and refitted with page two and so on. It was much more complicated than that, and at 774,746 words, the task was monumental. That represents millions of individual letters the compositor must negotiate. Error was inevitable. Add to that a kind of chaos in Barker's print shop at Northumberland House at Aldersgate, and the result is sadly predictable.

No copy of that original 1611 Bible matched any other copy.

Some of the printer errors were actually deliberate. Being understaffed and underpaid opened up a gate for anarchy, and to a compositor or a pressman it is still a community of words and an occasional stab of pungent text was common. For instance, in the first edition, Psalm 119:161, which is supposed to read "Princes have persecuted me without a cause," came out as "*Printers* have persecuted me without cause" (emphasis mine). David Norton suggests that this is due more to employee dissatisfaction than actual error. Editorial correctness was in the domain of the printer. As detailed and as meticulous as the Translators were, once it left their hands it was in the keeping of the printing house.

In one of the Gospels, *Judas* was substituted for *Jesus*. *Hoopes* for *hookes*, *ashes* for *asses*, *sunnes* for *sonnes*, *plain* for *plague*. Some of the errors were hidden errors that slipped by a proofreader unnoticed, only because it tended to make sense, as an error of gender or number might. Some corrections of hidden errors from the first edition to later editions include the following sample.

"*And in you*" of John 15:4 was corrected to "*and I in you.*" Malachi 1:8: "*if hee offer*" should be "*if ye offer.*" In 1 Corinthians 15:6: "*and that*" is corrected to "*after that.*" Psalm 69:32: *good* should be *God.* Ezra 2:22: *children* should be *men.* And Hebrews 11:23: "*they not afraid*" is corrected in a later edition and becomes "*they were not afraid.*" There were scores of other hidden errors.

Letters in the form tended to get inverted at times; the *u* and *n* for instance, so the word *and* becomes *aud* or *against* becomes *agaiust, concerning coucerning.* Then there is the neglectful and the indiligent *Beeer-sheba, accor-ning, fobreare, flatterech, felfe* (self), *lob* for *Iob* (Job), *powerfulll, looosed, brighnesse, Anocrynha* (Apocrypha), *bowles* for *bowels,* and so on. It is frightfully similar to our modern text message.

Years later, the errors became more amusing, though not for Barker. In 1631, he pressed what came to be known as the "Wicked Bible." It was given this odious title because Exodus 20:14 was short one word. It read, "*Thou shalt commit adultery.*" It does make the imagination run wild, I suppose, but Barker, continually pressed for cash, was fined £300 pounds for the error. All the copies were recalled.

Not long after the printing began, Barker reportedly lamented, "I do groan under the burden of this book."[7]

In the nineteenth century, Dr. Frederick Scrivener made an effort to collate all existing editions of the King James Bible in circulation. In doing so he found twenty-four thousand variations among them. That means "no one such thing as 'The King James Bible' agreed, consistent, and whole has ever existed."[8] As variable as its king.

Still, the 1611 King James Bible, in spite of the blemishes, was a wonder to behold. It "swept forward with a majestic stream of editions"[9] in folio (16 x 10 inches) and in smaller versions, the quarto and the octavo.

THE
HOLY
BIBLE

Conteyning the Old Testament
AND THE NEW:
Newly Translated out of the Originall
Tongues & with the former Translations
Diligently compared and revised by his
Maiesties speciall Commandement.
Appointed to be read in Churches.
Imprinted at London by Robert
Barker, Printer to the Kings
Most Excellent Maiestie
ANNO DOM. 1611

It was glorious. It reeked with majestie, with every detail, the jointure of heaven and earth, the contract itself. Cornelius Boel, an artist from Antwerp, engraved the title page. Like every other bit of Jacobean excess, the page is overgrown with meaning. It was a spectacle. It was also a portal. Invitation was scrawled into the detail. The tone of the entire page could be an opening by Beethoven (not Mozart). And the large animated spirit behind it all was all James.

Was God in the detail? That was their intention—find him a home. One with an English address.

The Pan King

> Second to the right, and straight on till morning.
> That, Peter had told Wendy, was the way to the Neverland;
> but even birds, carrying maps and consulting them at windy
> corners, could not have sighted it with these instructions.
> Peter, you see, just said anything that came into his head.
>
> —J. M. BARRIE, *Peter Pan*

TO THIS DAY it is still called the Authorized Version of the Bible (AV), though it was never truly authorized, at least not with any legal blessing.[1] Which is just like James. These are the little watermarks, the traces of him where we find his most personal signature, where he is the most himself. I am not sure if it was an oversight, or if some bigger picture suddenly comes into view. Like so many of his innovations, his larger dreams, what authorization the King James Bible had was in the king himself. And, as names do, after so many years it just seemed to stick.

We will, with all probability, continue to call it the Authorized Version though no such authorization exists. In perspective, and with this odd solitary figure behind it, I can think of no better title. We dare not call it anything else, even with the evidence we have. Why? Well, because it's the AV. It is all in the carriage.

The idea of *Great Britain* was authorized much the same way, that is, within the person of the king. James just did it. Time being what it is, it wasn't until the last Stuart monarch, one hundred years later, in the reign of Anne of Great Britain (Act of Union 1707), that the kingdoms of Scotland and England were officially joined. But like the AV, the authorization was long in play. James called himself "King of Great Britain" because that's how he heard it in his head.

In exploring the life of James Stuart, I have excluded the details of his life beyond 1611. Fascinating in moments, pitiable in others, his last days are not germane to our text. After the first printing of the Bible, our story no longer really needs him. Truth is, he's just not that interesting after that. All his happy thoughts have long materialized—the King James Bible, Great Britain, tranquility of the realm, the Union Jack. And who wants to see Peter Pan get old? Like Shakespeare after 1611, his volume just goes down. What's left is a kind of evanescence, which is hardly ever that attractive in a king.

Still, a few last notes about Jack.

Once upon a joust

The AV says, "Better is the end of a thing than the beginning thereof."[2] In most cases, this happens to be true. He still blurs for the camera, only at a much slower pace. A series of bad parliaments (they were ignored, shut down, or prorogued, that is, discontinued without dissolution). We hear more sermonizing about divine right and royal prerogative. He sends Walter Raleigh to find *El Dorado*, the city of gold. Raleigh does not find the fabled city, of course, and loses his head for his troubles.* Other than that, James just gets lazy,

---

*Raleigh was a particular target for James. He was scheduled for execution twice. The first time for treason (1603 in a farce called the Main and Bye Plot). When Sir Walter was on the gallows, James ordered a stay of execution at the last possible minute. The king was amused. Raleigh was not. Years later, James sent him on an expedition to find

hunts a lot, loses more teeth, makes more speeches and one grand fool of himself.

Unfortunately, any treatment of the final years of James Stuart has little choice but to include the twin disasters known as his "favorites," whom I feel obligated to mention only for roundness of this text. Our good king becomes the doting fool, "your old dad," as he wrote to them. And be warned, labels do not stick.

Antonia Fraser calls them the "fatal favorites." We have already been introduced to Esme Stuart, his Scot/French cousin, a man twenty-four years older than the love-deprived prepubescent king. In 1607, with the translation buzzing away in the background, James enjoys a leisurely afternoon at the tiltyard,[3] when a young man catches the king's eye. A lovely young man, a Scot. And once upon a joust, the lovely young man falls off his horse and breaks his leg. James tends to the lovely young man himself, and by the time the leg heals, the lovely young man is an earl.

Robert Carr (English spelling of Kerr, his Scots surname), for the price of a broken bone and an afternoon's joust, has a definite change of fortune and becomes the most powerful man in the kingdom next to the king (pun intended). Antonia Fraser describes him as "astonishingly good looking."*

El Dorado (1618), the lost city of gold, near the mouth of the Orinoco River in South America. On this trip, Raleigh lost his son Watt while engaging in battle with the Spanish, an action that had been forbidden by James. But instead of escaping free and clear when he had the chance, Raleigh returned to England and went back to the king. James put Raleigh back in the Tower and later had him executed.

*Alison Weir, in her book *Mary Queen of Scots and the Murder of Lord Darnley*, describes Lord Darnley, the king's father, as "astoundingly good looking" (p. 62). In all of James's romantic imaginations (as an adult) there is a subtle connection with his father. Each attachment shares a similar dynamic, particularly with regard to age, beauty, and perhaps the tone of the language observed between them. I have chosen to consign this thought to the footnotes. It belongs in the marginalia, a suggestion for further consideration, nothing more.

Beyond what is public and conspicuous, or the occasional "Oh man, do I have to watch that" kind of behavior with his favorites (and to the disdain of Queen Anne), history is mute. Unfortunately, conjecture and speculation are not, and the king's reputation has long suffered for it.

And no one notices the ghost who wanders in. Esme Stuart. But there is a reversal of roles. James is now the older, and Carr the younger. It is the younger who is beautiful, royal in awe and attribute. It is March 1607. James/Esme is forty. Carr/James is twenty. James gives Carr a great name, and makes him ugly rich, and at a time when the exchequer is gasping for life, as it did often with James.

This relationship, as it did with Esme Stuart, ends in disaster. A PR disaster for James and serious jail time for Carr, not to mention a whole list of enemies at court. Carr marries high, but badly. Both Carr and his wife, the lovely and extremely dangerous Frances Howard, are indicted for murder. She is let off. Carr spends some time in the Tower. James loses interest and before you can hear anything hit the ground, he is rapt with someone else. *George.*

George Villiers. Same story. It is always the same story. There is only one ghost. Only one imprint was made. James gets all stupid with love, but much worse. Villiers, an "untitled and penniless son of a Leicestershire squire,"[4] brings out the doting idiot in the king. It's not as if we haven't seen it before, but James makes a statement to his Privy Council that ends all doubt. Concerning his relationship with Villiers, James says, *"Jesus Christ had his John. I have my George."*[5]

Be cautious when judging him. His way of love is not the way of the adult. The lover image is just not our king. Like his gait, it is distracted, uneven, and will lead in the wrong direction. History is slowly giving James some breathing room for his entanglements, his odd psychology of attachment. Anyway, to judge him by any twenty-first-century scale is not only to be misled, it is to be wide of the point.

James would never imply that Jesus was sexually involved with his beloved disciple. As shocking as it might seem to you and me, it was an honest assessment of his affections, just how deep they ran. Was he sincere? Must we really ask?

Shakespeare's *The Merchant of Venice* is one play we know the king favored. He was so pleased with it he actually asked for a repeat performance. We are given no reasons why. One source suggested it was Portia's sagacity in the courtroom. While that is possible, I can't help but think that the relationship between the older Antonio and the younger Bassanio revived a deep memory in the king, that indelible print. Antonio's love for his friend is honorable, it is warm, true, selfless, and sacrificial. It is not romantic. It is not sexual. Such relationships between men were not uncommon in Early Modern England. I offer this to provide ballast, knowing how contrary our current judgments might run.

George Villiers outlived the king and was assassinated not long after. Of course he was.

As might be anticipated, Villiers and Carr both became spoiled, and ungrateful. The creature Majestie was the ruin of both of them. The lovely young men stepped too close and without sufficient awe or seasoning, paid the wrong kind of homage to Leviathan and were consumed.

James loved his family warmly and passionately—his sons, his daughter, his wife. For the same reasons he refused to attend Henry's funeral, he could not attend Anne's when she died in 1619, though it was not for want of love.

At last what can we say of the king? I could write him a thousand different ways and he still comes out James. For all the ignominy and all the bad press, there is much more that is truly glorious to be accounted for. The years between 1604 and 1611, the years of the translation, were doubtless his finest. The reign of James Stuart was the reign of empire. Colonial America was settled in 1607. Like the King James Bible, America itself was a Jacobean enterprise.

Poet William Carlos Williams rightly attributes the discovery and true spirit of America to Sir Walter Raleigh, the anti-James. With my affection for the great man, the true Renaissance man, I must agree. Perhaps El Dorado was not the myth we thought it was.

Scriptura erectus

Other than linguistic issues, the difference in tone, mood, the depth of its rhapsody, the stateliness, and perhaps age, the major difference between the King James Bible and all other Bibles is that the KJB is the only Bible that has the seal and imprimatur of a king. Other translations may have an organization behind them, a movement, a single personality, maybe even a corporation, but nothing quite like a king, and definitely nothing quite like James.

If this book preaches anything, it preaches election, the peculiar appointments of a sovereign God, an absolutist God, a monarchist who tolerates only one head, a God whose choices don't often make sense. For all of his unloveliness, for all the negative spin that has followed him throughout history, for all his crude Broad Scots, James Stuart was the right king at the right time for the right historical event. Only James could have given us the Bible he did, and only by the conditions that existed in culture—the brooding aesthetic, the powerful linguistic genius of the times, the ambivalence (the going national neurosis), the roll and pitch of the English language. And that discernible hum.

The Bible was meant to relieve us of the burden of ourselves, to hold up a mirror that is clear, articulate, accessible, and above all beautiful. And to do so with rhapsody. It should be stately, elevated, fluid, *other*. How are we to set ourselves adrift otherwise? There *should* be a certain amount of reach involved. It should touch us to the very quick, if indeed we are penetrable.

The only condition is surrender, as one must when dominion is present.

Majestie is, or should be, that presence that halts us, that stops us in our tracks, that sticks in the throat for want of words. Taking liberties with majestie, and as distracted as current appetites can be, the modern translator is tempted to disguise majestie, restrain or soften it, to muzzle it. As if Leviathan were a pet.*

Majestie is somewhat circumspect in a disenchanted age, an age of entitlement. But there is something else.

The King James Bible is infused with certain aspects of its bene-factor—the highness, the authority, the elevation, the necessity of deep and immovable belief, its "thine is the kingdom and the power and the glory" resonance, the power to inspire and to effect change, and yes, the absolutism, that touch of impervious majestie. James was an absolutist king in a time when the fabric of absolutism was beginning to wear thin, being held together with patches and bits of old thread. Western culture was growing up. Reason and intellection were on the rise.

My father would use no other translation than the King James. Nor would his father before him. It was a mild refusal, but a refusal nonetheless. You knew it was old somehow, generations deep. This refusal suggests a kind of instrinsic absolutism, a spirit of the book. A phrase like "King James only" reflects this absolutism. I bring this up simply because it fascinates me. To read judgment in my words is to read me incorrectly. Toxicity is an altogether different issue, and as it is with any movement, it lies at the extremes.

---

*Like many of the dualities explored in this book, the image of Leviathan serves a dual purpose. One, the creature Majestie, as we have witnessed in the text. But Leviathan is useful also as an image of the majestie of scriptures. Because the Word of God is alive ("living and active" according to Hebrews 4:12) it too must be approached, as the prologue warns, "with awe and dread." It is beautiful. It is mysterious. It is not penetrable by the usual means of examination. It asks for much more than that. It has free movement within us, even as it has an invisible presence in the subtext of this book.

Beyond those considerations of invested authority, if there is a charm about the King James Bible that other translations lack, it begins with the language, with that brief flash of linguistic virtuosity and vitality that shaped it, and moved it forward into time.

Admittedly, for the modern taste the KJB can be a piece of work. If you add the block print of its first editions and the insufferable presence of the *S*s that look like *F*s, it can come out sounding a bit like Daffy Duck or Sylvester the Cat. Read the following aloud.

But he that received the feed into ftony places, the fame is he that heareth the word anon with joy and recieveth it. Yet hath he not root in himfelf but endureth for a while: for when tribulation or perfecution arifeth becaufe of the word, by and by he is offended. (Matthew 13:20–21)

In the evolution of the English Bible, the King James Bible stood upright. It was *scriptura erectus*, owing a greatness to those evolutionary states that preceded it. The KJB threw an eclipse over all former translations, and yet did so, as English does, by absorbing them, giving them a newer, higher gloss. Tyndale never sounded so sweet.*

One more thought about Shakespeare. His cousin, Robert Southwell, was a Jesuit priest, which made him an outlaw under Elizabethan rule. Actually, Southwell was the Queen's Public Enemy Number One.[6] He was not only a Jesuit, but also a poet, a writer, and that made him dangerous. In 1592, he wrote a book of poems called *St. Peter's Complaint*. In the dedication he said the duty of poets was

---

*It is William Tyndale we have to thank for the retention of *thees* and *thous*, *spakes* and *begats*, the *-th*, and *-eth* endings and the like. This form of speech was out of fashion by 1604, and yet the King James Translators, perhaps out of some reverence for Tyndale, chose to keep them. The high tone adds gravity to the music of the text, and ages it a bit (a reverence they purposely chose to leave in).

to glorify God. The poet, he said, should not waste his gifts on popular theatre or romance. The dedication was addressed *"To My Worthy Good Cosen, Maister W. S."*[7]

Did the "Worthy Good Cosen" take the priest-poet's advice? Hardly. We know the poet went his own way, and became William Shakespeare, a name that looms so large above and around us even now, we hardly need attach superlatives to it.

But here is another *what if* to consider. If Shakespeare had *any* influence over the translation of the King James Bible, even remotely, would this influence not satisfy his cousin's exhortation? Could we not say that the poet indeed glorified God and that he did so by simply being himself, that is, by nurturing and applying the gifts God had given him in the first place? Did he not tap that deep inward spring and bring to English something English had not heard before?

Not to mention that after 1611 Shakespeare is done. The great flame that burned wild and white-hot during the years of translation is now but a snuff, a smoldering wick. Beyond 1611 he writes two more plays, lesser plays, *Henry VIII* and *The Two Noble Kinsmen*, collaborations, and hardly his old form. *The Tempest* (1610–11) is his valediction, his exit, his last great play with its sorcerer's drowned book and its broken staff. According to the Revels Accounts, it was performed before King James at Whitehall on Hallowmas, 1 November 1611.[8] The year of publication of the KJB.

> But this rough magic
> I here abjure [renounce], and, when I have required
> Some heavenly music, which even now I do,
> To work mine end upon their senses that
> This airy charm is for, I'll break my staff,
> Bury it certain fathoms in the earth,
> And deeper than did ever plummet sound

I'll drown my book.

—William Shakespeare, *The Tempest*, V, i, 50–57

Some heavenly music, indeed. The presence of James triggered something powerful in the playwright, something that burned for a bright season. During the years of translation the poet operated at capacity, in apex. The same could be said of James as the English king. His first years were his best years, his brightest, his most electric.

Would Shakespeare have made a decent priest? Maybe. With his instincts anything is possible. But I somehow doubt it. We might never have heard the name Shakespeare at all. But left to the elements, to the conditions of culture, left to the movement of his particular genius, and to the hidden orchestration of a great and omnipotent God, he became what he became. And in doing so, fulfilled a commission he was totally unaware of. It is just a thought, but a delicious one, one that offers whole new possibilities for the rest of us.*

Enough.

By the way, Robert Southwell was arrested, racked, and tortured by Elizabeth's sadistic handyman Richard Topcliffe. He was hanged, drawn and quartered at Tyburn (1595), a martyr. It was said that when Elizabeth read his book she wept.

For me, as a child, King James had no presence as a real king, as someone who occupied a real throne, or commanded a realm. It was simply a name I associated with an old way of speaking that no one

---

*The word *delicious* applies as well to the mystery of Psalm 46. In the 1611 King James Bible, if you count 46 letters from the beginning of Psalm 46 (do not count the words in the title) you will come to the word *shake*. Count 46 letters in reverse from the end of the psalm and you come to the word *speare*. Is this "an amazing freak of chance," as one writer asserts? (J. Michell, *Who Wrote Shakespeare*). Or is it something else? I chose to bury this riddle in the footnotes. It is rather appetizing, I admit. Shakespeare was 46 in 1610. It would make a great detective story, but one that belongs in another book.

really used anymore except at church, before a meal, or at a funeral. I also grew up thinking we dare not speak to God any other way.

It was the language of homage, of unquestioned reverence. I was hardly aware of its beauty, and yet, even for a boy there was something absolute, something final in the very sound of the words, though I lacked the capacity to understand or comment. It was strange in its antiquity, charming in its way, but distant. *King James* was little more than an imprint made in gold leaf on my father's leather Bible.

I still have that Bible sitting on my shelf, and not unlike our king, much of the gold has been rubbed clean with time. The gloss has been "slubber'd," as they would say in the vernacular. But true majestie is always absolute. It is immune to time and to a distracted posterity, immune to bad press and the strange appetites of future ages. Often, there is a shift in perception. The window opens. The shell breaks. The curtain draws back. I can only hope I have done such a service to this great king.

Second star to the right, and straight on till morning

I am almost certain Ben Jonson had no such thing in mind, but I think there is no better image to capture James than the so-very-English Peter Pan. James is the orphaned boy, the lost boy, the unscrubbed child who never quite grew up, nor had any mind to. Like his great book, he is a bit timeless.

He is intensely charming in a crude sort of way, and he loves to hear himself talk.

The puritan won't like him.

He prefers the open wood and the wildness of the chase to a life at court among the fawning multitudes. He has pirates all around him, and has claimed a land across the sea with real Indians. Granted, Pocahontas is no Tiger Lily, but she will have to do.

He is also at peace with Leviathan, the creature Majestie. Not exactly the big crocodile with time or a pirate in its belly, but close enough.

Best of all, King James had within him the power of flight and more than that, he did not hoard his flight, but had the ability and the willingness to make others around him fly. The Shakespeares, the Bacons, the Donnes, the Andrewes, the Overalls, the Saviles. I'm sure it is a matter of belief, of thinking the right thoughts. A bit of fairy dust might even help.

At his death, 27 March 1625, an autopsy revealed that "all the vitals were sound, as also was his head, which was very full of brains; but his blood was wonderfully tainted with melancholy."[9] Wonderfully.

And that's it. That's James. *Pan Pacificus.* More the artist than the administrator, more the visionary than the clerk, more the dreamer than the shopkeeper; where he dreamed he dreamed big, rather like a king. Where he loved, there were no half measures. Where he failed, he was absolutely magnificent. As only true greatness does, he offered the power of flight to those who, like him, had flight within themselves. In the end, it is always a matter of belief. Always.

APPENDIX A

Chronology

1558

- → John Knox publishes "The First Blast of the Trumpet Against the Monstrous Regiment of Women."
- → Mary Queen of Scots marries Francis Valois, Dauphin of France.
- → Mary Tudor dies (Mary I of England or "Bloody" Mary).
- → Elizabeth Tudor proclaimed Elizabeth I of England.

1559

- → Francis Valois crowned Francis II of France. Mary Queen of Scots becomes queen consort of France.

1560

- → Francis II dies at age sixteen.

1565

- → Mary Queen of Scots marries Henry Stuart, Lord Darnley.

1566

- → Lord Darnley and associates murder David Rizzio in the queen's bedchamber at Holyrood Palace on 9 March.
- → James born 19 June at Edinburgh Castle between nine and ten in the morning.
- → James baptized 17 December—Charles James, Prince and Steward of Scotland; Duke of Rothesay; Earl of Kyle, Carrick, and Cunningham; Lord of the Isles; and Baron of Renfrew.

1567

- → Lord Darnley murdered at Kirk o' Field.
- → Mary Queen of Scots marries James Hepburn, Earl of Bothwell.
- → Mary imprisoned at Lochleven Castle.
- → Mary forced to sign voluntary demission (abdication).
- → James Stuart crowned James VI of Scotland at Church of the Holy Rood.

1570

- → King James VI begins education under George Buchanan and Peter Young.
- → Papal Bull (Pius V) proclaiming Elizabeth I, "the pretended queen of England," a heretic, releasing all Catholic subjects from allegiance to her.

1571

- → James's first appearance in public as king (five years old). Addresses Scottish parliament.

1579

- → Arrival of Esme Stuart, Sieur d'Aubigny.

1580

- → Esme Stuart created earl, and soon after, duke of Lennox.

1581

- → James Douglas, fourth Earl of Morton, the last Regent of Scotland, executed for alleged complicity in the murder of Lord Darnley.
- → James assumes rule of Scotland.

1582

- → Mary Queen of Scots proposes and drafts the Association, a contract making Mary and James corulers of Scotland. In spite of his protests otherwise, James never signs the contract.

1584

- → Sovereignty Act of 1584 (Black Acts) establishes James VI as head of church in Scotland. Reestablishes episcopacy.

➤ *Ane Metaphoricall Invention of a Tragedie Called Phœnix*

➤ *Essays of a Prentise, in the Divine Art of Poesie*

1587

➤ Mary Queen of Scots beheaded at Fotheringay Castle.

1588

➤ English defeat the Spanish Armada.

➤ *Ane Frvitfull Meditatioun contening ane plane and facill expositioun of ye 7.8.9 and 10 versis of the 20 Chap. Of the Reuelatioun in forme of ane sermone.*

1589

➤ James VI marries Anne of Denmark in Oslo, Norway.

1590

➤ Witch trials begin in Scotland.

➤ Anne crowned Queen of Scotland.

1591

➤ *His Maiesties Poeticall Exercises at vacant hours*

1594

➤ Henry Frederick Stuart, future Prince of Wales, born 19 February.

1596

➤ Elizabeth, princess, future Elizabeth of Bohemia, born 19 August.

1597

➤ *Daemonologie*

1598

➤ *The Trew Law of Free Monarchies*

1599

➤ *Basilikon Doron*

1600

➤ Charles Stuart, prince, future Charles I of England, born 19 November.

1602

➤ Robert Stuart, prince, born 18 January, dies 27 May.

1603

→ Elizabeth I of England dies. James VI of Scotland proclaimed James I of England.

→ Millenary petition presented to James.

→ Shakespeare's troupe the Lord Chamberlain's Men become the King's Men by order of the king.

→ Outbreak of plague.

→ Coronation of James and Anne.

1604

→ Hampton Court Conference

→ Parliament refuses union of Scotland and England.

→ James prorogues parliament.

→ Somerset House Conference ends twenty-year war with Spain.

→ *A Counterblaste to Tobacco*

1605

→ The Gunpowder Treason and Plot

→ Mary Stuart, princess, born 8 April.

1606

→ James meets Robert Carr, first English "favorite."

→ Shakespeare's *Macbeth* completed and performed for James at Whitehall.

1607

→ Jamestown settled. First official English settlement in America.

→ Sophia Stuart, princess, born June 1607. Dies within 48 hours of birth.

→ Mary Stuart, princess, dies 16 December.

1609

→ *An Apologie for the Oath of Allegiance*

1610

→ Henry Savile publishes works of John Chrysostom.

1611

→ First edition of the King James Bible published.

1612
- Henry, Prince of Wales, dies at age eighteen.
- Robert Cecil dies.

1613
- The Globe Theater burns down during a performance of *Henry VIII.*

1614
- James meets George Villiers, soon to be earl (1617), marquis (1619), then duke of Buckingham (1623). Replaces Carr as king's favorite.

1616
- James forbids further editions of the Geneva Bible. King James Bible becomes the only English Bible.

1617
- Native American princess, Pocahontas, visits James at Whitehall.

1618
- Walter Raleigh sent on expedition to find El Dorado.

1619
- *A Meditation on the Lord's Prayer*
- Queen Anne dies 19 March.

1620
- *Mayflower* sails for America.

1625
- James dies 27 March.

Note: Published works of King James are in italics and listed by date of publication.

WILLIAM SHAKESPEARE PLAYS DURING THE TRANSLATION OF KJB (1604–1611)*

Measure for Measure	1604
Othello	1604
King Lear	1605
Macbeth	1606
Antony and Cleopatra	1606
Coriolanus	1607–08
Timon of Athens	1607–08
Pericles	1607–08
Cymbeline	1609–10
The Winter's Tale	1610–11
The Tempest	1611

*Dates according to Harold Bloom, *Shakespeare: The Invention of the Human*, p. xv.

APPENDIX B

The Stuart Succession

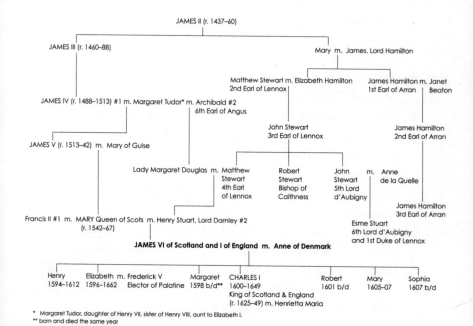

JAMES II (r. 1437–60)

JAMES III (r. 1460–88)

Mary m. James, Lord Hamilton

Matthew Stewart m. Elizabeth Hamilton
2nd Earl of Lennox

James Hamilton m. Janet
1st Earl of Arran | Beaton

JAMES IV (r. 1488–1513) #1 m. Margaret Tudor* m. Archibald #2
6th Earl of Angus

John Stewart
3rd Earl of Lennox

James Hamilton
2nd Earl of Arran

JAMES V (r. 1513–42) m. Mary of Guise

Lady Margaret Douglas m. Matthew
Stewart
4th Earl
of Lennox

Robert
Stewart
Bishop of
Caithness

John
Stewart
5th Lord
d'Aubigny

m. Anne
de la Quelle

James Hamilton
3rd Earl of Arran

Francis II #1 m. MARY Queen of Scots m. Henry Stuart, Lord Darnley #2
(r. 1542–67)

Esme Stuart
6th Lord d'Aubigny
and 1st Duke of Lennox

JAMES VI of Scotland and I of England m. Anne of Denmark

Henry
1594–1612

Elizabeth m. Frederick V
1596–1662 Elector of Palatine

Margaret
1598 b/d**

CHARLES I
1600–1649
King of Scotland & England
(r. 1625–49) m. Henrietta Maria

Robert
1601 b/d

Mary
1605–07

Sophia
1607 b/d

* Margaret Tudor, daughter of Henry VII, sister of Henry VIII, aunt to Elizabeth I.
** born and died the same year

The Rules

(The rules to be observed in translation)

1. The ordinary Bible read in the Church, commonly called the Bishop's Bible, to be followed, and as little altered as the Truth of the original will permit.

2. The names of the Prophets, and the Holy Writers, with the other Names of the Text, to be retained, as near as may be, according as they are vulgarly [commonly] used.

3. The old ecclesiastical words to be kept viz. the Word Church not to be translated Congregation.

4. When a word hath divers Significations, that to be kept which hath been most commonly used by the most of the Ancient Fathers, being agreeable to the Propriety of the Place and the Analogy of the Faith.

5. The Division of the Chapters to be altered, either not at all, or as little as may be, if Necessary so require.

6. No Marginal Notes at all to be affixed, but only for the Explanation of the Hebrew or Greek Words, which cannot without some circumlocution, so briefly and fitly be express'd in the text.

7. Such Quotations of Places to be marginally set down as shall serve for the fit Reference of one Scripture to another.

8. Every particular Man of Each Company, to take the same Chapter,

or Chapters, and having translated or amended them severally by himself, where he thinketh good, all to meet together, confer what they have done, and agree for their Parts what shall stand.

9. As one Company hath dispatched any one Book in this Manner they shall send it to the rest, to be consider'd of seriously and judiciously, for His Majesty is very careful to this point.

10. If any company, upon the Review of the Book so sent, doubt or differ upon any Place, to send them Word thereof; note the Place, and withal send the Reasons, to which if they consent not, the Difference to be compounded at the General Meeting, which is to be of the chief Persons of each Company, at the end of the Work.

11. When any Place of special Obscurity is doubted of Letters to be directed, by Authority, to send to any Learned Man in the Land, for his Judgment of the Place.

12. Letters to be sent from every Bishop to the rest of his Clergy, admonishing them of this Translation in hand; and to move and charge as many as being skilful in the Tongues; and having taken Pains in that kind, to send his particular Observations to the Company, either at Westminster, Cambridge, or Oxford.

13. The Directors in each Company, to be the Deans of Westminster and Chester for that Place; and the King's Professors in the Hebrew or Greek in either University.

14. These translations to be used when they agree better with the Text than the Bishop's Bible: Tindall's [Tyndale's], Matthews, Coverdale's, Whitchurch's [otherwise known as the Great Bible, used in the time of Henry VIII, identified by Whitchurch, the publisher], Geneva.

15. Besides the said Directors before mentioned, three of four of the most Ancient and Grave Divines, in either of the Universities, not employed in Translating, to be assigned by the Vice-Chancellor, upon Conference with the rest of the Heads, to be Overseers of the Translations as well Hebrew as Greek, for the better Observation of the 4th Rule above specified.

Notes

Prologue

1. Ackroyd, *London*, 362.
2. Bragg, *Adventure of English*, 2.
3. Akrigg, *Jacobean Pageant*, 158.
4. Weldon (1583–1564), *The Court and Character of King James*. While Sir Anthony's report is for the most part accurate, it is held suspect by many biographers and historians as a primary source because he had been denied some favor at the court of James and therefore had somewhat of a chip on his shoulder.
5. De Lisle, *After Elizabeth*, 45.
6. Willson, *King James*, 48.
7. Akrigg, *Jacobean Pageant*, 86.
8. Genesis 32:24–30.

Chapter 1: Mom and Dad (or An Evening with the Macbeths)

1. Shakespeare, *Henry V*.
2. Macleod, *Dynasty*, 25.
3. Willson, *King James*, 15–16.
4. Ibid., 14.
5. Fraser, *Mary Queen of Scots*, 293.
6. Both Antonia Fraser (*Mary Queen of Scots*) and Alan Stewart (*The Cradle King*), like me, question the troublesome event, and therefore use the convenient word "alleged."
7. Mary had elevated Lord Darnley before they married, creating him Baron Ardmannoch and Earl of Ross. Being an English subject, Elizabeth could have interpreted Darnley's acceptance of these titles as an act of treason.

8. Willson, *King James*, 18.

9. Guy, *Mary Stuart Queen of Scots*, 431.

10. McElwee, *The Wisest Fool in Christendom*, 30.

11. Guy, *Mary Stuart*, 15.

12. Weir, *Mary, Queen of Scots*, 29.

13. Jane Austen, *The History of England from the reign of Henry the 4th to the death of Charles the 1st. By a partial, prejudiced, & ignorant Historian.* Written when the author was 16.

14. Macleod, *Dynasty*, 94.

15. Melville, *Memoirs*, 1549–93, quoted in Weir, *Mary Queen of Scots*, 65.

16. Bingham, *Making of a King*, 22.

17. Weir, *Mary, Queen of Scots*, 62.

18. *regiment*—the rule or government over a person, people, or country; *esp.* royal or magisterial authority. Now *rare* (very common *c* 1550–1680). *(Oxford English Dictionary).*

Chapter 2: A Fawn Among Jackals

1. Letter from Thomas Randolph to William Cecil.

2. Macleod, *Dynasty*, 103.

3. Stewart, *Cradle King*, 7.

4. Herries, *Historical Memoirs*, 77.

5. Adam Blackwood, *History of Mary Queen of Scots*, 9–10, quoted in Stewart, *Cradle King*, 7.

6. Fraser, *Mary Queen of Scots*, 246.

7. Rizzio's guitar can be seen presently at the Royal College of Music in London.

8. Herries, *Historical Memoirs*, 75.

9. Weir, *Mary, Queen of Scots*, 119.

10. *"Justice! Justice! My Lady! Save me! Save me!"* Another source adds, "I am a dying man, my Lady!"

11. *". . . our life."* Its official name is the *majestic plural* (Latin—*pluralis maiestatis*). Royalty thought of themselves as one person with dual natures, that is, both human and divine. Of course, this is perhaps the more hidden or symbolic reason for the *royal "we"* as it is sometimes called. The more conspicuous meaning is that being sovereign, his or her voice is the voice of the state itself, therefore plural. It was all part of the royal idiom.

12. Claude Nau, *Memorials of Mary Stewart*, 4.

13. Fraser, *Mary Queen of Scots*, 254.

14. McElwee, *Wisest Fool*, 22.
15. Claude Nau, *The History of Mary Stuart*, 17.
16. Labanoff, *Lettres*, 351, quoted in Fraser, *Mary Queen of Scots*, 257.
17. Fraser, *Mary Queen of Scots*, 257.
18. Bingham, *Making of a King*, 26.

Chapter 3: Rockabye Sweet Baby James
1. Herries, *Memoirs*, 132.
2. Stewart, *Cradle King*, 14.
3. Ibid.
4. Herries, *Memoirs*, 79, quoted in Willson, *King James*, 13.
5. Ibid.
6. Stewart, *Cradle King*, 14.
7. A reference from *Hamlet*. A *petard* is an explosive that makes a loud noise.
8. Willson, *King James*, 13. *"Because his father has broken to me."* That is, all bets are off. We're done here.
9. Herries, *Memoirs*, 133.
10. Bingham, *Making of a King*, 27.
11. *caul* [Latin: *caput galeatum*, literally, "head helmet"] The amnion or inner membrane inclosing the ftus before birth; *esp.* this or a portion of it sometimes enveloping the head of the child at birth, superstitiously regarded as of good omen, and supposed to be a preservative against drowning *(Oxford English Dictionary)*. To be "born in the caul" simply means a child is born with the amniotic sac or membrane still intact around the body. Famous "caulbearers" include Sigmund Freud, Napoleon, and the poet, Byron.
12. From his address to Parliament following the failed Gunpowder Treason and Plot of November 5.
13. Willson, *King James*, 17.
14. McElwee, *Wisest Fool*, 17.
15. Ibid., *23*.
16. Stewart, *Cradle King*, 31.
17. David Willson, *King James*, 19.
18. Stewart, *Cradle King*, 31.
19. Macleod, *Dynasty*, 117.

Chapter 4: The Most Valuable Life in Scotland
1. McElwee, *Wisest Fool*, 32.
2. Ibid.

3. Coronatio, Ja.6. In Castro Striuelensi. 29 Juli 1567. Dalyell, *Fragments of Scottish History*, appendix XIII.

4. Bingham, *Making of a King*, 35.

5. Ibid., 36.

6. Weir, *Mary, Queen of Scots*, 21.

7. Bingham, *Making of a King*, 37.

8. Ibid.

9. Fraser, *King James*, 29.

10. Bingham, *Making of a King*, 37.

11. Stewart, *Cradle King*, 34.

12. Ibid.

13. Willson, *King James*, 19.

14. Fraser, *King James*, 26.

15. Macleod, *Dynasty*, 131.

16. McElwee, *Wisest Fool*, 41.

17. Ibid.

Chapter 5: Greek Before Breakfast, Latin Before Scots

1. Bingham, *Making of a King*, 57 ("Diurnal of Occurrence," 242).

2. Stewart, *Cradle King*, 36.

3. Bingham, *Making of a King*, 57.

4. Stewart, *Cradle King*, 36.

5. McElwee, *Wisest Fool*, 36.

6. Fraser, *King James*, 26.

7. McElwee, *Wisest Fool*, 40.

8. George Buchanan, *Song of Songs* (Dedication).

9. *British Quarterly Review*, vol. 66, "George Buchanan's Detectio Mariae Reginae Scotorum," by Robert Vaughan, Henry Allon, 1877.

10. Willson, *King James*, 25.

11. George Buchanan, *De Jure Regni Apud Scotos*.

12. George Buchanan, Dedicatory letter in *Rerum Scoticarum Historia*, (Edinburgh, 1582).

13. George F. Warner, "The Library of James VI", *Misc. of the Scottish History Society* (Edinburgh, 1893), I, ix–lxxv. *Misc. of the Maitland Club* (Edinburgh, 1840), I, 1–23. Allan F. Westcott, *New Poems by James I of England* (NY, 1911) xv11–xxiv, quoted in Willson, *King James*, 23.

14. McElwee, *Wisest Fool*, 24.

15. Stewart, *Cradle King*, 41.

16. Ibid., 44.
17. Fraser, *King James*, 35.

Chapter 6: A Timid, Friendless Boy
1. Willson, *King James*, 26.
2. McElwee, *Wisest Fool*, 39.
3. Ibid., 42.
4. M. Fontenay, Hatfield House MSS, III, quoted in Willson, *King James*, 53.
5. McElwee, *Wisest Fool*, 43.
6. Fraser, *King James*, 36.
7. McElwee, *Wisest Fool*, 44.
8. Weldon, *Court and Character of King James*, 55.
9. Nicolson, *"God's Secretaries: The Making of the King James Bible,"* Cambridge University Podcast.
10. Fraser, *King James*, 36.
11. McElwee, *Wisest Fool*, 46.

Chapter 7: Speak of Me As I Am
1. Bingham, *Making of a King*, 122.
2. Willson, *King James*, 32.
3. McElwee, *Wisest Fool*, 47.
4. Bingham, *Making of a King*, 46.
5. Fraser, *King James*, 37.
6. Letter from Henry Wadryngton to Sir Francis Walsingham, May 1582, *Border Papers*.
7. Bingham, *Making of a King, 129.*
8. That is, "storm and stress," a phrase coined by G. Stanley Hall on the psychology of adolescence.
9. Willson, *King James*, 36.
10. Ibid.
11. McElwee, *Wisest Fool*, 36.
12. Macleod, *Dynasty*, 130.
13. Ibid.
14. Bingham, *Making of a King*, 137.
15. Ibid., 138.
16. Ibid., 142.
17. Calderwood, *History*, 559, quoted in Bingham, *Making of a King*, 141.
18. Willson, *King James*, 41.

19. Ibid.
20. Bingham, *Making of a King*, 90.
21. Melville, *Memoirs*, 145.
22. McElwee, *Wisest Fool*, 50.
23. Fraser, *King James*, 38.
24. Melville, *Memoirs*, 283–285.
25. McElwee, *Wisest Fool*, 52.
26. Bingham, *Making of a King*, appendix A, letter from Esme Stuart to James VI.
27. Melville, *Memoirs*, 285.
28. Bergeron, *King James*, 49.
29. Fraser, *King James*, 38.
30. Bingham, *Making of a King*, 130.

Chapter 8: You Don't Know Jack

1. Fontenay to Nau (letter), 15 August 1584, *Calendars of State Papers—Scotland* 7: 274–5, quoted in Stewart, *Cradle King*, 77.
2. Akrigg, *Letters*, letter 10, 55.
3. Willson, *King James*, 54.
4. Obtained from the *OPSI, The Office of Public Sector Information* (UK).
5. Stewart, *Cradle King*, 138.
6. Willson, *King James*, 123.
7. Ibid., 50.
8. Ibid., 71.
9. Ackroyd, *Shakespeare*, 413.
10. Fraser, *Mary Queen of Scots*, 413.
11. Labanoff, *Lettres*, 368.
12. Macleod, *Dynasty*, 118.
13. Fraser, *Mary Queen of Scots*, 494.
14. Lee, *Great Britain's Solomon*, 33.
15. Labanoff, *Lettres*, vol. VII, p. 36, quoted in Fraser, *Mary Queen of Scots*, 506.
16. Ibid., vol. VI, 438.
17. Fraser, *Mary Queen of Scots*, 517.
18. Ibid., 520.
19. Ibid., 528.
20. Ibid., 529.
21. Ibid.

Chapter 9: Mum

1. Fraser, *Mary Queen of Scots*, 531.
2. Ibid., 534.
3. Ibid., 539.
4. Moysie, *Memoirs*, 60.
5. Willson, *King James*, 78.
6. Ibid.
7. Ibid.
8. Calderwood, *History of the Kirk of Scotland*, 611, quoted in Stewart, *Cradle King*, 88.
9. Stewart, *Cradle King*, 81.
10. *gossip* [godsip, godsib, gossipp, etc.]—"One who has contracted spiritual affinity with another by acting as a sponsor at a baptism. a. In relation to the person baptized: A godfather or godmother; a sponsor. Now only *arch.* and *dial*" (*Oxford English Dictionary*).
11. Akrigg, *Letters*, 87–88.

Chapter 10: The Age Was Lousy with Poets

1. Willson, *King James*, 86.
2. Ibid., 94.
3. Ibid., 191.
4. Sounds like *noxious*, doesn't it?
5. Willson, *King James*, 85.
6. De Lisle, *After Elizabeth*, 52. ADHD is an acronym for *Attention Deficit Hyperactivity Disorder*. Those who suffer ADHD have a problem with inattentiveness, over-activity, impulsivity, or a combination of these.
7. Willson, *King James*, 89.
8. McElwee, *Wisest Fool*, 67.
9. Stewart, *Cradle King*, 108–109.
10. William Asheby to Francis Walsingham (Letter), 24 September 1589, Calendar of State Papers Scotland, 10:157, quoted in Stewart, *Cradle King*, 109.
11. Willson, *King James*, 89.
12. James to Anne (Letter), c. 2 October 1589. *Warrender Papers 2*: 109–110, quoted in Stewart, *Cradle King*, 108.
13. Akrigg, *Letters*, October 1589, 97.
14. Ibid., letter dated 22 October 1589, 98.
15. Melville, *Autobiography and Diary*, 277.

16. Moysie, *Memoirs*, (Edinburgh: Bannatyne Club, 1830), 80–81, quoted in Stewart, *Cradle King*, 112.

17. Melville, *Memoirs*, 277.

18. Stewart, *Cradle King*, 117.

19. Ibid., 119.

20. *Papers Relative to the Marriage of King James Sixth of Scotland, with the Princess Anna of Denmark*; *A. D. M.D. LXXXIX. And the Form and Manner of Her Majesty's Coronation at Holyroodhouse. A.D. M.D.XC.*, ed. J. T. Gibson Craig (Edinburgh: Bannatype Club, 1828), quoted in Stewart, *Cradle King*, 119.

Chapter 11: Double, Double, Toil, and Trouble

1. James VI of Scotland, *Daemonologie*, 44.

2. Willson, *King James*, 103.

3. *Newes From Scotland*, ed. by G. B. Harrison (London, 1924), 15.

4. Willson, *King James*, 105.

5. Ibid., 103.

6. Ibid., 104–105 (3 preceding quotations).

7. *necromancy*—"the art of predicting the future by supposed communication with the dead; (more generally) divination, sorcery, witchcraft, enchantment" *(The Oxford English Dictionary)*.

8. James VI of Scotland, *Daemonologie*, 19.

9. Stewart, *Cradle King*, 179.

10. Willson, *King James*, 179–180.

11. Garber, *Shakespeare After All*, 697.

12. Fraser, *Faith and Treason*, 289. (Also in the film *V for Vendetta*, Warner Brothers, 2006.)

13. Bloom, *The Modern Scholar, Shakespeare: The Seven Major Tragedies*, Recorded Books, 2005.

Chapter 12: The Supremest Thing on Earth

1. James I of England, *Speech to Parliament*, March 1607.

2. Andrew of Wyntoun (early 15th century) *Orygynale Cronykil of Scotland*. Also, Fergus brought the Stone of Scone with him from Ireland. He was succeeded by a son named Dúngal.

3. George Walton Williams, *South Atlantic Review*, "Macbeth: King James's Play," vol. 47, no. 2, 12–21.

4. Guy, *The Queen of Scots*, 25.

5. Genesis 28:10–22.
6. Fraser, *King James*, 123.
7. Ibid., 120.
8. Willson, *King James*, 63.
9. Ackroyd, *London*, 359.
10. John Aubrey, *Brief Lives*, ed. A. Clark, II, 186.
11. *Basilikon Doron*.
12. Lacey, *Sir Walter Ralegh*, 324.
13. McElwee, *Wisest Fool*, 133.

Chapter 13: 1603
1. Weir, *Life of Elizabeth I*, 479.
2. Akrigg, *Jacobean Pageant*, 89,
3. Nicolson, *God's Secretaries*, 10.
4. Weir, *Life of Elizabeth I*, 484.
5. Willson, *King James*, 155.
6. Lee, *1603*, 25.
7. Ackroyd, *London*, 97.
8. *Memoirs of Robert Carey*, quoted in Christopher Lee, *1603*, 106.
9. Lee, *1603*, 107.
10. Ibid., 112.
11. Willson, *King James*, 158.
12. Ibid., 90.
13. McElwee, *Wisest Fool*, 90.
14. Willson, *King James*, 171.
15. Historical Manuscripts Commission, *Salisbury MSS.*, XV: 28.
16. McElwee, *Wisest Fool*, 116.
17. Lee, *1603*, 132.
18. Ibid., 149.
19. *York Corporation House Books*, 154.
20. Lee, *1603*, 136.
21. Ashton, *James I*, 65.
22. *The True Narrative of the Entertainment of His Royal Majestie, from the Departure from Edenbrough; till his Receiving at London* (London, 1603).
23. De Lisle, *After Elizabeth*, 166–167.
24. Nichols I: 113-4=114, 139-140. [Nichols, John, ed., *The Progresses, Processions, and Magnificent Festivities of King James the I*, 4 vols. (London: J. B. Nichols, 1828].

25. Starkey, *Monarchy*, audiobook.
26. Willson, *King James*, 168.
27. Ibid.
28. Ibid., 170.
29. Ibid., 174.
30. Ibid., 166.
31. Ackroyd, *London*, 194.
32. McElwee, *Wisest Fool*, 115.
33. Lee, *1603*, 139.
34. Ackroyd, *Shakespeare*, 417.
35. Ibid., 418.
36. Ibid., 425.
37. Willson, *King James*, 165.
38. Arthur Wilson, *The History of Great Britain, being the Life and Reign of King James the First* (1653). 12–13. [Willson]
39. Willson, *King James*, 165.
40. Ibid., 252.
41. Nicolson, *God's Secretaries*, audiobook.
42. Patterson, *Reunion of Christendom*, ix.
43. Ibid.
44. John Harington, *Tract on Succession*, quoted in de Lisle, Leanda, *After Elizabeth*, 45.

Chapter 14: The Hampton Court Conference

1. Excerpt from the *Millenary Petition*, as quoted in Bobrick, *In the Beginning*, 150.
2. Willson, *King James*, 201.
3. Starkey, *Monarchy*, audiobook.
4. Ackroyd, *Shakespeare*, 407.
5. According to the *Oxford English Dictionary*, the term "Roman" Catholic was first introduced in the reign of James I in 1605. Later, in 1623, in negotiating with Spain on the marriage of Charles to the Infanta, the Spanish insisted that the English Catholics be called "Roman" Catholic. The term was officially adopted at that time.
6. *absorb, ability, foreign*, and *absorb*, definition and etymology from *the Oxford English Dictionary*.
7. Bragg, *Adventure of English*, 10.
8. Nicolson, *God's Secretaries*, 44.

9. Bobrick, *Wide as the Waters*, 209.

10. Ibid., 210.

11. Ibid.

12. Nicolson, *God's Secretaries*, 50.

13. Ackroyd, *Shakespeare*, 367.

14. Nicolson, *God's Secretaries*, 47.

15. Ibid., 123–124.

16. Ibid., 44.

17. Ibid., 254.

Chapter 15: With All the Lightness of an Afterthought

1. Nicolson, *God's Secretaries*, 53.

2. *State Trials*, Vol. 2, p. 7, [ed. William Cobbett, London, 1809], quoted in Benson Bobrick, *Wide as the Waters*, 211.

3. Akrigg, *Letters*, 221.

4. Bobrick, *Wide as the Waters*, 211.

5. William Barlow, *The Summe and Substance of the Hampton Court Conferenc*e, 79, 83. James issued his famous synopsis of the Puritan agenda—"No Bishop, no King"—in this attack on Reynolds.

6. Bobrick, *Wide as the Waters*, 214.

7. Nicolson, *God's Secretaries*, 56.

8. Norton, *A Textual History*, 4.

9. Bobrick, *Wide as the Waters*, 214.

10. McGrath, *In the Beginning*, 163.

11. Nicolson, *God's Secretaries*, 65.

12. Ibid., 66.

13. Bobrick, *Wide as the Waters*, 216.

14. Bruce, *History of the Bible*, 19.

15. Rule #14 (Rules of Translation) These translations to be used when they agree better with the Text than the Bishop's Bible: *Tindall's* [Tyndale's], *Matthews, Coverdale's, Whitchurch's* [otherwise known as *the Great Bible*, used in the time of Henry VIII, identified by Whitchurch, the publisher], *Geneva.*

16. Bobrick, *Wide as the Waters*, 237.

17. Shakespeare, *Romeo and Juliet*, from Prologue.

18. Nicolson, *God's Secretaries*, 215.

19. Pelikan, *Whose Bible Is It?*, 16.

20. Nicolson, *God's Secretaries*, 145.

21. Bobrick, *Wide as the Waters*, 239.

22. A. W. Pollard, *The Holy Bible: A Facsimile in a Reduced Size of the Authorized Version Published in the Year 1611* (Oxford: Oxford University Press, 1911), 27, quoted in Norton, *A Textual History*, 11.

Chapter 16: The Elizabethan Aesthetic

1. Elizabeth I of England, "The Queen's speech at Tillbury Camp (9 August 1588)," *Folger Shakespeare Library: Selected Works of Queen Elizabeth I*, 77.

2. *lingua franca*—a language that is adopted as a common language between speakers whose native language is different *(Oxford American Dictionary)*.

3. Ackroyd, *Shakespeare*, 368.

4. Ibid., 371.

5. *Hamlet*, II, ii, 274.

6. T. S. Eliot, "Hamlet and his Problems," 57.

7. The Modern Scholar, *Shakespeare: The Seven Major Tragedies*, Lecture 3 (Hamlet, Part I).

8. William Shakespeare, *Hamlet*, III, i, 160–162.

9. Shakespeare stood as godfather to Jonson's son.

10. McGrath, *In the Beginning*, 255.

Chapter 17: All the King's Men

1. Nicolson, *God's Secretaries*, 27.

2. Bobrick, *Wide As the Waters*, 218.

3. John Aubrey, *Brief Lives* (ed. O. L. Dick, London, 1949), 7, quoted in Bobrick, *Wide as the Waters*, 219.

4. Nicolson, *God's Secretaries*, 30.

5. Ibid., 31.

6. William Shakespeare, *Love's Labours Lost*, III, i, 34.

7. Nicolson, *God's Secretaries*, 31.

8. Ibid.

9. Anonymous, quoted in Bobrick, *Wide as the Waters*, 224.

10. Nicolson, *God's Secretaries*, 99.

11. Opfell, *King James Translators*, 47, quoted in Bobrick, *Wide as the Waters*, 226–227.

12. Paine, *Learned Men*, 28, quoted in Bobrick, *Wide as the Waters*, 227.

13. Bobrick, *Wide as the Waters*, 236.

14. Ibid., 280.

15. Nicolson, podcast.
16. Nicolson, *God's Secretaries*, 164.
17. Ibid., 167.
18. Ibid., 166.
19. Allen, *Translating for King James*, 141–142.
20. Nicolson, *God's Secretaries*, 125.
21. Bobrick, *Wide as the Waters*, 232.
22. Ibid.
23. Nicolson, *God's Secretaries*, 126.

Chapter 18: The Lost Bois

1. Nicolson, *God's Secretaries*, 151.
2. Anthony Walker, *Life of John Bois*, ch. 5, p. 6, found in Allen, *Translating for King James*, 139.
3. Nicolson, *God's Secretaries*, 208.
4. Allen, *Translating for King James*, 147.
5. Ibid.,141.
6. Nicolson, *God's Secretaries*, 209.
7. Ibid.
8. *Oxford American*, *euphony*.
9. Ackroyd, *Albion*, 312.
10. Butterworth, *Literary Lineage*, 235.
11. Allen, *Translating the New Testament Epistles*, *xxiv*.
12. Norton, *English Bible As Literature*, 72.

Chapter 19: To the Chief Musician

1. "*A man for all seasons*" was a token of praise for Thomas More written by Robert Whittington (1480–1553) in *Vulgaria*, 1520. It is also the title of a play by Robert Bolt that was made into a movie in 1966 starring Paul Scofield. The play was originally performed at Shakespeare's Globe Theatre in London. The play/film features Sir Thomas More as a man of principle who stood against King Henry VIII (on the break with Rome) and eventually lost his life. More must be respected on that wise. He was brilliant and he was a man of deep conviction. For these elements of his character Whittington coined the phrase. On the other hand, More was an unrelenting hunter of "heretics." He burned his share of them. His loathsome enemy was William Tyndale, who, by the way, could give as good as he got.

2. Bragg, *Adventure of English*, 80.

3. Henry Hart Milman (1791–1868), Dean of St. Pauls, quoted in Ackroyd, *Albion*, 305.

4. Wild, *Romance of the English Bible*, 99.

5. *glory* has an interesting English beginning. According to the *Oxford English Dictionary*, it was used first by William Langland, Geoffrey Chaucer, and John Wycliffe. All three forms of *glory* are different. Langland used the term in 1362 and its usage was more akin to *vainglory*, or a "boastful spirit." Chaucer's usage (1385) was limited to *human glory*, the "glory of a person or a thing." Wycliffe was the first to use the word in relation to God. These three men were contemporaries. In all likelihood they knew one another and trafficked the same circles. All three were literary. Langland may have been a *Wycliffite*. He and Wycliffe shared similar concerns about spiritual matters. A curious reference is cited in *Piers the Ploughman*. Will describes himself as a "loller," living in the Cornhill area of London. Possibly rel. to Lollard. Also "ploughboy" is a possible reference to both Wycliffe and Tyndale.

6. Moynahan, *God's Bestseller*, xi.

7. Bobrick, *Wide as the Waters*, 73.

8. Wild, *Romance of the English Bible*, 139.

9. Moynahan, *God's Bestseller*, 28.

10. Bobrick, *Wide as the Waters*, 90.

11. Roger Scruton, *England: An Elegy*, 99, quoted in Ackroyd, *Albion*, 307.

12. Moynahan, *God's Bestseller*, 184–185.

13. McGrath, *In the Beginning*, 79.

14. Nicolson, *God's Secretaries*, 223.

15. *iamb*—a metrical foot consisting of one short (or unstressed) syllable followed by one long (or stressed) syllable (*Oxford American Dictionary*).

Chapter 20: Finishing Touches

1. Ward Allen, *Epistles*, xvii, referenced in Norton, *Textual History*, 13.

2. Bobrick, *Wide as the Waters*, 248.

3. Ibid., 248.

4. Ibid.

5. Nicolson, *God's Secretaries*, 216.

6. King James Bible 1611, "Dedicatory Epistle to the King."

7. Southwell and Shakespeare may not have been actual blood cousins, although there is evidence that they were so related on the playwright's

mother's side (Arden). The word *cousin* could be an indication of intimate association. Henry Wriothesley, the third Earl of Southampton, was at one time Shakespeare's patron. Southwell was the priest associated with the Southampton coterie. As it is with much of Shakespeariana, we must employ the word *speculative* to any assumptions between the priest and his "worthy good cosen."

8. Bobrick, *Wide as the Waters*, 251.
9. Nicolson, *God's Secretaries*, 226.
10. Lupton, *Welcome Joy*, 185, quoted in Bobrick, *Wide as the Waters*, 253.

Epilogue: The Pan King

1. Bobrick, *Wide as the Waters*, 257. "No known act of Parliament or Convocation, royal proclamation or Privy Council decree ever officially authorized or sanctioned its use."
2. Ecclesiastes 7:8 KJB.
3. *tiltyard*—"a yard or enclosed space for tilts [jousts] and tournaments" (*Oxford English Dictionary*).
4. Akrigg, *Letters*, 365.
5. James's declaration to his Privy Council, 1617, quoted in Willson, *King James*, 384.
6. Wood, *Shakespeare*, 153.
7. Harrison [ed.], *Complete Works of William Shakespeare*, 1471.
8. Fraser, *King James*, 211.

Bibliography

Ackroyd, Peter. *Albion: The Origins of the English Imagination*. New York: Nan A. Talese [Doubleday], 2003.

———. *London: The Biography*. New York: Nan A. Talese [Doubleday], 2000.

———. *Shakespeare: The Biography*. New York: Nan A. Talese [Doubleday], 2005.

Aikin, Lucy. *Memoirs of the Court of King James the First*. London: Longman, Hurst, Rees, Orme and Brown, 1822. [Google Books].

Akrigg, G. P. V. *Letters of King James VI & I*. Berkeley and Los Angeles: University of California Press, 1984.

———. *Jacobean Pageant: The Court of King James I*. New York: Atheneum, 1967.

Allen, Ward. *Translating For King James*. Nashville: Vanderbilt Univesity Press, 1969.

———. *Translating the New Testament Epistles 1604–1611: A Manuscript from King James's Westminster Company* [Lambeth MS 98]. Nashville: Vanderbilt University Press, 1977.

Anderson, William. *The Scottish Nation*. Edinburgh: Fullerton & Company, 1862. [Google Books].

Ashton, Robert. *James I: By His Contemporaries*. London: Hutchinson. 1969.

Avis, Paul. *God and the Creative Imagination*. London and New York: Routledge, 1999.

Barrie, J. M. *Peter Pan*. London: Penguin Books Ltd., 2008 [first published 1911].

Barroll, Leeds. *Politics, Plague, and Shakespeare's Theater: The Stuart Years*. Ithaca and London: Cornell University Press, 1991.

Bergeron, David. *King James & Letters of Homoerotic Desire*. Iowa City: University of Iowa Press, 1999.

Bingham, Caroline. *The Making of a King: A Biography of the Young Man Who Became James VI*. New York: Doubleday, 1969.

Bloom, Harold. *Hamlet: Poem Unlimited*. New York: Riverhead Books, 2003.

———. *Shakespeare: The Invention of the Human*. New York: Riverhead, 1998.

Bobrick, Benson. *Wide as the Waters*. New York: Simon & Schuster, 2001.

Bragg, Melvyn. *The Adventure of English*. New York: Arcade Publishing, 2003.

Bruce, F. F. *History of the Bible in English*. Oxford, UK: Oxford University Press, 1978.

Burgess, Anthony. *A Mouthful of Air*. New York: William Morrow and Company, 1992.

———. *Shakespeare*. New York: Knopf, 1970.

Butterworth, Charles C. *The Literary Lineage of the King James Bible*. New York: Octagon Books, 1971.

Calderwood, David. *History of the Kirk of Scotland*, 8 volumes, Wodrow Society, Edinburgh, 1849.

Crystal, David. *Pronouncing Shakespeare*. Cambridge, UK: Cambridge University Press, 2005.

———. *Think on my Words*. Cambridge, UK: Cambridge University Press, 2008.

Daniell, David. *The Bible In English*. New Haven & London: Yale

University Press, 2003.

———. *William Tyndale: A Biography*. New Haven & London: Yale University Press, 1994.

De Lisle, Leanda. *After Elizabeth*. New York: Ballantine Books, 2005.

Dunn, Jane. *Elizabeth and Mary: Cousins, Rivals, Queens*. New York: Knopf, 2004.

Faris, John T. *The Romance of the English Bible*. Philadelphia: Westminster Press, 1911.

Fraser, Antonia. *Faith and Treason: The Story of the Gunpowder Plot*. New York: Nan A. Talese, 1996.

———. *King James VI of Scotland, I of England*. New York: Knopf, 1975.

———. *Mary Queen of Scots*. New York: Delacorte Press, 1969.

Garber, Marjorie. *Shakespeare After All*. New York: Anchor Books, 2004.

———. *Shakespeare and Modern Culture*. New York: Pantheon Books, 2008.

Goldberg, Jonathan. *James I and the Politics of Literature*. Stanford: Stanford University Press, 1989.

Guy, John. *The True Life of Mary Stuart Queen of Scots*. New York: Houghton Mifflin, 2004.

Harrison, G. B., ed. *The Complete Works of William Shakespeare*. New York: Harcourt, Brace, and World, 1952.

Herries, Lord. *Historical Memoirs of the Reign of Mary, Queen of Scots, and King James VI. Abbotsford Club, no. 6*. Edinburgh, 1836.

Kenyon, J. P. *The Stuart Constitution*. Cambridge, UK: Cambridge University Press, 1969.

Kermode, Frank. *The Age of Shakespeare*. New York: Modern Library, 2004.

Labanoff, Prince (A. I. Lobanove-Rostovsky). *Lettres et Memoires de Marie, Reine e'Ecosse. 7 Volumes*, 1844.

Lacey, Robert. *Sir Walter Ralegh*. New York: Atheneum, 1974.

Lee, Christopher. *1603*. New York: St. Martin's Press, 2004.

Lee, Maurice Jr. *Great Britain's Solomon: James VI and I in His Three Kingdoms*. Chicago: University of Illinois Press, 1990.

Lupton, L. *Welcome Joy*. London, 1988.

Macleod, John. *Dynasty: The Stuarts 1560–1807*. New York: St. Martin's Press, 1999.

May, Steven W., ed. *Queen Elizabeth: Selected Works* (Folger Shakespeare Library). New York: Washington Square Press, 2004.

McElwee, William. *The Wisest Fool in Christendom*. New York: Harcourt, Brace, and Company, 1958.

McGrath, Alister. *In The Beginning*. New York: Anchor Books, 2002.

McIlwain, Charles Howard, ed. *The Political Works of James I*. Cambridge: Harvard University Press, 1918.

McWhorter, John. *Our Magnificent Bastard Tongue*. New York: Gotham Books, 2008.

Melville, Sir James. *Memoirs of His Own Life*, 1549–93. (London, 1683; ed. D. Wilson, London 1752; ed. A. Francis Steuart, London, 1929; ed. Gordon Donaldson, The Folio Society, 1969).

Moynahan, Brian. *God's Bestseller*. New York: St. Martin's Press, 2002.

Nicolson, Adam. *God's Secretaries*. New York: Harper Collins, 2003.

Norton, David. *A History of the English Bible as Literature*. Cambridge, UK: Cambridge University Press, 2000.

———. *A Textual History of the King James Bible*. Cambridge, UK: Cambridge University Press, 2005.

Opfell, O. S. *The King James Translators*. London, 1982.

Paine, G. S. *The Learned Men*. New York, 1959.

Patterson, W. B. *King James VI and I and the Reunion of Christendom*. Cambridge, UK: Cambridge University Press, 1997.

Pelikan, Jaroslav. *Whose Bible Is It*? New York: Viking, 2005.

Ramsbotham, Richard. *Who Wrote Bacon*? Forest Row, UK: Temple Lodge Publishing, 2004.

Rowse, A. L. *The England of Elizabeth*. Madison: University of

Wisconsin Press, 1950.

Shapiro, James. *A Year in the Life of William Shakespeare, 1599.* New York: Harper Collins, 2005.

Starkey, David. *Monarchy.* New York: Harper Collins, 2000, audiobook.

———. *Elizabeth: The Struggle for the Throne.* New York: Harper Collins, 2000.

Stevenson, Joseph, ed. *The History of Mary Stewart: From the Murder of Riccio Until her Flight Into England* (by Claude Nau Her Secretary). Edinburgh: William Paterson, 1883. [Google Books]

Stewart, Alan. *The Cradle King.* New York: St. Martin's Press, 2003.

Turnbull, William, trans. *Letters of Mary Stuart Queen of Scots.* London: Charles Dolman, 1845. [Google Books].

Weldon, Sir Anthony. *The Court and Character of King James.* London: Printed by R. J. and are to be sold by John Wright, at the King's Head in the Old Baily. [Google Books].

Weir, Alison. *The Life of Elizabeth I.* New York: Ballantine Books, 2003.

———. *Mary, Queen of Scots and the Murder of Lord Darnley.* New York: Ballantine Books, 2003.

Wild, Laura H. *The Romance of the English Bible: A History of the Translation of the Bible into English from Wyclilf to the Present Day.* Garden City: Doubleday, Doran & Company, Inc, 1929.

Williams, William Carlos. *In The American Grain.* New York: New Directions, 1956 [originally published 1925].

Willson, David Harris. *King James VI & I.* New York: Oxford University Press, 1956.

———. *A History of England.* New York: Holt, Rinehart, and Winston, 1972.

Wood, Michael. *Shakespeare.* New York: Perseus Books Group, 2003.

Acknowledgments

A FIRST THANKS to Joel Miller at Thomas Nelson, who gave me room to imagine. A close second are the amazing biographers and historians whom I drew this story from: Adam Nicolson, Benson Bobrick, Peter Ackroyd, Antonia Fraser, Alison Weir, the four Davids—David Willson, David Starkey, David Norton, and David Daniell. The three Williams—McElwee, Shakespeare, and Tyndale. Melvyn Bragg, Caroline Bingham, Christopher Lee, G. P. V. Akrigg, Alan Stewart, Alister McGrath, Marjorie Garber, Ward Allen, and others. I do not pretend to be of their kind.

To my agent, Bucky Rosenbaum, and his unstoppable heart.

With a more immediate gratitude, my warmest to editors Kristen Parrish, Janene MacIvor, and Heather Skelton.

At last, and always, Benita.

About the Author

DAVID TEEMS is the author of *To Love Is Christ* (Thomas Nelson, 2005) and *And Thereby Hangs a Tale: What I Really Know About the Devoted Life I Learned from My Dogs* (Harvest House, 2010). His next book, *The Poet and the Morning Star*, a twin biography of John Wycliffe and William Tyndale, is due for publication in 2011 by Thomas Nelson. David and his wife Benita live in Franklin, Tennessee, with their Dalmatian, Sophie. For more: www.davidteems.com

Index

T–U